SEX AND THE S

After studying physics at St. Step
Kirpal read law at the University of Oxford and did his master's in law at the University of Cambridge. He worked briefly with the United Nations in Geneva before returning to Delhi. He has been practising law at the Supreme Court for well over two decades and has appeared in a range of matters involving fundamental rights. His clients cross the political and ideological spectrum. He was the counsel for Navtej Johar, Ritu Dalmia and others in the case that led to the striking down of Section 377 of the Indian Penal Code.

Praise for the book

'*Sex and the Supreme Court* is an important contribution towards understanding the role of the Supreme Court as an agent of social change in the context of its decisions on gender and sexuality.'

– *Telegraph*

'Lucidly written and with little legal jargon to impede the non-initiated reader, the book shines because Kirpal takes pains to set up the broad points of the law, what's at stake and the delicate balancing act that is required of judges when deciding on questions of rights and community, and on religious edicts vs individual freedoms or autonomy.'

– *Hindustan Times*

'For the layperson interested in law and public policy around gender in India, *Sex and the Supreme Court* excellently summarises some of the significant debates.'

– *Feminism in India*

'Some of the articles emerge as powerful stories that help the reader go along on a corporeal and emotional journey from uncertainties to celebrations, and are not just absorbing and amusing, but also stimulating, stirring and thought-provoking. A must-read book.'

– *Tribune*

SEX AND THE SUPREME COURT

How the Law Is Upholding the Dignity of the Indian Citizen

Edited by
SAURABH KIRPAL

First published in hardback in India in 2020 by Hachette India
(Registered name: Hachette Book Publishing India Pvt. Ltd)
An Hachette UK company
www.hachetteindia.com

This edition published in 2022

SRD

Hardback edition ISBN 978-93-89253-00-9
Paperback edition ISBN 978-93-91028-06-0
Ebook edition ISBN 978-93-89253-01-6

Hachette Book Publishing India Pvt. Ltd
4th & 5th Floors, Corporate Centre,
Plot No. 94, Sector 44, Gurugram – 122003, India

Typeset in Berling LT Std 10/13.5
by Jojy Philip, New Delhi – 15

Printed and bound in India
by Manipal Technologies Limited, Manipal

Contents

Sex and the Workplace

Sex and Religion

Introduction

The law is ubiquitous. Yet, most of us go about our daily lives not realizing the full import of the law. From the contracts we enter into when we purchase groceries,[1] to the traffic rules we obey when we drive to work, every aspect of our lives is touched by the law. Given the important role that law plays in our lives, we are curiously oblivious to its functioning. It is something as real as breathing and yet equally far from our conscious minds.

The attempt of this book is to explain and examine the impact that the law has had on different aspects of sex, sexuality and gender. The agency through which this impact has been felt most clearly is the Supreme Court. This book explores the relationship between the law, that is, the Constitution, the rights of an individual, and how these rights are enforced by the Supreme Court.

An examination of the nature of the Indian Constitution, and the rights and principles contained therein, reveals that the Court has to perform a delicate balancing act between social practices and personal rights. The Supreme Court has been performing this task since its inception nearly 70 years ago. However, it is only in the relatively recent past that it has woken up to the enormous task ahead of it in relation to issues of sex, sexuality and gender.

The judgements, starting from the Vishaka judgement,[2] which concerns sexual harassment at the workplace, to the recent judgements on Section 377,[3] the transgender community,[4] interfaith marriages[5] and allowing women into the Sabarimala temple,[6] have one thing in common: They place the individual at the centre of the constitutional firmament. In the tug of war between the demands of the traditional conception of society and the rights of an individual to their identity and dignity, the Supreme Court has come down firmly in favour of the individual.

It is a matter of some debate whether these judgements have had the desired impact on the systemic inequalities faced by women and sexual minorities. There is also the vexed question of the legitimacy of the Court in making these decisions, which some believe should be in the domain of Parliament. These aspects will be examined in this essay, as well as in other essays in this anthology. However, given the current moral authority enjoyed by the Court, there is no doubt that the judgements handed down by it shape public discourse and play an important role in transforming society.

THE LAW AND SOCIAL CHANGE

Perhaps one of the most fundamental ways in which the law shapes us is in how we identify ourselves. Wife, mother, employer, lover...each of these roles is not merely a societal construct but a societal construct backed by a complex set of legal rules. A whole ecosystem of laws and regulations governs the interactions we have in such positions, with each other and, inevitably, with ourselves.

Our very sense of identity is shaped by the law. For instance, to be a Hindu wife before 1956 meant that the husband could have other wives as well, and children from those wives.[7] A woman's right to property and inheritance was heavily restricted; she was merely seen as chattel.[8]

These laws not only determined the legal status of a woman but inevitably devalued her self-worth. When people all around you tell you that you are less than equal, coupled with the sanction of the law, it is certain that a large number of women will start internalizing and believing that. Men will, with no apparent sense of irony about the gendered laws drafted by them, rely on those very laws to seek to establish the second class status of women.[9] To change the position of women as well as sexual and other minorities, it is necessary to change these laws.

The law, of course, is not static. Usually, the law reflects and encapsulates the social and moral values of a society. It is precisely for this reason that the law is an extremely important tool for social change. Law and society have a symbiotic relationship. The law is shaped by society and in turn shapes it. When a society is hidebound by tradition and social stasis, any reform has to come through the agency of the law.

The problem with changing the law is that the law is framed by the very people who represent society. The representatives of the people in Parliament are unlikely to think beyond that which is desired by the vocal majority (or sometimes even a socially powerful vocal minority). Even though women can hardly be called a minority, given the systemic suppression of their socio-political rights, they have virtually ceded political power to the largely male members of Parliament.

How will the law then, as an engine for social change, deliver? In the Indian context, at least in the recent past, the answer has almost always been the Supreme Court. As the essays in this book will examine, the Supreme Court has entered the field in a multitude of areas relating to sex, gender and sexuality. All these interventions have the backing of what is possibly the soul of the Constitution – the fundamental rights.

Part III of the Constitution contains the fundamental rights of every citizen. These rights are the legal armoury deployed by the courts in the judgements delivered by them. In our system of law, as in most systems governed by a written constitution, there is a chapter that contains the fundamental rights possessed by a citizen. But it is important to remember that this need not necessarily be the case. Britain, the country from which our

Constitution derived the greatest inspiration, does not have such a set of rights.

The chapter on Fundamental Rights in the Constitution was shaped by the experiences of the freedom struggle. All the members of the Constituent Assembly as well as the Drafting Committee had been connected in some way to the freedom struggle. They had lived life under a set of rules where no right was guaranteed, and every person was at the mercy of the British. The framers of the Constitution did not wish to replace the dictatorship of the sovereign with the dictatorship of the majority. So, an elaborate set of rights was framed.[10] These rights were deemed fundamental in nature inasmuch as they stem from the basic aspects of life, which an individual needs to maintain for a dignified and meaningful existence.

The fundamental rights are both 'positive' as well as 'negative' in nature. Negative rights are those that limit state interference on the freedom of an individual. However, the fundamental rights are more than a defence system against an overactive Executive. Instead, these rights, coupled with the Directive Principles of State Policy contained in Part IV of the Constitution, exhort the State to act positively in the furtherance of those rights. The State and all its institutions, which include the courts, have the responsibility under the Constitution to ensure the welfare of all individuals. It is through the positive intervention of the agencies of the State that the full potential of each individual can be realized. One of the most important means of accomplishing that is through the enforcement of the positive fundamental rights.[11]

This aspect of the Constitution is particularly clear in the case of discrimination based on the grounds of sex. While most rights are couched in negative language, restricting the power of the State to act to the detriment of a particular right of a citizen, Article 15 of the Constitution is worded in a manner that casts an obligation on the State to frame laws restricting even private individuals from discriminating against women (amongst other groups). The Directive Principles of State Policy are even clearer.[12] They lay down an obligation upon the State to ensure that men and women have an equal right to an adequate means of livelihood, a right to equal pay for equal work, rights to humane conditions at work, and maternity relief. This is the spirit and the soul of the Constitution.

THE HOLY TRINITY OF RIGHTS

If the chapter on Fundamental Rights is the soul of the Constitution, then three fundamental rights are the arch-anchor of that soul.[13] These are the right to equality (Article 14), the right to freedom (Article 19) and the right to personal liberty (Article 21). Each of these rights has its own facets, which have been used to protect the rights of women and sexual minorities. However, these three rights are often used together as a framework to protect personal autonomy and dignity.

The Right to Equality

Three Articles together form the framework of equality. Article 14 is the basic right to equality, which prohibits discrimination by the State in general. Article 15 prevents discrimination specifically on the grounds of religion, caste, race, sex or place of birth.[14] Article 16 extends the protection against discrimination to matters of public employment.[15]

The fundamental right to equality contained in the Constitution seems to be quite clear. There appears to be no room for any form of discrimination as is evident from the text of the document. Then why does it require the Supreme Court such a long time and such a vast number of judgements to achieve full equality – why has equality not already been achieved? It is one thing to say that society requires time to change, but surely that change can come about immediately in a formal legal system such as ours, by the one declaration of equality contained in the Constitution?

This question hides in itself the nuanced debate about the nature of 'equality' and the nature of discrimination. For instance, the personal laws of any community are rarely ungendered simply because society itself is in the grip of patriarchy. Yet, in the exercise of personal law, there is a claim to freedom of religion. There is then a conflict of rights – the right to equality versus the right to profess the freedom of religion. The most obvious example of this, of course, is the case of the triple talaq,[16] which pitted the rights of equality (since women could not divorce men in the same manner as men could) versus the claimed right to freedom of religion.[17]

In other cases there may be facial neutrality but substantive inequality. What this means is that a law may be applicable to all persons and hence seem neutral. Yet, the position of different segments of society would be different, so the law might impact them disproportionately and hence be discriminatory. An instance of this is the Section 377 case. The law had criminalized all forms of sodomy – generally understood to at least include all forms of anal penetrative sex.[18] It was argued that the law treated homosexual and heterosexual couples equally by banning the same sexual conduct for both classes of persons. However, since only the sexual interaction between homosexuals would constitute sodomy, effectively all sexual intercourse between homosexuals was made criminal. This amounted to discrimination against the LGBTQ community at large.

It is because of these nuances and insidious forms of discrimination that the Court has to constantly come to the aid of those discriminated against, and hence protect the equality guaranteed in the Constitution.

The Right to Freedom

The right to free speech is part of a broad panoply of rights under the umbrella of Article 19, the right to freedom. These rights include the right to free speech,[19] the right to assemble peacefully, to form associations,[20] the right to move freely and reside through the country[21] and the right to practise any profession and carry on any trade and business.[22] These rights are possibly the closest to the traditional conception of civil and political rights. The very words 'right to freedom' embody the idea that these rights are meant to protect the freedom of a citizen[23] from encroachment by the State. Indeed, that is precisely how the Article is structured.

The most precious of these rights is possibly the right to free speech contained in Article 19 (1)(a). It is obvious that for a democracy to thrive, free speech is necessary. However, this right has another interesting facet, which has just begun to be used by the Court. Article 19 (1)(a) is not merely a right to free speech; it is a right to 'free speech and expression'. This right to expression is not just an oral or visual form of conveying thought and ideas. Expression can also be a tacit assertion of one's beliefs and identity. In the Section 377 case, the Supreme Court has held that the right to live an open and dignified life and the ability to express a same-sex relation freely is protected by this right. This dimension of the right will surely be used in the future to expand an individual's rights to enable a full and unhindered expression of their personality and identity, subject, of course, to the restrictions stipulated in Article 19 (2).[24]

The Right to Life

A close reading of the fundamental rights in the Constitution shows them to be drafted in language far more limited in scope than is commonly understood by people. For instance, the pivotal right to personal liberty, the so-called 'right to life', merely states that 'no person shall be deprived of his life or liberty except according to procedure established by law'. This seems like a most tenuous protection. It seemingly gives the Legislature powers to take away any personal liberty as long as it makes a law on the subject.[25]

However, Article 21 has proved to be the gift that keeps on giving because of the imaginative interpretation of the Article by the Court. This has been done through the process of reading the words 'life' and 'liberty' so widely as to breathe life into even the most sterile sounding words.

The US Supreme Court held that when the Constitution protected liberty, it protected more general rights that were 'implicit in the context of ordered liberty'.[26] The US Supreme Court held that, 'Although the Court has not assumed to define "liberty" with any great precision, that term is not confined to mere freedom from bodily restraint. Liberty under law extends to the full range of conduct which the individual is free to pursue, and it cannot be restricted except for a proper governmental objective.'[27]

The Indian Supreme Court has followed this mode of reasoning and held that the word 'life' used in the Article is not a mere inhibition on the State from killing people. The word includes in its fold a wider manifestation of the concept of 'life'. The Court has said that the words 'life' and 'personal liberty' 'are used in the Article as compendious terms to include within themselves all the varieties of life that go to make up the personal liberties of a man and not merely the right to the continuance of a person's animal existence.'[28] The right to life through this mode of expansive interpretation now protects a host of other rights, e.g. the right to health,[29] the right to a good environment,[30] the right to privacy,[31] and so on.

THE CONSTITUTION AND THE COURT

When there are rights, there also has to be a mechanism for the enforcement of those rights. The Constitution has ultimately reposed faith in the courts, and particularly the Supreme Court, to enforce the rights.[32] The mode and manner of the enforcement, of course, depends on the nature of the right. No right can be absolute, for instance, no one can claim a freedom to incite hatred and violence against a particular community. Generally speaking, rights have to be weighed against other considerations, for instance, the maintenance of public order or the sovereignty and security of the nation.[33]

The task to protect the rights of the individual and to perform a balancing act between the fundamental rights and larger societal interests falls upon the constitutional courts. Typically, a judge will have to decide on the validity of a social policy that impinges on a personal right – for instance, the policy of reservation mentioned above vis-à-vis the right to equality. Of course, the judge will also have to determine the converse, that is, the assertion of a personal right that seeks to displace or invalidate a pre-existing social policy. The debate relating to the right to equality of women versus the socio-religious exclusion of women of a certain age from entering the temple at Sabarimala is an example of such a task.[34]

The balancing done by the Court is an inherently political task performed by unelected judges. A question often asked is how this can be countenanced in a democracy. The answer is constitutionally simple but socially difficult to understand. Constitutionally, the power to determine the constitutionality of any law is given solely to the courts.[35] They also have the power to enforce the fundamental rights through the issuance of writs.[36] Thus, the Constitution specifically empowers the judges to strike down legislation in case it runs afoul of any fundamental right.

The more problematic question is how society countenances even controversial decisions by the unelected Court. I believe that it stems from a fundamental commitment of the citizen to the idea of the Indian State. Simply put, even if a citizen disagrees with a particular judgement of the Court, they would probably respect the Constitution, which gives the Court the right to determine the question. A citizen may not like the outcome, but will respect the determination because they largely believe in the legitimacy of the institutions of the State.

This then brings one to the next question: What is it in the Indian Constitution that compels citizens to respect it? After all, we are a country of notorious divisions. Yet, almost all people express a faith and allegiance to the Constitution. This can only be so if the citizen, knowingly or otherwise, feels bound to and connected with the values contained in the Constitution.

This is because the Constitution has become a document embodying all that is aspirational in the Indian imagination. Faced with injustice on a daily basis, citizens point to the Constitution as the harbinger of all that is fair and just. The Constitution is their ally; it is only the politicians, bureaucracy, police and the other instruments of the State that have let us down, or so it is believed. Consequently, citizens routinely invoke the constitutional jurisdiction of the Court to seek redress for the wrongs inflicted upon them.

Rohit De argues that it is through the people's use of the Constitution as a tool that the Indian State has developed in the manner it has. An interesting finding of his is that the minorities and subaltern groups were over-represented in litigation before the Court possibly because they 'took the State's obligations to protect them seriously'.[37] Another explanation might well be that it was the minorities and the subalterns who needed the most judicial protection against an overreaching Executive.

RIGHTS AND SOCIETY

The Constitution is not merely a charter of rights. At the time of its drafting it was seen as a text promising social revolution. For a deeply poor colonized country there was an urgent need to uplift the community at large, and the historically oppressed communities in particular, to ensure the stability of the newly born union. There were calls to put the interests of the community over that of the individual. A person no less than Mahatma Gandhi did not support election by direct suffrage, preferring instead the indirect method of creation of the Panchayati Raj system.[38]

In this paradigm, the State was almost to disappear rather like in the Communist system. The philosophy was that 'the State that governs the best, governs least'. In such a system, the individual was to be the master of his or her own destiny, with the role of the State being kept to a minimum. Every person was to be largely responsible for their own empowerment and well-being. The community in the village was to be the engine of social reform.

However, such a view was rejected by, amongst others, people like Dr B.R. Ambedkar. Dr Ambedkar believed the village to be a 'den of ignorance, narrow mindedness and communalism'. He famously said that 'unlike a drop of water which loses its identity when it joins the ocean, man does not lose his being in the society in which he lives. He is born not for the development of the society alone, but for the development of his self'. Perhaps this was the result of his experiences of oppression faced in the village.

Be that as it may, in the conflict between the two opposite ideals of the relationship between the State and the individual, and the role of the individual within the State, it was Dr Ambedkar's view that prevailed. Our Constitution then gave the fundamental rights to the individual and recognized his or her autonomy and dignity. It also enjoined the State to ensure that those rights would be protected and furthered to enable a person to achieve their full potential in life.

The story of the enforcement of fundamental rights in the last few years then has been the story of the assertion of the right of the individual to their dignity and autonomy against the actions of the State and society. The chapters in this book are fundamentally connected in that manner. They cover different aspects of the sense of self and identity of the individual, and their interaction and interplay with different social constructs, that is, the community, religion, autonomy and the workplace. These are not watertight compartments just as no one part of the personality is fully distinct. The narratives, both judicial and personal, of any of these aspects are bound to be interwoven. However, a rough division and examination of each of these strands of the human condition is still possible and desirable.

The Individual and Autonomy

Autonomy implies the right to choose and decide the course of one's life for oneself. That freedom, however, is meaningless without the ability to act upon it. For instance, a person may identify themselves as a homosexual, but if the law prohibits homosexuality, that identification is merely a chimera.

The Supreme Court affirmed the autonomy and dignity of the individual as well as the rather fluid nature of sexuality when it delivered the transgender judgement in 2014. Justice Madan Lokur's essay dwells not merely on why the Supreme Court judgement was delivered but also discusses the political and institutional developments since the judgement. The essay notes that it is the southern Indian states which have taken the greatest impetus from the judgement, and put in place policies for the advancement of the constitutional rights of transgender people.

However, the essay also notes the recent Transgender Person (Protection of Rights) Act, 2019 passed by Parliament and notified into law. The Act appears to dilute the judgement of the Supreme Court inasmuch as there is a watering down of the principle of self-identification of gender. This is a classic instance of a step forward by the Court and then a step back by Parliament.

It is not merely the Government that can take a step back though. As the essay on Section 377 notes, the bitter battle for decriminalization of sodomy was a tale of the courts taking a step forward and then taking a massive jump back. The essay recounts the history of how the Delhi High Court initially decriminalized homosexuality in 2009 only to recriminalize it in 2013. It is only recently that the Supreme Court has undone the historic wrong done to the members of the LGBTQ community and delivered a judgement that holds the promise of justice and equality to the community by striking down Section 377.

The judgements of the Supreme Court have been delivered, but have they made any difference to the lives of the people? The compelling personal essays in this anthology narrate the experiences of three individuals, each of whom come from very different socio-economic positions. Zainab Patel was born a Catholic male in a conservative family. She transitioned, and is today a powerful and independent transwoman and an activist fighting for the rights of the larger transgender community.

Ritu Dalmia, noted chef and restaurateur, tells her story about what compelled her to file the case that eventually led to the decriminalization of Section 377. Keshav Suri writes as a gay man who has actively fought for the economic empowerment of the transgender community through initiatives like the PureLove campaign. He works with his LaLiT Group of Hotels to make it an inclusive and welcoming environment for sexual minorities.

The common feature in all these essays is the idea that the journey towards self-acceptance has been furthered by the judgements of the Supreme Court, but there is also the recognition that the path towards full equality is still a long way away. For instance, sexual autonomy is not achieved merely through decriminalization. Other issues faced in various areas of one's life also need to be addressed. In matters of employment, health and personal relationships, there is still a lot of discrimination against sexual minorities. It is only when these problems are adequately addressed will a person be able to enjoy full autonomy.

The Individual and the Community

The right to choose or act upon your sexuality has meaning and purpose only if society allows you to be with the person you love. But who decides whom you can love? And if you can love the person you choose, can you marry him or her? The community often imposes its rules in the choice of a spouse by citing public interests and claiming that those trump the freedom of the individual. Caste and religious groups seek to deny people the freedom to marry, claiming that these individual actions have a deleterious impact on them.

In recent years, the issue of love jihad has captured the imagination of the media and also the country at large. There has been fearmongering alleging an ostensible and concerted practice of religious conversions of women. Women are sought to be protected against allegedly predatory men whose only intention is to propagate their religion through duping innocent women into religious conversions.

The fact that this fear requires an immensely sophisticated, and as yet undiscovered, mastermind does not allay the doubts of the conspiracy theorists. Even the sheer statistical improbability of making any change in the religious make-up of the community through these inter-religious marriages does not detract the alarmists. Of course the first victims of this love jihad are women since they are the pawns in the game that men play in the name of religion.

The essay titled 'Love and Marriage' examines this issue as well as the decision in the case of khap panchayats. It traces the idea of marriage through history. Marriage has been a subtle social tool that has often been used for the subjugation of women rather than simply being a social contract recognizing the love between two people. It is for this reason that society has sought to control marriage by imposing various restrictions – the prohibition of intra-caste and inter-religious marriages. The courts have had to come to the aid of young couples whose only crime is to seek to marry for love rather than for societal reasons.

The essay examines Hadiya's case – where a young woman from Kerala converted from Hinduism to Islam and sought to marry a man of that faith. In the face of outrage by Hindu groups, the Supreme Court finally ruled that Hadiya was an adult and hence entitled to change her faith and marry whosoever she wanted. Also discussed here are the attempts by social groups, which routinely try to block inter-caste or intra-gotra (a form of endogamy) marriages. The courts here have to come to the aid of young people who have to flee from societal oppression in order to marry for love.

Nowhere is the concept of marriage as a social tool more apparent than in the crime of adultery. The law on adultery till 2018 viewed a woman as the chattel of a man, the criminal law being used to protect the man's property, i.e. the woman. This was because Section 497 of the Indian Penal Code stated that 'whoever has sexual intercourse with a person who is and whom he knows or has reason to believe to be the wife of another man, without the consent or connivance of that man, such sexual intercourse not amounting to the offence of rape, is guilt of the offence of adultery.'

Implicit in this offence is the idea that the wife is the property of the husband and the lover who has sex with the wife of the other man impinges on that man's proprietary rights. The essay by Menaka Guruswamy and Arundhati Katju examines the decision of the Supreme Court in the case of *Joseph Shine*,[39] the case that struck down this section. The judgement is important not merely for the striking down of the section but also for recognizing the importance of choice and autonomy within the framework of marriage. This, of course, will probably be a precedent that will be used when the matter in relation to the prohibition of marital rape is ultimately heard by the courts. The essay notes that the judgement was not merely about the right to equal treatment, but concerned the larger issue of a woman's sexuality within marriage.

Both these essays ultimately focus on a larger issue in the public domain relating to same-sex marriage. Once the courts recognize the foundational values of marriage as well as the autonomy inherent in every individual, making the case for same-sex marriage is the logical next step.

The Individual and the Workplace

Jesus is said to have told the Devil that 'man shall not live by bread alone but by every word that comes from the mouth of God'. That might well be true, but it is tough to imagine being able to lead the constitutionally guaranteed dignified life without bread or, in more recent times, money. Having access to adequate income is almost a necessary condition to be able to lead a fulfilled life. For most people that income comes from the work that they do.

The right to work is thus a means to achieve the fulfilment of one's autonomy. Of course, for most people, the ability to work also has an intrinsic value. The work that people do defines them and often gives their life meaning and purpose, and even if it doesn't most people wish that they can do work that interests them.

For women though, there is a double whammy. First is the patriarchal bias against women, which results in them getting lower paid jobs. Secondly, even when they do get the jobs they look for, there is the ever-present possibility of sexual harassment. The Supreme Court has had occasion to deal with these aspects in the cases relating to equality of pay as well as sexual harassment at the workplace. However, Namita Bhandare's essay on the MeToo movement elaborates that changing the law is not sufficient. She traces the history of the movement and finds its origins, in India at least, in the Vishaka case, where the Supreme Court first laid down guidelines in relation to sexual harassment at the workplace.

The law, however, has often been a hindrance than an aid for women. This essay notes that powerful men use and abuse the very system of law that is supposed to come to the aid of the disempowered. The MeToo movement was thus born partly as a consequence of disillusionment with the traditional forms of justice. It is through the use of alternative mechanisms, including social media, that justice is sometimes delivered.

It is true that some men will use all the legal loopholes to avoid accountability. Yet, even in these instances, the law is still required. Crimes against women cannot simply be condemned in WhatsApp groups or on social media. They need to be adjudicated upon in the courts of law. This essay is thus also a call for the speedy delivery of justice in matters that are pending before the courts.

The Individual and Religion

Religion has been said to be the opium of the masses. As one of the oldest societal constructs, it is also one of the most powerful and insidious means through which society itself has been shaped and controlled. It is on the battleground of religion that the clash between the individual and society is at its most stark.

The issue of marriage, as noted above, is an instance of men asserting their power over women. When religion is added to the mix, it becomes a heavy and intoxicating cocktail. In that instance, the fight is not merely portrayed as one between an individual and society, but as one between an individual and God. The litigation relating to the prohibition on instant triple talaq, as examined by Madhavi Divan in her essay, was just such a case. An argument was raised that triple talaq was an 'essential religious practice' of the Muslim community.

Thus, even though the practice was discriminatory against women, it was constitutionally protected because it was part of the freedom of religion. Two of the five judges in the Supreme Court Bench accepted this argument. However, the majority verdict struck down this practice, even though the theme of gender equality is noticeably absent from a large part of the judgement. The essay notes that the Court did not fully engage with other forms of gender discrimination in Muslim law, for instance, polygamy or other forms of unilateral divorce, and confined itself to the 'low hanging fruit' of instant triple talaq.

The reason for judicial deference appears to be the reluctance to delve into matters of personal law through judicial intervention.

A slightly different view on the issue of instant triple talaq has been proposed by Justice Badar Ahmad in his essay. He points out that the Shariah is far more malleable than has been suggested and thus gender justice may be achieved within the community through reforming the law. This is important because perceived injustices to women are often cited as a reason for the imposition of a Uniform Civil Code upon a community, which may be able to redress issues through internal reform.

Balancing the rights between gender justice and religious faith is a delicate task. To always rule in favour of the former may, in some cases, severely prejudice the latter. One such instance is the case of the entry of women into the Sabarimala temple. Women between the ages of 10 and 50 have not been allowed to enter the temple. This impinged on the rights of women and, accordingly, the matter went to the Supreme Court. On the other hand, it was contended that the devotees of Lord Ayyappa constituted a separate religious denomination. It was also claimed that this denomination had an essential religious practice whereby women were not allowed to see the deity since it was a 'naishtik brahmacharya' or 'eternal bachelor'.

These claims were rejected by the Supreme Court. Mukul Rohatgi in his piece argues that the Court erred in this ruling. To always expect rationality in religion, which is essentially a matter of faith, might be a tough task. His essay traces the history behind Lord Ayyappa's temple in Sabarimala. Ultimately, it notes that the followers of Lord Ayyappa are a distinct denomination or a subset of Hinduism. Maintaining the sanctity of the idol as an eternal celibate can only be achieved by restricting the entry of women. This religious belief has to be constitutionally protected. While supporting the entry of women might be a reformative act, it could disturb the pluralist nature of the Constitution.

CONCLUSION

The cases that form the subject matter of this book are the result of the adjudicatory process of the Supreme Court. In a way, the Court, the Constitution and the judicial decision-making process are inextricably linked. The Constitution proclaims grand fundamental rights. However, these rights take shape and have a practical impact only when applied by the Court on a case-by-case basis. How the Court reads and interprets those rights is a result of the extremely malleable judicial process. The methodology employed for the interpretation of the written text of the Constitution determines the outcome of the case.

The wordings of the fundamental rights, like the rights contained in many constitutions across the world, are majestically vague.[40] The text of the right is the same for all to see, but what it means for a particular case depends vastly on the person reading it. As the persons reading and applying those rights change, so does the content of that right, even though the words remain static. Judges will often hold in their judgements and say that they are merely declaring the law as it is and not creating any new laws.

However, that does gloss over the inherent creative component in the interpretative process. As Justice Arjan Sikri observes in his essay on the concept of 'dignity', the underlying theme of the recent jurisprudence of the Court has been the attempt to flesh out a concept of dignity that values autonomous choices and the right to self-fulfilment. Justice Sikri notes that the right to dignity, which all of us take for granted, is not actually specified as a fundamental right at all in the Constitution but has been read into it through a process of interpretation. This is really creation through the means of interpretation.

But how does this creation really occur? Interpretation does not happen in a vacuum. Typically, the process of interpretation would require the text of the Constitution to be read in conjunction with the precedent. This process of reading a law in the context of other laws is not unique or recent, but is a fundamental feature of all judicial reasoning.

Yet, in a modern, organic constitution, precedent alone will not determine outcome. The Constitution has to be read in the context of its underlying egalitarian principles, that is, through the prism of what is now called 'constitutional morality'. This overarching principle of constitutional morality finds a mention in most progressive judgements and has been used to imbue rights with greater meaning than their literal text might suggest.

This has been possible largely because the Supreme Court enjoys a unique prestige and legitimacy in India. There are few other institutions that are respected as much as it is, even if one disagrees with its decisions. It has therefore been able to expand the fundamental rights by relying on the moral authority it has. The Court regularly intervenes in matters of public interest through its judgements and orders. In fact, these days, even casual observations of judges on the Bench make front-page news.

However, the actual judgements of the Supreme Court and their impact on society are not fully understood or appreciated by the general public. Information about the Court's judgements are heavily edited by newspapers and electronic media, or in some cases completely misinterpreted on social media. In the process of dissemination of information to the public, there is almost a game of Chinese whispers. The powers of the Court and what it actually decides gets transformed into something quite different from what the Court actually held.

It is hoped that this book will help the general public better appreciate the issues at stake and how the Court shapes the discussion around them. This is important because the reformation of society is a largely unfinished task. Many challenges lie ahead and it is only through the understanding of the working of the institutions of change that we can see a road map for the future. The voices in this book are not merely those of legal experts. These are voices that have personally experienced or seen discrimination at close quarters. Positive change will only happen when the legal universe inhabited by the judges listens to these voices and acts in furtherance of the promises contained in the Constitution.

Sex and the Individual

Pride versus Prejudice

The Struggle against Section 377

SAURABH KIRPAL

What does it mean to be human? What is the relationship between the State and the individual? These are not merely metaphysical questions meant to be discussed and debated in classrooms and lecture halls. They have a real and immediate impact on how people live, how society is organized, and the health and happiness of millions. Nowhere is this more apparent than in the case of the criminalization of 'carnal intercourse contrary to the order of nature',[1] or homosexual acts.

Section 377 of the Indian Penal Code made homosexuality an offence. It made criminal a sexual act that was founded on homosexual love, for which a person could be incarcerated for life. The Indian Penal Code, enacted in 1860, was a legacy the British left us. We had to wait till 2018 when, finally, the Supreme Court declared that consensual acts of homosexual sex would not be a crime. This judgement was passed in the case of *Navtej Singh Johar v. Union of India* or the 'Navtej judgement'.[2]

In a way, Section 377 was not only about a sexual act. It was about so much more. By prohibiting homosexual sexual acts, the very identity and sense of self-worth of an individual was stripped away and negated. One was, in a sense, dehumanized. The State, through the means of coercive criminal law, imposed its version of morality and its conception of how an individual should behave. Criminalization was a signal by the State that a homosexual was not an equal citizen of the country, but was the child of a lesser god – a deviant.

In reading down Section 377, the Supreme Court has sought to restore the dignity of the individual and also hold that the State has no business interfering with the most intimate aspects of a person's behaviour and way of living. The judgement is thus not just a charter of freedoms for the LGBTQ community but also a beacon of hope for every person who has borne the brunt of oppression.

This essay will trace the history of the rather odious provision and its ultimate reading down in the case of the Navtej judgement.

The Navtej judgement resulted in four separate judgements, all agreeing with the final decision to read down Section 377. Yet each judgement had its own philosophy and ethos, which encapsulated different arguments and issues surrounding the LGBTQ community. They each tell a story that relates to the history of the effort to decriminalize homosexuality, the constitutional analysis of the issues involved and the future of the community. The theme of each judgement is neatly captured by a memorable quote, mentioned in each judgement, ranging from the literary to the metaphysical, from the political to the emotive.

So much has been written about the judgement, yet there has not been an analysis of the judgements separately to explain and understand the variation of the judicial reasoning contained in it. Judgements, like judges, are not a monolithic whole. They are, to use an appropriate analogy, multicoloured like the rainbow. Till we understand and appreciate this, we cannot fully envisage the future course of judicial action. This essay is an attempt to understand the variations in the judicial reasoning. Deconstruction of the judgements will make us realize that the cases that arise in the future will also be deeply influenced by the beliefs of the judges hearing the cases.

A BRIEF HISTORY OF THE 'CRIME'

Criminal law in ancient India was never uniformly codified and applied by a central authority figure through the use of coercive state power. Even though Islam and later Christianity had come to Indian shores by the 12th and the 15th century respectively, given the lack of a cohesive state, no uniform criminal code existed.

In the Hindu tradition, there was no clear cut proscription of homosexual acts, much less criminalization. The *Kama Sutra*, possibly the authoritative text on matters relating to sexual desire, categorizes various forms of sexual activities. Sutra 36 of the text is particularly informative. It talks of oral sex between males in connection with the word 'sadharana', which means 'ordinary'. This indicates that sex between males was considered ordinary rather than a form of deviance.

Certain scholars have remarked that the *Kama Sutra* was not a symbol of sexual liberation and that same-sex relations were 'accommodated rather than authorized'.[3] Be that as it may. Accommodation is a form of tolerance and certainly not an attempt to criminalize. Similarly, stories of gender fluidity abound in the scriptures and the Puranas. No less than Lord Shiva and Lord Vishnu 'in the avatar of Mohini', the greatest gods in the Hindu pantheon, were said to have had intercourse through which a child was born. Shikhandi, a man born in a woman's body, was a central character in the Mahabharata and was responsible for Bhishma Pitamah's death (Arjuna used Shikhandi as a shield to short him). Such stories show that in Hindu mythology, homosexuality was not seen as a perversion requiring imprisonment.

All this changed not through the evolution of cultural or religious mores, but through the imported prejudice of the Victorians. In 1833, during the rule of the British East India Company, it was decided to set up an Indian Law Commission chaired by Thomas Babington Macaulay. The draft for the penal code was revised repeatedly, finally presented to the Legislative Council, and passed in October 1860. As an aside, it is interesting to note that in 1860, the Legislative Council consisted of members elected by the Board of Directors of the East India Company, and certainly had no Indian members.

Lord Macaulay claimed himself to be a man of great precision. In a letter to Lord Auckland, the Governor General in Council, he claimed that the two qualities of a law were precision and intelligibility. The letter said that 'a law, and especially a penal law, should be drawn in words which convey no meaning to the people who are to obey it, is an evil. On the other hand, a loosely worded law is no law, and to whatever extent a legislature uses vague expressions, to that extent it abdicates its functions, and resigns the power of making law to the Courts of Justice.'[4]

One would have thought that given this devotion to precision, the offences contained in the Act would have been drafted carefully and clearly. Indeed this was the case. However, there was one class of offences that Macaulay found so abhorrent that it was left delightfully vague. This was the provision that became Section 377.

In the introductory report, Macaulay stated:

> [the acts] relate to an odious class of offences respecting which is it desirable that as little as possible should be said... [We] are unwilling to insert, either in the text or in the notes, anything which could give rise to public discussion on this revolting subject; we are decidedly of opinion that the injury which would be done to the morals of the community by such discussion would far more than compensate for any benefits which might be derived from legislative measure framed with the greatest precision.

Macaulay's opinionated homophobia led to a blanket refusal to phrase the law with precision for fear that it may lead to a discussion in society.[5] Mere discussion appeared to be an abomination in the mind of this esteemed law maker. And the wording of the section was even more curious. The section stated that 'whoever voluntarily has carnal intercourse against the order of nature with any man, woman or animal, shall be punished with imprisonment for life, or with imprisonment of either description for a term which may extend to ten years, and shall also be liable to fine.' What is therefore almost amusing is that a law targeted against homosexuals cannot even bring itself to use the words homosexual or sodomy.

What is now known as Section 377 did not explicitly target homosexuals. Its use was most common for the persecution of homosexual activity.[6] In the initial years, only acts of sodomy were prosecuted and even homosexual acts of oral sex between a minor and an adult was not seen as a crime as there was no sodomy involved.[7]

This view of the law changed in the early 20th century. In 1925, in a case titled *Khanu v. Emperor*,[8] a minor was forced to perform oral sex on an older man. The interpretation of Section 377 was expanded beyond the act of sodomy. The explanation that was given for the widening of the interpretation of this provision was that 'the sin of Gomorrah is not less carnal intercourse than the sin of Sodom'. This preoccupation with the act of sodomy and the kingdoms of Sodom and Gomorrah clearly indicates that this provision was to apply to homosexuality first and perhaps other issues as an afterthought. More importantly, the origins of the 'crime' in the Bible were laid bare.

The criminalization of homosexuality was now complete. All forms of sexual intercourse between members of the same-sex were now punishable. But the discrimination against the community did not end there. In 1871, another law called the Criminal Tribes Act was passed, with the explicit purpose of 'registration, surveillance and control of...eunuchs'.[9] Eunuchs who were 'reasonably suspected of kidnapping and castrating children' or committing offences under Section 377 (virtually every transgender person) were required to be registered with the local government and also furnish details of their property![10] Penalties were imposed on registered eunuchs who appeared in female clothes, danced in public or performed for hire.[11]

The Criminal Tribes Act was eventually repealed at Independence. However, the colonial legacy of Section 377 continued. Even though the former colonial masters decriminalized sodomy in Britain,[12] no such move ever gathered much traction in India. It was as though we had forgotten our rich cultural tradition of tolerance, and fully imbibed the worst facets of colonial prejudice. Even though the 172nd report of the Law Commission of India recommended the amendment to Section 377, the report was met with the same dusty file room future as most progressive Law Commission reports.

However, though the law stood still, society did not. Unfortunately, in this case, society seemed to fall further in its regressive outlook to the issue of homosexuality. The '80s and early '90s were the times of the beginning of the AIDS epidemic. A bill called the AIDS Prevention Bill was introduced in the Rajya Sabha in 1989. The provisions of the Bill were extremely draconian and required medical practitioners to inform the local health authority of the presence of an AIDS patient; the Bill also allowed the health authority to question, test and isolate the patient in hospital. Further, the provision permitted the Government to seek information about all past sexual partners of the patient. Though the Bill was eventually dropped in 1991, discrimination against patients with HIV/ AIDS has remained rife.

The LGBTQ community was ostracized even by other disempowered groups. In 1994, the Sakhi Collective, a lesbian organization, wrote that they had not received any support from an Indian feminist organization.[13] Some self-proclaimed feminists are supposed to have said that there were no lesbians in India!

This hatred of the LGBTQ community extended to the political groups as well. The National Federation of Indian Women, an organization associated with the Communist Party of India, condemned the holding of the South Asian Gay Conference, and asked the Prime Minister 'not to follow Bill Clinton's immoral approach to sexual perversions'.[14] An MLA of the Shiva Sena also wrote a warning letter against the conference.

In 1994, a group of physicians recommended that condoms be distributed in Tihar jail due to the high reportage of homosexuality. The prison authorities, however, refused to allow condoms to be distributed because it would have amounted to an explicit recognition and even condonation of homosexual acts, and this would be in contravention of Section 377, IPC. This led to an NGO, the AIDS Bhedbhav Virodhi Andolan (ABVA), filing a Public Interest Litigation before the Delhi High Court, calling for the repeal of Section 377 on the grounds that it violated the right to privacy.[15]

But even though the case was filed almost 25 years before the Navtej judgement, the grounds raised in the petition were almost prescient. At a time before the Supreme Court had held that there was a fundamental right to privacy, the petition urged the Court to strike down the section on the basis that the privacy rights were inherent in the right to life and liberty recognized in Article 21 of the Constitution. The petition also alleged that the section was arbitrary and violative of the equality clause of the Constitution, particularly since it was drafted in 1833 and was archaic.

The petition came up for hearing in 2001 and, by then, the movement had lost some of its momentum. Since the ABVA is run by unpaid volunteers and since it did not have a full-time paid lawyer, when the matter finally came up, it failed to appear. The case was, therefore, unfortunately, dismissed.

THE DELHI HIGH COURT VERDICT

It has been said that in India, the high courts often do more to protect the civil rights of the citizens than even the Supreme Court.[16] This was clearly the case, at least initially, in the case of Section 377. After the dismissal of the petition filed by the ABVA, it took another courageous NGO to file a petition before the Delhi High Court.

The Naz Foundation was set up in 1994 by Anjali Gopalan and a few others. The main focus of their work was HIV/AIDS prevention and care. This being the '90s, it led them to work closely with the gay community. In 2000, a young man came to see them and recounted his horrific tale: He had been forced to receive electro-shock therapy at a government hospital to be cured of his homosexuality. When Naz tried to register a complaint with the National Human Rights Commission, they were rebuffed as it was pointed out that Section 377 made homosexual acts a criminal offence.[17]

This led the NGO to file a petition in the Delhi High Court challenging this interpretation. The petition was dismissed at one point of time by the High Court, which said that since Naz was not personally affected by the provision, it had no standing to challenge it. This decision was reversed by the Supreme Court, which directed the High Court to hear the matter.[18]

The case was finally heard by the Delhi High Court in 2009 by a bench comprising Chief Justice Ajit Prakash Shah and Justice Muralidhar. The first interesting feature in the case was the contradictory stand taken by the Union of India. Those of us who practise in the courts are not particularly surprised by this. The government is not a single entity and it sometimes seems that its various branches act in virtual ignorance of one another.

The Ministry of Home Affairs filed an affidavit in the Court supporting the retention of Section 377. The Home Ministry argued that homosexuality was against public morality and hence should remain criminal. The National AIDS Control Authority (NACO) filed quite a different affidavit, signed by the Under-secretary to the Ministry of Health and Family Welfare. NACO stated that AIDS was difficult to prevent and treat since the criminalization of homosexual conduct was pushing everything underground. It therefore sought for decriminalization of Section 377. In the end result, the High Court, in an erudite judgement, read down Section 377 and said that consensual homosexual conduct in private was not a crime.[19]

The sensitivity displayed by the High Court in its ultimate judgement was possibly fashioned by its reaction to the abhorrent allegations of sexual abuse against the LGBTQ community that had been placed before it. In this regard, the Delhi High Court judgement is different from even the Navtej judgement of 2018, which does not explicitly discuss the tremendous violence against members of the LGBTQ community.

Two particularly striking examples of sexual violence were mentioned in the High Court judgement. In July 2001, the police in Lucknow were investigating a complaint under Section 377. They went to the headquarters of a local NGO called the Bharosa Trust, which was engaged in the area of HIV/AIDS prevention amongst the gay community. There they seized educational material, which they claimed to be pornographic material, and sex toys. This false story was published with great relish in the local newspapers. The police then arrested the director and other employees of the Trust (as well as officers of the Naz Foundation, which had an office in Lucknow) and alleged that a sex racket was being run.

The arrested persons were allegedly beaten up by the police and their offices were sealed.[20] They spent 47 days in jail before being granted bail by the High Court. The Chief Judicial Magistrate as well as the District and Sessions Judge had earlier denied them bail and held that 'the work of the accused is like a curse on society'. The prosecution had urged that the accused 'were a group of persons indulging in these activities and are polluting the entire society by encouraging young persons and abetting them for committing the offence of sodomy'.

Then there was an instance of custodial torture of LGBTQ persons. In Bangalore in 2004, a eunuch was standing at a public place dressed in female clothing. A group of young men accosted her and subjected her to gang rape, forcing her to have oral and anal sex. She was later taken to the police station where, rather than being given protection, she was stripped naked, handcuffed to the window, grossly abused and tortured.

With this background, the High Court rejected the argument of the Home Ministry as well as some private entities who had all sought retention of Section 377 citing largely religious reasons. The Court held that in the case of fundamental rights, if there was a clash between public morality and constitutional morality, it was the latter that would prevail. This was possibly the first time that the concept of constitutional morality was used by Indian courts. The elaboration of the concept of constitutional morality was greater in the Navtej judgement, and is hence discussed in greater detail later in the essay.

The Court also held that the right to privacy and dignity required that consensual sexual acts in the privacy of the home could not be proscribed by law. Of course, privacy did not merely imply a physical space but also the privacy of a person in the sense of their dignity. Quoting Justice Albie Sachs of the South African Constitutional Court, the High Court held 'for every individual, whether homosexual or not, the sense of gender and sexual orientation of the person are so embedded in the individual that the individual carries this aspect of his or her identity wherever he or she goes. A person cannot leave behind his sense of gender or sexual orientation at home. While recognizing the unique worth of each person, the Constitution does not presuppose that a holder of rights is an isolated, lonely and abstract figure possessing a disembodied and socially disconnected self. It acknowledges that people live in their bodies, their communities, their cultures, their places and their times. The expression of sexuality requires a partner, real or imagined. It is not for the state to choose or to arrange the choice of partner, but for the partners to choose themselves.'[21]

The High Court eventually read down Section 377 and held that consensual homosexual sex between two adults in private was not a crime.

THE KOUSHAL ABERRATION

The High Court judgement was pronounced on 2 July 2009. Its effect was electrifying. Anecdotal evidence aside, there was a substantive shift in the attitudes of persons to their own sexuality as well as that of society towards them. A study published in 2012 assessed the impact of the Naz Foundation judgement by interviewing members of the LGBTQ community.[22] It found that post the judgement, there was increased self-acceptance and confidence, reduction in police harassment and greater societal acceptance. The report, however, did find that there was no greater acceptance by the family.

The mood in society after 2009 therefore started changing. I believe the judgement did a lot to accomplish that, as did the activism of members of the LGBTQ community. Pride marches, seminars and other sensitization efforts resulted in society grudgingly accepting the judgement. This also had an effect on the Government. During the hearing before the High Court, the law officer of the Union of India had made outrageous and constitutionally completely infirm arguments in Court, for which he was duly chastised by the Court.[23] However, after the judgement, the Government decided to accept the verdict and not challenge it in appeal before the Supreme Court.

Though the Government decided not to challenge the High Court verdict, that did not deter self-appointed guardians of public morality from challenging it. One part-time astrologer by the name of Suresh Kumar Koushal sought the permission of the Supreme Court to challenge the verdict, and was permitted to do so. All sorts of religious groups then filed challenges – there was, in the case of the hatred of the LGBTQ community, a true unity in diversity. Even members of the minority community, without any sense of irony, actually petitioned the Court to emasculate the rights of another minority!

However, given the fact that the judgement of the High Court was so well written, the Government had not challenged it and public opinion had seemed to move on, there was hope that the Supreme Court would also come down on the right side of history and uphold the Delhi High Court verdict. That this would prove to be a false hope is clear from examining the proceedings before the Supreme Court.

When the case was being heard, one of the judges repeatedly asked whether a person could ask for a fundamental right to commit an act that was contrary to the order of nature. This barely disguised hostility showed the contempt of the Court towards an oppressed minority. In fact, this finally resulted in the Court giving gems of dictums in its final verdict when it held that 'In its anxiety to protect the so-called rights of LGBT persons and to declare that Section 377 IPC violates the right to privacy, autonomy and dignity, the High Court has extensively relied upon the judgements of other jurisdictions.'

The judges probably felt that the LGBTQ community had no rights, though how that would square with the most cursory reading of the Constitution truly baffles the mind. Perhaps if time had been spent reading Part III of the Constitution (the Fundamental Rights chapter) rather than expressing disdain on foreign scholarship, the decision might have been different.

Several other instances should have rung alarm bells. Mr P.P. Malhotra, the same learned Additional Solicitor General who had argued the matter before the High Court, now argued in favour of allowing the appeals even though the Government had decided not to file an appeal. This was clearly erroneous, and yet the judges do not seem to have questioned it. When the Attorney General asked another Additional Solicitor General to appear in Court and point this out, the judges got visibly upset and said that they would refuse to take cognizance of the Attorney General's instructions![24]

The judgement was reserved on 27 March 2012. Even though the hearing had had a few hiccups, the lawyers arguing for the reading down of Section 377 were hopeful. Surely the Supreme Court would not reverse course on its historic commitment to human rights. They would await the judgement.

However, that wait would prove to be very long indeed. The judgement did not come for weeks or even months. Then a year passed and there was still no judgement. One of the members of the Bench, Justice G.S. Singhvi, was due to retire on 11 December 2013. Had he failed to pronounce the verdict then, the matter would have had to be reheard. So, on that very date, almost 20 months after the verdict had been reserved, the judgement was pronounced.[25]

The judgement was read out in Court and there was stunned silence. The Supreme Court had reversed the judgement of the Delhi High Court and had made millions of Indians criminals again. The Court had not really decided any of the arguments based on fundamental rights (possibly because they had forgotten them given the huge delay). They merely held that it was not for the Courts but for Parliament to decide on the issue of decriminalization.[26]

The dejection that followed the judgement actually spurred further growth of the LGBTQ movement. Too many people had come out and tasted freedom after the High Court judgement. The activists who for decades had fought for the cause of the LGBTQ community, as well as the younger generation, got together to protest the decision of the Supreme Court. A social media campaign called 'no going back', which eventually morphed into a sort of an umbrella movement against the Koushal judgement, started.

The Central Government, which had permitted its Additional Solicitor General to make arguments in favour of the retention of Section 377, also finally woke up and filed a review petition before the Court. Since the author of the Koushal judgement had retired, by this point of time, the review petition was placed before another Bench comprising Justice H.L. Dattu[27] and Justice Mukhopadhyay. The review was summarily dismissed. Thereafter the lawyers for the case tried the ultimate legal recourse that they had – the filing of a curative petition.

A curative petition is a method devised by the Supreme Court to take a relook at a judgement that has been completely erroneously decided and is violative of all norms of justice, for instance, a judgement passed without hearing one of the parties.[28] The jurisdiction of the Court in allowing a curative petition is extremely restricted because the Court wishes to generally uphold the finality of its judgement; any other view will possibly open the floodgates of curative petitions. After all, every losing party probably thinks that there has been gross injustice in their case.

In order to discourage its use, the Supreme Court's rules require that a senior counsel certify that the curative petition needs to be filed. These certificates are not easy to come by. However, in a heartening move, there was a deluge of certificates from the top senior counsels of the Supreme Court in the 377 case. This showed a uniform displeasure of the Supreme Court bar with the decision in the Koushal case. Not only did the senior counsels give the certificates, they did another unprecedented thing: K.K. Venugopal, Ashok Desai, Mukul Rohatgi, Harish Salve, C.U. Singh, Meenakshi Arora, Shyam Divan and Anand Grover, to name a few top counsels (three of who were or are Attorney Generals of India), walked to the Chief Justice's Court. There they mentioned the matter of the curative petition to the Chief Justice and said that the matter related to the soul of both the Constitution and the Supreme Court, and ought to be heard in open court. One can only imagine that this had its required impact because a short order was passed by the judges in their chamber directing that the matter be listed in Court.

Two further developments had occurred after the decision of the Supreme Court in the Koushal case. Virtually contemporaneously, the Court had decided the NALSA case where the rights of transgender persons were given constitutional recognition.[29] This was in direct contrast with the decision in the Koushal case, which had failed to recognize these very rights. Secondly, the Supreme Court had given its ruling in the privacy case. In the privacy case, a bench of nine judges had virtually held the Koushal judgement to be bad law but had not performed the formal task of overruling the case since the curative petitions were at that time pending before the Court.[30]

Eventually, the curative petitions were referred to a five-judge bench.[31] However, there were two problems with the curative petitions. First, the jurisdiction of the Court in a curative petition is extremely limited. Even if the Court felt that the judgement was wrong, they could not correct it unless the error was of an extreme magnitude. Secondly, none of the petitions before the Court that were pending had been filed by any member of the LGBTQ community. This was possibly because when the petitions were first filed in the Delhi High Court in 2001, no member of the community was willing to come forward.

But things had changed by 2015. Five courageous individuals got together to file a Writ Petition before the Supreme Court directly, challenging Section 377, as it impacted their lives.[32] These individuals were not merely people of eminence, but were ordinary people who, through the dint of hard work, had become mainstream success stories. They gave a human face to the problems posed by Section 377. These people were Navtej Singh, classical dancer; Sunil Mehra, journalist; Aman Nath, hotelier, Ritu Dalmia, chef; and Ayesha Kapur, businesswoman.

The Navtej Johar case was listed in Court in June 2016. When the matter first came up before the Court, it noted that since the issue was pending in the curative petitions, the petition should be placed before the Chief Justice. The presumption was that the case would be heard along with the curative petition.

Even though the curative petitions were referred to a Constitution Bench in February 2016, not much seemed to have happened. However, almost suddenly and much to our surprise, the Navtej Johar petition was listed in the Chief Justice's Court in January 2018. At the hearing, the Court noted that the decisions in the transgender and the privacy case had cast some doubt on the correctness of the Koushal decision. The case was directed to be heard by a bench of five judges of the Court – the so-called Constitution Bench.[33]

Matters referred to the Constitution Bench of five judges are not often heard immediately. This is because of the tremendous backlog of cases. So, it was presumed that the case would take quite some time before it would be heard. However, the case was listed for hearing in Court shortly after the summer vacation in 2018. It was apparent that the Court was keen to deal with the issues as it was placed for hearing ahead of a raft of matters that had been pending in the Supreme Court for a much longer period of time.

The hearing of the case started and it was apparent from the beginning that the judges were quite sympathetic to the cause of the LGBTQ community. The Government's position was not clear as no affidavit had been filed in response to the petition. However, a day after the hearing of the case had started, the Government filed an affidavit in Court. Since the UPA government had been replaced by the NDA government, the stance that the Government would take was not certain. However, it was heartening to note that even the NDA government did not oppose the decriminalization of homosexuality.

The affidavit on behalf of the Government left it to the wisdom of the Court to decide the matter in the manner that it thought fit. There was a sting in the tail though; the affidavit stated that in case the Court was to decide any issue other than mere decriminalization (i.e. issues like gay marriage), the Government would file another affidavit in response to that.

The hearing of the case was completed on 17 July 2018. The wait for the judgement began. In complex constitutional matters, judgements are expected to take some time to be written, deliberated and discussed amongst the judges. However, Chief Justice Misra was due to retire from the Supreme Court on 2 October so the judgement had to be delivered before that time.

On 6 September, the judgement was finally delivered in a packed courtroom. The Chief Justice said that there were to be four judgements, all concurring in the outcome. As each of the judges read the judgements, the euphoria in (and outside) the Court was increasing. The judgements had not merely read down Section 377, but had proved to be a charter of rights for the LGBTQ community.

'I AM WHAT I AM'

Chief Justice Dipak Misra started his and Justice Khanwilkar's judgement by quoting the famous German poet and philosopher Arthur Schopenhauer, who said: 'I am what I am, so take me as I am.' The import of the poem, as well as that of the judgement, was to affirm the identity and individuality of members of the LGBTQ community. The thrust of the judgement of the Chief Justice was to recognize that a person of alternative sexuality had the right to choose their own partner.

In a series of earlier judgements, the Supreme Court had recognized the right of a woman to marry a man of a different caste[34] or religion.[35] This right to choose one's sexual partner was held to be part of the right to privacy and had its constitutional basis in Article 21 of the Constitution. The argument, which was accepted by the Court, was that to have the right to life implied the right to live life with dignity and autonomy. After all, it is meaningless to say that you have a right to live your life if that life is stripped of all freedom, individuality or choice. The right to life has to be meaningful and one of the most important aspects of that would be the right to live with a person of your own choosing.

Privacy and autonomy were ultimately parts or facets of the right to live with dignity. The Court had this to say about dignity:

> Dignity is that component of one's being without which sustenance of his/her being to the fullest or completest is inconceivable... The purpose of saying so is that the identity of every individual attains the quality of an individual being only if he/she has the dignity. Dignity while expressive of choice is averse to creation of any dent. When biological expression, be it an orientation or optional expression of choice, is faced with impediment, albeit through any imposition of law, the individual's natural and constitutional right is dented. Such a situation urges the conscience of the final constitutional arbiter to demolish the obstruction and remove the impediment so as to allow the full blossoming of the natural and constitutional rights of individuals.[36]

Though cast in ornate language, the passage contains the heart of the reasoning of the judgement. It basically says the following:

1. An individual has the right to live with dignity.
2. The right to dignity contains a right to make a free choice about one's self.
3. The law cannot curtail such a choice.
4. It is the obligation of the constitutional courts to ensure that any invalid restrictions on such choices are struck down.

'THE LOVE THAT DARE NOT SPEAK ITS NAME'

Justice Rohinton Nariman started his judgement by quoting the famous lines of Lord Alfred Douglas's poem 'Two Loves'. This poem was sought to be used as evidence against Oscar Wilde in his trial for gross indecency.[37] The poem is about an older man who sees two younger men, the first of whom claims to be Love, presumably between 'a boy and a girl'. The second man also calls himself Love, but is accused by the first man of not being love, but shame. At this point, the second man dejectedly says that he is not shame but love, but a 'love that dare not speak its name'. The poem, even though disavowed by Oscar Wilde, speaks of the ignominy of homosexuality that people dare not even mention its existence.

This poem captures the essence of the judgement of Justice Nariman – a judgement with rich historical context but at the same time one that looks towards the future. It is a judgement that neatly wraps its value judgements in constitutional theory and practice.

The judgement also brings out the argument that in our constitutional democracy, when ascertaining the content of any right, it is 'constitutional morality' that is the touchstone upon which any law is to be judged. The judgement holds as under:

> It must not be forgotten that Section 377 was the product of the Victorian era, with its attendant puritanical moral values. Victorian morality must give way to constitutional morality as has been recognized in many of our judgments. Constitutional morality is the soul of the Constitution, which is to be found in the Preamble of the Constitution, which declares its ideals and aspirations, and is also to be found in Part III of the Constitution, particularly with respect to those provisions which assure the dignity of the individual. Given...the right of every citizen of India to live with dignity and the right to privacy including the right to make intimate choices regarding the manner in which such individual wishes to live being protected by Articles 14, 19 and 21, it is clear that Section 377, insofar as it applies to same-sex consenting adults, demeans them by having them prosecuted instead of understanding their sexual orientation and attempting to correct centuries of the stigma associated with such persons... The fundamental rights chapter is like

> the North Star in the universe of constitutionalism in India. Constitutional morality always trumps any imposition of a particular view of social morality by shifting and different majoritarian regimes.

This elevation of constitutional morality as a legal tool finds its echoes in the other judgements in the 377 case too. Some commentators question the precise meaning of the term 'constitutional morality' and even go on to say that there is no sanction for such a concept in the explicit text of the Constitution. This ignores the fact that the Constitution is an organic document – a living text. Its meaning has to be developed and expanded with the changing times.

However, there are certain values that the Constitution always espouses. The ideas of justice, liberty, equality and fraternity contained in the Preamble and the fundamental rights chapter are just such values. They form the immutable core of the Constitution, and these values will always be enforced by the Court.

Another interesting point about Justice Nariman's judgement is the final order he passed. The judgement directed the Union of India to give the judgement 'wide publicity through the public media, which includes television, radio, print and online media at regular intervals, and initiate programmes *to reduce and finally eliminate the stigma associated with such persons*. Above all, all government officials, including and in particular police officials, and other officers of the Union of India and the States, be given periodic sensitization and awareness training of the plight of such persons in the light of the observations contained in this judgement.'

The judgement was thus forward-looking and not merely reactive. Unfortunately, however, it appears that this direction seems to have been ignored as no publicity, much less sensitization and awareness training, appears to have been undertaken by the Government since then.

DEMOCRACY IS COMING

Justice D.Y. Chandrachud used a song by Leonard Cohen to make a point about the issues in the case. The song, written by Cohen in 1992, goes a bit like this:

Democracy
It's coming through a hole in the air…
It's coming from the feel
that this ain't exactly real,
or it's real, but it ain't exactly there.

From the wars against disorder,
From the sirens night and day,
From the fires of the homeless
From the ashes of the gay:
Democracy is coming…

The precise meaning of the words is not exactly clear. One reasonable interpretation, however, is about the fact that democracy is not merely something that's imposed by a powerful state or organization. Instead, it is something that often comes through 'a hole in the air', that is, through the small acts of individuals whose lives need to change. The song seems to capture the idea of democracy as a participative concept rather than the majoritarian juggernaut that it is sometimes understood to be.[38]

The judgement is also a testament to the idea of the individual as the centre of the constitutional firmament who enables democracy through the protection and enforcement of fundamental human rights.

> Our Constitution, above all, is an essay in the acceptance of diversity. It is founded on a vision of an inclusive society which accommodates plural ways of life. The impact of Section 377 has travelled far beyond criminalizing certain acts. The presence of the provision on the statute book has reinforced stereotypes about sexual orientation. It has lent the authority of the state to the suppression of identities.

> The fear of persecution has led to the closeting of same-sex relationships. A penal provision has reinforced societal disdain…
>
> Above all, this case has had great deal to say on the dialogue about the transformative power of the Constitution. In addressing LGBT rights, the Constitution speaks – as well – to the rest of society. In recognizing the rights of the LGBTQ community, the Constitution asserts itself as a text for governance which promotes true equality. It does so by questioning prevailing notions about the dominance of sexes and genders. In its transformational role, the Constitution directs our attention to resolving the polarities of sex and binarities of gender. In dealing with these issues we confront much that polarises our society. Our ability to survive as a free society will depend upon whether constitutional values can prevail over the impulses of the time.

The above passage makes a statement as to the understanding of the interaction between an individual and the society, as well as the role of the Constitution and the Court in the course of that interaction. Each individual is an autonomous person who is entitled to live free from prejudice and inequality. Society is envisaged as a pluralistic society – one where we rejoice, rather than cower in fear of, variety and difference. It is not the role of society to make life impossible for those who stray from the norm, but instead, to be inclusive.

The Constitution is, so to say, the holy text; it does not merely confer rights on individuals but also has the power to transform the lives of oppressed people. And if the Constitution is the holy text, the judges would be the high priests. Without a sensitized and empathetic judiciary, the words of the Constitution would be empty promises. It was judicial indifference that resulted in Section 377 being retained on the statute books, and it was the clear presence of empathy that resulted in Section 377 being read down.

'HISTORY OWES AN APOLOGY'

Nowhere was the empathetic attitude of the Court as apparent as in the judgement of Justice Indu Malhotra. In the memorable concluding words of her judgement, she said this:

> History owes an apology to the members of this community and their families, for the delay in providing redressal for the ignominy and ostracism that they have suffered through the centuries. The members of this community were compelled to live a life full of fear of reprisal and persecution. This was on account of the ignorance of the majority to recognize that homosexuality is a completely natural condition, part of a range of human sexuality. The misapplication of this provision denied them the Fundamental Right to equality guaranteed by Article 14. It infringed the Fundamental Right to non-discrimination under Article 15, and the Fundamental Right to live a life of dignity and privacy guaranteed by Article 21. The LGBT persons deserve to live a life unshackled from the shadow of being 'unapprehended felons'.

This was the crux of the matter. The Court recognized that homosexuality was not some alien concept, but was part of the human condition and a normal variation of sexuality. Once sexuality is seen as an integral part of the identity of any person, to criminalize it is to dehumanize a person and to render them as a less than equal citizens. Every right that is available to an average person should also be available to a member of the LGBTQ community.

But these rights have always been there in the Constitution. What changed with this judgement was the empathy that the judges felt with the suffering and discrimination faced by the members of the community. Empathy enables a person to see the humanity in another person, and that is the first step to accord them the same rights and dignity that we show ourselves. The ability to place yourself in the shoes of another makes you understand how the shoe pinches.

CONCLUSION

Homosexual acts are no longer criminal offences as a result of the Navtej Johar judgement. It is tempting to be cynical and say that the lives of the people on the street have been largely unaffected by the judgement and that discrimination against the community is still rife. Another ground for the cynicism is the belief that the Courts cannot be consistently relied upon to rule in favour of the LGBT community when the need so arises.

What such a view fails to appreciate is that few changes in society are instantaneous. Homophobia was not built in a day and will not disappear with the flourish of a single judgement either. After all, judgements are not magic wands that make homophobes into empathetic individuals overnight. However, the moral force of the judgement will begin to chip away at the discrimination faced by the LGBTQ community.

Ultimately, however, the greatest hope for the community lies with the young. The Delhi High Court judgement made the LGBTQ community taste freedom. The Supreme Court judgement has granted the community self-confidence to come out and demand their rights. Pride marches and social gatherings, speeches and seminars across the country have seen the increased presence of out and proud youth. They are not likely to be pushed back into the closet, at least not without a fight.

Young people, using the power of social media, will change minds and attitudes of the next generation. In this interconnected world, images of LGBTQ people are no longer overwhelmingly negative. Across the world, the gay community is making strident progress. India will not be left behind.

We Will Always Be Who We Are!

KESHAV SURI

Judgement Day: 6 September 2018

It was bright and sunny as I looked out of my window. The sky was daubed in bright, beautiful hues as though to announce, 'This is a special day!' We had to go to the Supreme Court as this was the day of the judgement on Section 377. My husband, Cyril, and I were ready in record time, and reached The LaLiT New Delhi, my family-run enterprise.

I was very nervous. We had witnessed a long-drawn court case, and weren't sure if our basic rights would be returned to us, to the LGBTQ community in India. To have Cyril by my side gave me confidence. He was one of the main reasons that I stood where I did – on the precipice of history, fighting for true equality in our society. I will elaborate more on this later, but let's shift focus to the day at hand.

I, along with few close friends – Ishaan Sethi, Devdutt Pattanaik and advocate Neeha Nagpal, who wrote my writ challenging the criminalization of homosexuality, reached the Supreme Court. It is a short journey to the Court from The LaLiT, but it felt like years had passed by. We stepped out of the car, without an ounce of knowledge of what was going to transpire. But I told myself that no matter how the day went, I was who I was: a worthy human being.

Outside the courtroom, I met media persons, and they all had one question: Are you hopeful? In my mind, I knew there was no alternative. We had to win this. The arguments in Court had been powerful, and had spoken about a just and equal future. Who could say no to that? So I answered with a resounding 'yes'. I meant it. Was I anxious, I was asked. Yes, I was, but I never wavered in my conviction, believing wholeheartedly that we had the right to be equal in the eyes of the law and society.

I was supremely positive of the judgement going in favour of the LGBTQ community, and I had already planned a celebration at Kitty Su, my nightclub at the hotel. But even if that day's judgement went against us, I knew I would continue to fight for our rights till we got full equality in the country we call home. The freedom to love without the fear of persecution and judgement is a basic fundamental right. I had decided I would continue my work to make India more inclusive and to build an egalitarian world. I had my hotel and the Keshav Suri Foundation (more on that later) to ensure that marginalized communities could be aided to lead a respectable life.

We walked into the courtroom and took our place at the back. The room was packed and the atmosphere was electrifying. Outside, there were huge crowds, with journalists, community members and well-wishers filling the grounds. For a long time, I could only hear the sound of my own heart. I grabbed Cyril's hand and was utterly grateful he was there. I couldn't have done it without him and needed his support and positive vibes more than ever.

As the judgement was read out, I was stunned. It is one thing to have conviction in your dream, and quite another to experience the gratification of the same. I had known in my heart that it would be a favourable outcome, but what I hadn't expected was the kind of judgement that came out. I could hear the sighs and gasps in the quiet courtroom. I was grasping each and every word as it kept getting better, from one judgement to another. In my head I was doing somersaults. I was elated and relieved. I could have kissed everyone in Court that day, I was so happy. The verdict was delivered with such beauty and purity that it made all the struggle worth it.

The judges started with a profound quote by German philosopher Arthur Schopenhauer: 'I am what I am, so take me as I am. No one can escape from their individuality.' Even British philosopher John Stuart Mill was quoted: 'But society has now fairly got the better of individuality; and the danger which threatens human nature is not the excess, but the deficiency of personal impulses and preferences.'

It made my heart swell with joy. No one could make us ashamed any more. We didn't have to fear the law. The country's highest court was standing with us.

After all the judgements had been read, I walked out of the Court hand in hand with Cyril, relieved, ecstatic and feeling more alive than ever. Much to the delight of the shutterbugs, I kissed Cyril right on the steps of the Supreme Court. The picture made it to several front pages, including that of the *Indian Express*. In the hours following, my Twitter and Facebook feeds showcased the pride our nation felt at the Supreme Court's decision.

With mixed emotions, we headed back to The LaLiT, which was home to me. I wanted to celebrate the day with my team there, who had stood by me through the years of fighting for the rights of the LGBTQ community. The team members had always backed my ideas for awareness drives and innovative initiatives to encourage equality in society. They openly welcomed members of the LGBTQ community in the workforce and made them feel comfortable. It was finally time for celebration.

Unfortunately, my mother was not in town that day, but the

entire hotel staff was in the lobby of the hotel when Cyril and I walked in. They welcomed us with a flash mob, and a host of media channels and journalists recorded the action. The team broke into a song and dance that went viral on social media. We also hoisted the pride flag.

The celebrations continued into the evening. I had never experienced such a sense of liberation – yet the enormity of the judgement hadn't quite sunk in! It had been a long journey to get here, and the real work would now begin…

BEGINNING

I came from a privileged background, but it wasn't really all that different from the thousands of other children struggling with their sexuality. I went to an all-boys Catholic school in Delhi and was mocked for my mannerisms. I was called every name in the book. It isn't easy for a child to fathom why he is being targeted. I realized there was a perception about me being gay – even though there was no such vocabulary back then – as all the female roles in the school plays were given to me. I enjoyed playing Mother Mary and Goddess Sita as a young boy – it was my first experience with drag, with my destiny, which eventually led me to give birth to my drag alter ego, Kitty Su. Come to think of it, it was considered okay or 'natural' for my school to initiate us into cross-dressing, but it was not okay for them to accept homosexuality. Due to a lack of awareness and knowledge, most schools tend to have a homophobic stance. Mine did too, but it helped me develop a thick skin.

For my graduation, I went to Warwick, and that was probably the most closeted time of my life. I was battling with myself over my identity and also hiding it from the world. Going back, I want to give that boy a tight hug. Who knew he would come this far. Or, maybe, he always did! I then attended King's College for my master's degree. Those were better days – I had shed a lot of weight and become confident; however, it is hard to escape the impact of body-shaming if one is subjected to it for years.

Eventually, I went to the School of Oriental and African Studies (SOAS), London, for my Master of Laws degree. I think at this point I was also buying time before I returned to India, to my family. Taking that course turned out to be the best decision of my life. I felt right at home at SOAS. The experiences there opened my mind. I was ready to take on the world. What I like about being queer is that we get to choose our family; as queer people, we eventually find our tribe. I met mine at SOAS. For those who do not have family acceptance, let this be a reminder that you are not alone. Go seek the queer tribe: We are everywhere! I lost my father to a heart attack during the same time – it was a sore that will take me much longer to recover from. It was also the year I had come out to my family, and the innate sense of guilt after doing that never left me. To live with that kind of baggage is tough. With all my heart, I thank my mother and my sisters for all the support they gave me through that time.

The first few years of my work experience were basically to gain love and acceptance and prove to my team members that I was not sitting in the position I was due to privilege. Eventually, an idea took shape to start a nightclub that would provide a safe haven for people from the LGBTQ community. Thus, 'Kitty Su' was established. Over the years, the club has become a hub of thought-provoking change – the mecca of music and inclusivity. When I returned to India, I had decided that having a place like Kitty Su was important and necessary, due to many years of discrimination and lack of safe spaces for the queer community, especially in a mainstream venue like a hotel. Just like I found my tribe at SOAS, I wanted the queer youth in India to find theirs, by providing them with a safe space to be themselves.

THE TRIGGER

In 2009, the Delhi High Court decriminalized homosexuality and gave us our freedom, but in 2014 the Supreme Court Division Bench reversed that judgement and sent us back into the closet. The 2014 judgement of the Supreme Court haunted me. The words of one of the judges resonated with me for a long time and turned into my worst nightmare. He had asked who these minorities were, and called the LGBTQ community 'too miniscule to matter'.

I considered 2014 my spiritual and political awakening. The Supreme Court order couldn't be the norm. It had to be an aberration. To change the order of things, I had to do something to show this country that we mattered. I decided to raise awareness about homosexuality. I wanted people to wake up to the fact that sexual orientation was a natural state of being and not a 'bizarre' or 'sick' choice someone makes.

The first campaign to hit the ground was 'No Hate'. We used different accessories in the hotel to deliver the message. The walls were painted with slogans; coasters in restaurants were given a new look. The idea was simple. We wanted to let those who frequented us to know that hate for a community would take us nowhere. 'No Hate' was followed by the 'Straight but Not Narrow' campaign. This was about acceptance, where we wanted straight men and women to broaden their minds about the choices at hand for the LGBTQ community. This campaign also found a place in our hotels.

An incident that shook me to the core after the regressive 2014 judgement was the 2016 shooting at a gay club in Orlando in the United States by a homophobic bigot. I didn't consider myself an activist, but the killing of 49 people and wounding of another 50 set off something in me. I was shocked that something as pure as love could lead to such hatred. I decided it was time I accepted that unless we took drastic steps, such blatant hate would take over the world. Even through all the sadness, I was convinced that this could never transpire in India, but now I wanted to make sure it didn't even come close to such an incident taking place. I wanted to speak my heart out; I wanted to contribute towards changing perceptions.

I started with educating my team, as I needed them on board with my plans. We conducted several sensitization workshops across the hotels to ensure inclusivity was the norm. I began with spreading knowledge about sexual orientation and equality. Once my team was sensitized, we launched campaigns to tell people about our policies and initiatives. We started PureLove nights, where everyone was welcome. We dedicated Thursdays to promoting an inclusive environment at the hotel, where guests shared the space with members of the LGBTQ community. Our basic intent was to promote the hotel as a safe space for people from all walks of life.

We started drag shows, which are now a regular feature at Kitty Su. Our journey of intersectionality began with Violet Chachki, when she first came to perform for the sixth Kittyversary. More than 2,000 people turned up that evening. She was courageous to come over when homosexuality was still a criminal offence. Her act inspired many others, as many Indian queens who were closeted earlier began to perform regularly. Several international queens have also frequented the Kitty Su stage, and we are proud to have mainstreamed the art form in India. We also worked with other marginalized communities such as the differently abled and acid-attack survivors. We hosted powerwalks for acid-attack survivors and offered them internships and jobs. We also aided their surgeries and helped fund their dream projects. In May 2017, DJ Aamish, at the time India's only wheelchair-bound DJ, became a Resident Kitten. Kitty Su was thus gradually established as a haven.

I want to take this opportunity to talk about my team member Maahi. The name she had been given at birth was Humza. Humza joined our workforce at Kitty Su as an associate in 2014. Soon after, he confided in his colleagues that he wanted to undergo a gender transition. I am proud to say that he found the environment at The LaLiT safe enough to make one of the most difficult decisions of his life. Our endeavour to encourage The LaLiT staff to accept colleagues and guests without the bias of sexual orientation seemed to have worked. Humza felt confident that he would receive the support of his team.

As Humza's transition to Maahi began in 2016, he didn't once waver in his decision or develop a fear of society. His family was repulsed when he confided in them. They beat him up and things escalated to the point where he began to receive death threats. Without a support system in his family, The LaLiT took their place for Humza. During that period, I learnt what it meant to be treated with hormones, what it took to transition. Apart from the obvious risks that are associated with any treatment, hormone therapy induces changes in an individual's body. For instance, it aids the growth of breasts in trans women and prompts facial hair growth in trans men. Further, it is a mental battle for patients as they try to adjust to these changes.

During this challenging time for Maahi, we supported her financially and emotionally. We also learnt a lot through her. Her struggles prompted us to promote our inclusivity practices on a bigger scale. Time is the biggest healer, and as it progressed, Maahi found acceptance with her family. She has since moved on from The LaLiT, but she taught me an incredibly important lesson in life. Even in our darkest days, we should not stop loving ourselves and believing in ourselves. Today, there are more than 12 trans men and women, and more than 100 queer team members at The LaLiT, across functions and roles. I am proud of this army that we have!

One action led to another, and I realized I could contribute to this awakening among the masses. The truth is that heterosexual love isn't the only kind of romantic and sexual love that exists. It was this thought that gave birth to the PureLove campaign at The LaLiT in September 2017. All our initiatives to bring the LGBTQ community into the mainstream were part of this campaign. 'PureLove' meant we offered unconditional love, without judgement.

We started hiring people extensively from the LGBTQ community as representation is important. Depression is high among members of the community and one of the primary reasons for it is the inability to lead a normal life. Jobs and financial security are denied to people on the basis of their sexual orientation. The right to earn a livelihood is universal, and one should not be denied the same based on caste, colour, creed or sexual orientation. Helping marginalized groups find jobs was one of the biggest challenges I faced. The LaLiT welcomed marginalized and oppressed communities with open arms, and 'all-inclusive' became our primary mantra, though inclusiveness for me was never restricted to the LGBTQ community. We also built gender-neutral washrooms across our hotels, for guests as well as the staff. We encouraged our employees to take the LaLiT Equality Pledge, which states 'Respect for All'. I was thrilled to find that my team was proud of our zero-tolerance policy towards discrimination.

The efforts of The LaLiT were slowly catching on, and many reputed organizations and individuals floated proposals to join the fight for equal rights of marginalized communities. It took a lot of effort and several gender sensitization workshops, but The LaLiT had the distinction of being the only Indian hotel chain in an elite list of 32 global companies to endorse the United Nations' LGBTQ standards. Today, there are almost 300 such companies.

Our unrelenting pursuit of equal rights impressed the Saksham Trust for Pride in Chandigarh. We joined hands with the Trust for the pride parade in Chandigarh in 2018. This was the first instance when a corporate entity came on board as a partner for a pride parade.

Hope becomes a crucial element when talking about marginalized communities. In order to raise spirits, we constantly tried to bring on board successful individuals from marginalized sections of society to inspire others. Chef Chris Trapani was one such inspirational figure. The celebrated chef and champion of LGBTQ rights flew down to India and shared his experiences with an audience at The LaLiT. As the first transgender chef to appear on American television, Chef Tripani spoke about transitioning from a female to a male, and inspired all by sharing anecdotes on running a successful food truck company. We also set up a Mediclaim initiative for the LGBTQ community. Regular interactions with them had made me realize the need for a change in insurance policies, and we went all out to make it happen.

I am particularly proud of The Elphie Books series for children commissioned by The LaLiT. Through this series, we targeted the written medium and collaborated with content creators. The purpose of these books was to help mould the minds of the younger generation, and make them aware of the ideas of respect, equality and inclusivity. Elphie is a rainbow-coloured, gender-agnostic character who faces challenges on the path of understanding and acceptance. Shaping the thoughts of the next generation can go a long way in changing perceptions in society.

INSPIRATION

Having someone to look up to makes one's journey easier. Through the course of my life, I have met several people who have motivated me. Their stories have given me the confidence to pursue my dreams and accept myself.

Cyril has been a big inspiration for me. In 2014, he and I had known each other for five years, and were beginning to understand each other, but didn't know where our relationship was headed. Marriage was clearly not on the cards. As the years passed, our relationship grew from strength to strength, but we were still circling around the 'M' word. I hadn't filed the Writ Petition yet. We were happy and 'gay', and I was constantly trying to drill it into Cyril's head that we didn't need a certificate; our love didn't need a licence. And, more importantly, it was not legal in India. Cyril said to me, 'It is illegal in *your* country, not mine!'

This remark opened up a Pandora's box. Cyril loves India, but I couldn't challenge the fact that our love made us criminals in my country. It made me think deeply about our relationship and about the LGBTQ status in India. But Cyril pushed me further. He wanted me to acknowledge the fact that complaining wasn't getting us anywhere. It's not like I was doing anything to change our status.

I was defensive. What about all the initiatives I had undertaken at The LaLiT to spread the message of inclusivity? What about Kitty Su, where we regularly hosted events to bring the plight of the LGBTQ community forward? PureLove nights had been one of the biggest success stories, and I was proud of the drag nights. But Cyril wanted me to look beyond The LaLiT. What had I done to change anything at the national level? I was living in a cocoon happy in the thought that my efforts at The LaLiT would bring about a change in the mindsets of people across the country. This hit me really hard. I promised myself that I would look beyond The LaLiT. So I started attending conferences and visiting other corporates to steer them towards inclusivity for the LGBTQ community.

In August and September 2017, Cyril and I met lawyers and finally decided to file the writ. The other part of the story also had a happy ending. Cyril gave me an ultimatum that December: We either got married or broke up. So, of course, we flew to Paris in June 2018, had the most beautiful ceremony, and I got myself a husband I will love and cherish for life.

Cyril and I wanted to spend this huge moment in our lives with our immediate family and close friends. We went to Goa in November 2018. The timing couldn't have been better. There were dual celebrations for our nuptials and the Supreme Court finally striking down Section 377, recognizing that loving someone wasn't a crime, irrespective of sexual orientation. Our wedding celebrations were an intimate affair with a lot of meaning, not only for us but also for our loved ones who had witnessed our journey over 10 years. Our families are very important to us, and they were all there to share the most beautiful day of our lives. Our respective sisters walked us down the aisle, with one of them playing the dhol. The ceremony was officiated by our mothers, along with India's first ever transgender high priestess. Cyril and I exchanged vows on the beach with the sunset in the background, and there were happy tears all around. The night after the wedding, my family had organized a drag night, with all of us in our best drag outfits, reliving the '80s! I performed a dance with my mother. As she smiled and danced elegantly with me, I realized how fortunate I was. To get the kind of love, support and blessings Cyril and I have received is not something we will ever take for granted.

It may be a cliché, but I wouldn't be here without my mother and three sisters. They say that parents love their children unconditionally but it surely can't come easy. My mother, Dr Jyotsna Suri, has always been by my side. In my hour of need, in my darkest hours, she has stood by me like a rock and helped me through troubled waters. My work and approach to conventional living didn't bother her. She wanted nothing more than my happiness and accepted me just as I was.

My mother's acceptance wasn't just of me, her son, but also of the cause, the movement. She pushed and supported my every endeavour and worked towards my inclusive ideology. She is my icon, and the centre of my calm. And then there is my band of sisters – Divya, Shradha and Deeksha. They have been a part of every major decision in my life, and I wouldn't have had the strength to embrace and love myself if I didn't have their unconditional love. While I couldn't be happier in my personal life, it does not escape me that everyone isn't as lucky. In India, you cannot be with someone you love even though Section 377 has been struck down recently. Gay marriage is still a far-off dream as the Indian legal system does not yet recognize same-sex marriages.

I was supremely impressed by the petitioners in the first Writ Petition filed in the Supreme Court: Navtej Johar, Sunil Mehra, Aman Nath, Ritu Dalmia and Ayesha Kapur. They understood their position as influencers in society, and had decided to use it for the larger community. But the first petitioner against Section 377 was Anjali Gopalan, a human rights and animal rights activist, and the founder of the Naz Foundation, an NGO dedicated to fight HIV/AIDS in India. The Naz Foundation filed a writ against Section 377 in 2001. She led the cause when few thought about it. A powerhouse of energy, she continues to be a source of inspiration and support to many.

Navtej Singh Johar, a Sangeet Natak Akademi awardee and Bharatanatyam dancer, was the first to take the plunge in 2014. Highly skilled and respected in the LGBTQ community, he wanted to be the voice of change. Sunil Mehra, a senior journalist, storyteller and yoga instructor at Studio Abhyas, joined the fight for basic human liberties with his partner Navtej. Celebrity chef Ritu Dalmia also decided to become a voice for change in India. Ayesha Kapur was a successful businesswoman. The co-founder and co-chairman of the Neemrana Hotels, Aman Nath, was a mate from the same industry. It was an added benefit that I had known him for most of my life. I looked up to him in a lot of ways and drew inspiration from his choices. Together, we have been comrades-in-arms in our fight for the cause.

THE IMPACT

I launched the Keshav Suri Foundation with a mission to empower and bring into the mainstream the LGBTQ community. For the launch event, 'Queering the Pitch', we collaborated with the Federation of Indian Chambers of Commerce and Industry (FICCI) to reach out to corporates and a larger audience. This tie-up would never have been possible before the judgement, but now a door was open.

Since its inception, the Foundation has been working tirelessly to raise awareness about the plight of the LGBTQ community. We also have on board counsellors who help individuals and families during the tricky phase of their coming out, and any other psychological support they need as they navigate their sexuality.

Raising awareness, though, is only the first step. The Foundation also works closely with members of the community to empower and aid their quest of being incorporated into mainstream society. Financial independence is the first step towards this goal. It may be miniscule, but we are offering scholarships to transgender students at our hospitality school. We want people to stand on their feet, and we want to do our best to help as many people as possible earn a respectful livelihood. At The LaLiT we have hired, worked with and skilled more than 100 queer people, and Kitty Su continues to be the only platform to have mainstreamed drag.

WHAT NEXT?

I have always felt that love is too beautiful to be hidden in a closet. We have still not destroyed the boundaries but, thanks to the Supreme Court judgement in 2018, we have surely blurred them. Each step we take towards an equal society helps blur the boundaries between 'us' and 'them'. It's taken time, the blood and sweat of thousands of people, uncountable hours in courtrooms, but the verdict made me and countless others *free*. I am no longer labelled a criminal for the purest of acts: LOVE. It is strange that a country that is home to the

Kama Sutra took so long to grant LGBTQ people their basic civil liberties. But now I no longer have to live under the fear of being falsely prosecuted by the law. We no longer have to wake up feeling like criminals. One can't imagine the toll this law has taken on the mental health of the LGBTQ community and their families.

The sixth of September 2018 will always be celebrated as a day of pride in India. Chief Justice Dipak Misra's iconic words from his landmark verdict have laid the foundation for an inclusive society. But we have only just scratched the surface, and there are miles to go before we sleep. The battle ahead is more personal and complicated. It is a battle for acceptance, for equal rights. The challenge now is to change individual perceptions. A law or government ruling can't force the society into acceptance. Women fought a long time for equal rights, and continue to do so.

One big thing the verdict helped us with, though, was acceptance *within*. The story of Dutee Chand is a powerful one. She is an incredible talent on the Indian athletics circuit and has already fought a long battle to compete as a woman because of her androgen levels. The Supreme Court verdict helped her come out of the closet. She became the first Indian athlete to acknowledge being in a same-sex relationship. It requires immense guts to tell the world the truth, especially for someone coming from a rural background. Dutee's status as a role model will inspire many to do the same. Her rural roots also helped spread the story beyond the tier I, II and III cities. We hit the regional masses with her revelation, and that is the next step – we need to penetrate the masses and not let the narrative be restricted to the elite and urban communities.

There has been a tremendous amount of support in the last few years, but it is still too early to gauge the impact of decriminalizing homosexuality. Further, a lot needs to change when it comes to marriage, health care, family care, adoption, inheritance and property rights for LGBTQ people. That is where change is needed next.

While the courtroom battle was essential and got the ball rolling, the real one begins now. Our struggle moves from the bedroom, as it were, to the kitchens and the boardrooms. The Supreme Court in its verdict asked for respect for the LGBTQ community, and highlighted the freedom of choice. If basic civil liberties are granted to the LGBTQ community, then the next logical step is economic freedom. LGBTQ people need equal opportunities in jobs, and should not be rejected on the basis of their sexual orientation.

To ensure inclusion comes to the corporate sector, we have set up the Diversity and Inclusion (D&I) Task Force in collaboration with FICCI. For the first time ever, FICCI has opened its doors to two openly queer people as chairs for this purpose – Radhika Piramal and me. With a threefold agenda – gender diversity, inclusion of people with disabilities, and notable representation from the LGBTQIA+ community, the D&I Task Force is sure to bring a positive change into the corporate world.

I strongly feel corporate India needs to step up to empower the community and bring it into the mainstream. The LaLiT has been supporting job fairs like RISE and Q-rious to help more and more LGBTQ youth to get employment. My foundation has also collaborated with Stonewall UK and Pride Circle to bring the Workplace Equality Index to India. These are small but strong steps and I am sure they will go a long way in bringing about economic equality.

The most important and trickiest of all, though, is the right to marry the person you love. Marriage equality is critical when one mentions choice. If you are given the freedom to choose your partner, then you should have the freedom to share the most beautiful day of your life with them too. I can personally vouch for the intimate joy that is experienced when saying 'I do' to the person you love. Unfortunately, I couldn't do it in my own country. I had the means to get what I wanted, but not many can do the same. It is going to be a challenge, one that is perhaps even tougher than the last. But I have hope and faith. I plan to continue my fight to be regarded as an ordinary citizen enjoying every fundamental right that the Constitution gives me.

I Am a Chef Who Happens to Be a Lesbian

RITU DALMIA

Perhaps our greatest distinction as a species is our capacity, unique among animals, to make counter-evolutionary choices.

– Jared Diamond

There are certain scenes from my childhood that stay with me till today. They are of the time that everyone called me a boy. I remember how happy it made me feel, although I did not understand why I felt this way.

I don't remember ever playing with dolls, although Barbie dolls were quite the rage then. Wearing skirts and dresses was always a struggle, and I used to fight with my mother when she wanted me to wear them. She could not understand why a 10-year-old was not interested in dolls or pretty frocks. I had short hair, loved stealing my brother's clothes, wore flat shoes, and my aunts would say, 'How unladylike.'

My brother would tease me and laugh when I was with my girlfriends; he called us 'lesbians' and 'Sita aur Gita'. I would giggle right back, not understanding what his remarks meant. Now, when I look back, I guess he had reasons to do so, for I would wait by the phone for hours for my best friend to call, and when she was over at our house, I did not want anyone else around us.

As I grew older, my attachment to women started bothering me. I started dating men; I would go out with them and sleep with them. I grew my hair and wore a salwar kameez every day. I wasn't quite sure why I was doing all this; all I knew was that I did not want anyone to call me a 'dyke', a word that people would use quite often to tease me.

Thankfully, this phase did not last long. After about a year of trying to be something I was not, I decided that I didn't care what others thought of me; I would do what felt right to me. I knew I was very comfortable with my womanhood, and I did not need to prove myself to anyone or try and fit into a stereotype.

But I regret my behaviour during this phase of my life; in fact, it has been my biggest regret. For instance, I did things like sleeping with men not because I was in love with them but because I was too afraid to see the truth: I was running away from myself. It took me time to understand why I had done the things I'd done.

***

I've been asked when I realized I was a lesbian. In a way it is strange when people ask you that, because it is not like you just wake up one day and discover your sexuality. When I look back now, I realize that the clues had been there all along. I've already shared with you some childhood memories. When I was a teenager, I used to write poems about girls I had crushes on, and I remember aching over a friend who had stopped talking to me. I must have been experiencing my first love, except that I did not have the vocabulary for my feelings. Growing up in Delhi in the '80s, I did not know any gay women, nor were there movies or books to help me, so I had no reference point or a way to figure out what I was feeling.

I was 23 when I met my future partner, a client at my restaurant. The first time I met her, my heart raced, I was dizzy and I knew then that I had met my Waterloo. Soon after, I had to move to London for my work, while she continued to live in Delhi. I remember staying up every night aching for her. I did not know how to define what I felt for her; all I knew was that my phone bills nearly led me to bankruptcy, and whenever I came back home I would spend every minute with her!

Finally, when we both mustered up enough courage to voice what we felt, it was like a dam of emotions had just burst open. I embraced what I felt, and found myself in a same-sex relationship. I was happy and accepted it. I finally felt good enough about myself to be my authentic self. I stopped worrying about what anyone thought about my identity and whom I loved and had sex with. It was an unfamiliar sense of happiness, a sense of relief, a sense of freedom.

My close friends knew about my relationship, but it was very important that my parents knew about it as well. I was financially independent and emotionally strong. I was not looking for their acceptance or approval, but I needed to share with them that I was happy, that I had found someone whom I loved and who loved me back. I told my mother about the woman in my life casually over a meal one day, and did not get any reaction whatsoever; in fact, she was very quiet. She did not talk to anyone for two days and then, on the third day, a box of mangoes was sent to my partner. This was her way of telling us that she was happy for us.

My father, on the other hand, never talked to me about it although he knew about my relationship from my mother. He always made an effort to speak with my partner whenever she was over. This was the only way he knew how to react. My dad passed away two years ago, and although he never mustered up the courage to speak about it, I knew he had accepted my truth.

We continued our long-distance relationship for three years. Then, I came back to Delhi to be with my beloved in 2000. And life changed. When I was living alone in London, we had the freedom to be ourselves with each other. I would not get awkward when I held her hand in public, for instance. Delhi, on the other hand, was a completely a different story. Homosexuality was a criminal offence in India. We were not free to love each other.

It made me very sad that I had to be careful expressing affection for my partner in public in ways that I did not have to worry about when I was with a man. I had never thought twice about holding hands or being affectionate with a man when I identified as straight. Now when I was out anywhere with my girl friend, I always had to think if we were in a place safe enough to even hold hands. Could I call her 'honey' when we were in a store without getting any strange looks? I hoped that this reality would change in my lifetime, but it seemed impossible at the time.

A dismal fact of being gay in India is that women are more closeted then men. I was running a restaurant in Delhi and we saw many male couples coming in for a meal, but seeing two women together was a rarity. (Yes, I can spot two women or men who are 'together'!)

It is a common belief that it is much easier for two women to be together than it is for two men. But I believe the reverse is true. I feel women have more difficulty accepting their sexuality than men do, and social conditioning makes things tougher for them. So it's harder for women to come out. I have met many men who lead double lives, who married to please their families, and live secret lives with their male lovers.

Strangely, 'lesbian' has always been a dirty word. Our society is patriarchal and declaring yourself a lesbian is basically saying that you don't need a man, and that goes against everything we have been taught. The protection of a man, starting from fathers and brothers and moving on to husbands, has been given paramount importance. So to be a 'lesbian' is sacrilege to all that Indian society stands for.

When my partner and I started living together in Delhi, we could hear a lot of whispering around us, well, behind our backs.

I trained myself to rise above this. I was not going to let it bother me. But then came the time to face some practical problems, for example, when I took on a life insurance cover and wanted to name my partner as my beneficiary. I was not allowed to do that; only a spouse or blood relative could be a beneficiary, I was told. Then, we wanted to open a joint account for running our home but oops, we couldn't do that either. Over time, we had many properties which belonged to us jointly, and our business was together, yet there were no clear methods to protect each other's rights and assets.

These were small issues that bothered me. Still, I was oblivious to the law and did not care about it; how did it matter to me? I was safe, living in my own world, where my friends and family accepted and even celebrated who I was. To them, my partner was just that – my partner, someone I loved and who loved me back, and gender didn't change anything.

In 2008, I was introduced to a group of lesbians by a friend. These women were involved in the first pride march in Delhi. They casually mentioned that it would be nice if I came and marched with them. A part of me wanted to go so badly but another part of me was petrified. I was already a well-known chef in the country and I did not want to be labelled. My partner was dead against it, yet something in me just wanted to be a part of that march.

I finally went with two straight friends, and loved it. It was the first time I saw so many people from the LGBTQ community gathered together. Of course, the next day I was on the first page of the newspapers. But maybe the march was also the beginning of a change within me.

This newspaper article caused a lot of trouble on the home front. And suddenly, all my colleagues at work looked at me differently. My partner was still not out, and she was very upset about her family and friends joining the dots. I had the media calling me not to ask for my favourite recipe but to ask who I was sleeping with. I had never been closeted but, at the same time,

I was not going around wearing a T-shirt saying 'I like women'. I was a chef who happened to be a lesbian, not a lesbian who happened to be a chef!

I was stressed and upset, yet at the same time there was something in me that had woken up. Around this time, I met two women from Jharkhand who had been beaten black and blue by their parents for being in love. Another young girl had been molested by relatives so that she could be 'cured' of her lesbianism. Suddenly, the rules of the society started mattering to me.

Funnily enough, during this time I saw a movie called *If These Walls Could Talk* about two women who have lived their lives together, and when one of them passes away, the other has no right on their property; she is not even able to make medical decisions about her lover. I bawled like a baby that night, terrified and wondering if that is where my partner and I were heading.

I knew I had to do something, however small; I needed to do my bit. It started with donating money for the case that was being fought in the Delhi High Court by the Naz Foundation, and just keeping myself abreast of what was happening around me, rather than living in my safe and sheltered life, oblivious to the reality of the LGBTQ community in India.

Today, when I think about it, I was very lucky that I could accept my sexuality, for my partner had a much harder time doing so. At that time, I could not understand why she felt uncomfortable, but I think I am a lot wiser today and believe each one has their own personal journey in this matter, and there is no right or wrong. However, when the law is also against it, it just makes it that much harder.

Our relationship couldn't take the strain that we had been experiencing, and my partner and I eventually separated in 2011. Yet, my mother still has her own relationship with her. She, who never even finished middle school, and came from a very conservative Marwari background, accepted her daughter's choice and was even happy about it. On the other hand, I know of so many friends whose parents are educated and liberal in their thinking, and have gay friends, yet struggle to accept their own child's sexuality.

* * *

In July 2009, the Delhi High Court passed a judgement decriminalizing homosexuality. Suddenly, my restaurants were full of same-sex couples, no longer afraid. Between 2009 and 2013, I met more gay people than I had in my whole life, all was well, and over the next few years I forgot all about Section 377. I started having more and more people from the LGBTQ community applying for work at my restaurants; they were no longer fearful of being persecuted. Soon we had a basketball team, which later grew into a cricket team, and all was well with our world.

In December 2013, however, the Supreme Court overruled the 2009 judgement. We were all criminals once again – the Court declared that homosexuality was a crime. All the happy same-sex couples who were out and about went deep into their closets once again. I was angry, helpless and frustrated. I did not know what I could do to help the situation.

Around the same time, I was introduced to Menaka Guruswamy and Arundhati Katju for another legal matter of mine. Soon they were not just my lawyers but also my friends. One day in 2015, Menaka and I found ourselves on a flight back from Goa, and we started talking about Section 377. She suddenly asked me how I would feel about being a petitioner. One statement that Justice Singhvi had made, which had shocked everyone, was that 'he had never met a gay person in his life'. So far all the petitioners were NGOs, school teachers and parents; there was not a single gay or a lesbian who had filed the petition.

I said yes right away, without thinking. I was very angry at that point in my life. On the one hand, I was being asked by the Government to come and receive various honours bestowed upon me for the work I was doing as a chef, and yet at the same time they were making me a criminal. I felt terrible at this hypocritical charade. I could be arrested for just being me and wanting to love a woman. I could no longer sit on the fence – I really felt that I had to take a stand.

When I spoke about this plan with my family and friends, everyone begged me not to do it. I was told: 'Support them financially, but don't put your name to it...do you realize you are declaring yourself a criminal?' Someone else said to me: 'You are running a business and you are on a board of directors, this may not go too well for you.'

I turned to Ella, a dear friend – and now my partner – for advice. Ella had always encouraged me to embrace my sexuality and be open about it. She was very blunt with me. 'You have been moaning and complaining about the law in the country for years, and now that the time has come, either you do something about it, or don't ever complain again.' My decision was made. I am many things, but a coward I am not.

There had to be a certain number of petitioners and I started calling everyone I knew to see if they would file this petition with us. It was unbelievable to see how much fear people had. No one was willing to join the petition and it was all due to fear. Ayesha Kapur, my colleague at work and also a very dear friend, was a rare woman who agreed to file the petition with me. Today, if I respect anyone, I respect her: She had not come out to her father, being an extremely private person, yet she understood what this meant and took it on without caring about the consequences. That took a lot of courage and I really admire her for that as I know how difficult it was for her.

The next two years were strange for me. I had a constant barrage of nasty messages being posted on my Twitter account. Up till now, I was only used to getting fan mail, and to read such hateful messages really threw me off balance. I had the word 'lesbian' sprayed on my car window, a stone was hurled at me, a man spat at me at the Delhi airport in front of everyone... I was no longer the darling chef of the country but the dirty lesbian who had the cheek to file this petition.

Yet, on the other hand, I received so many amazing letters, notes from boys and girls from all over the country thanking me and hoping one day they too would be able to come out of the closet. At one point, all this also became overwhelming. For instance, I had strangers writing to me telling me that they were contemplating suicide because they could not live with their homosexuality, and I was not ready to take on this kind of responsibility.

Yes, there were times when I regretted my decision, when I wondered if I had acted foolishly. There was this whole country full of LGBTQ people: Why did I have to be the one to do this? I wondered whether I was being foolish like my friends and family had told me. Perhaps I should have taken an easier route and supported the movement by giving financial assistance without putting myself out there, open to attack and abuse. The strange part was that after a few agonizing hours of self-doubt, I always arrived at the same answer: I had done the right thing by filing the petition, and if I didn't do anything I had no right to complain, like Ella had said to me.

Finally, the hearing was scheduled in July 2018. I was in Mumbai but I was not going to miss this for anything, so I cancelled all my travel plans and was in Court every morning sharp at ten.

The next few days were very emotional for me, hearing Menaka Guruswamy and Saurabh Kirpal present their arguments. Through each hearing, I sat there laughing and crying at the same time. It was very moving and extremely emotional to be there in Court each day. When Menaka gave her closing statement, I do not think there was a single dry eye in the entire courtroom. This case was not about an absurd and irrelevant law; it was about people whose lives were being affected on a daily basis, and the brilliant team of lawyers managed to show that to the panel of judges who were thankfully sensitive and receptive.

There was hope again, and I dared to have faith in our judiciary once more. There was the legal aspect to the case but more than that there was a human aspect, and the legal team fighting for us were speaking for each and every member of the LGBTQ community. We were fighting for our right to be treated like everyone else and not be declared criminals because of whom we chose to love. The fight felt bigger than me – than all of us. We weren't just fighting for ourselves but for thousands that feared persecution because they dared to love someone of the same sex.

6 September 2018: It was 6 a.m. in London – where I was on work – when the judgement was read out in the Supreme Court of India. I was stunned, shocked and so happy that my jaw started hurting because I just could not get rid of my smile.

When I had decided to file this petition, I truly did not believe that I would see a change happening in my lifetime. And on this day, two years after filing the petition, history was finally being rewritten. I am not an activist and never wanted to be one; yet for me this was my life's biggest accomplishment and nothing else in my life had ever given me this sense of pride.

In the months after the judgement, I had chefs working with me who had the courage to come out to me. I would get stopped by strangers on the road to tell me that they had embraced their sexuality after the judgement. Parents thanked me for changing their views and helping them accept their children's choices. Chocolates and gifts started pouring in at my restaurants with thank-you notes… I had done this for myself, for my pride and for my dignity, without even realizing the impact it would have on people.

Just the other day, I was reading about Dutee Chand, the fastest Indian sprinter, who came out of the closet recently and in one of her interviews said that the judgement of September 2018 helped her overcome her fears and come out gay and proud. Now something like this is what needs to be marvelled at: She is a young girl from a small village in Odisha, and a national star. If someone like her has found the courage to declare that she is a lesbian, as a result of that incredible day in the Supreme Court and the striking down of Section 377, I believe there is a lot of hope for change in the coming years.

We all need to do our bit to help make the inclusion of gay people into the mainstream easier. We need to feel safe, whether in our homes, workplaces or society at large. We shouldn't be treated as lesser beings because of whom and how we love. I think what everyone wants is not to be treated differently. The LGBTQ community needs to just feel like everyone else. They want to work, pay their taxes and just live normal lives. But for that to happen the community needs the same opportunities as everyone else and not be discriminated against because of their sexual orientation. I have always said that there should not be any discrimination on the basis of sex, religion and also sexual orientation. But that also means that there shouldn't be any special status either and that everyone should be treated in the same way.

Today, we have come a long way from the time when we were treated like criminals for just loving whom we did. But while we have been successful in getting Section 377 struck down, we still have a long way to go before everyone from the LGBTQ community in India feels safe and equal to all.

As I write this, I cannot help but smile to myself, feeling proud and content knowing I had a tiny role to play in this change.

Transgender Rights and Wrongs

JUSTICE M.B. LOKUR

Why did the Beatles sing 'Sweet Loretta Martin thought she was a woman, but she was another man'? Did they have a transgender person in mind or did they feel it had a nice ring to it? No one knows for sure today, except perhaps Paul and Ringo.

Now, decades later, the rights of transgender people in India are quite the focus of discussion. A significant decision was taken by the Supreme Court in 2014,[1] and there was expectation and hope that the judgement would be implemented in letter and spirit. Unfortunately, it seems that some of that hope has been dashed by the passage of the Transgender Persons (Protection of Rights) Act, 2019.

Looking back, how did the issue of the rights of transgender people even reach the court? And, looking ahead, how has the Supreme Court's Transgender Persons Act of 2019 impacted the previous decision of 2014? Further, what is still needed to bring the transgender community into the mainstream? We have answers for a few questions, but there are other questions on this subject for which there are as yet no meaningful answers. A legal perspective is certainly necessary, but that is not the only manner of looking at transgender rights and concerns.

A broad-based social process, including one of integration, must be set in motion for the desired results. To achieve these results, society in general and the Government in particular must take a few forward steps, otherwise transgender people will regress to where they were in the times of the Ramayana and the Mahabharata, and 'get back to where you once belonged' will become a cruel reality.

* * *

The National Legal Services Authority (NALSA) is undoubtedly the most important statutory body for providing legal aid and services to disadvantaged, underprivileged and marginalized sections of our society. The NALSA Annual Report of 2018 records that a large number of deserving persons have benefited through its various schemes. The beneficiaries include persons in custody, and women in need of legal assistance. There is a category of 'others' (unspecified beneficiaries), and during the year, almost 2,00,000 such persons have benefited including, I would imagine, many transgender persons.

Parliament enacted the Legal Services Authorities Act, 1987 and Section 3 thereof constituted the Central Authority, of which the Chief Justice of India is the Patron-in-Chief and, usually, a judge of the Supreme Court is the Executive Chairman. Of course, there are other members too. The Government of India has constituted the National Legal Services Authority to exercise the powers and perform the functions conferred on, or assigned to, the Central Authority under the Act.

One of the more important functions of the Central Authority is to initiate social justice litigation of special concern to the weaker sections of society. The first such litigation initiated by NALSA related to the protection of the fundamental rights of abandoned and destitute women/widows in Vrindavan, Uttar Pradesh, and to prevent abandonment by their children/relatives.[2]

Why did NALSA decide to take up the cause of transgender persons? No record for the decision is available in the public domain. But an intelligent guess would lead to the conclusion that NALSA was of opinion that transgender persons constitute 'weaker sections' of society in that they too are deprived of their fundamental rights, which are ordinarily available to males and females. The more significant of these fundamental rights include equal treatment under the law (Article 14) and the right to a life of dignity (Article 21).

Because of their circumstances, transgender people are often shunned or disowned by their family and friends, denied participation in social and cultural events, and denied access to education, health services and public spaces. Certain other rights are also denied or restricted, such as the right to marry, denial of equal livelihood opportunities such as through employment, obtaining something as uncomplicated as a driving licence or possessing an identity card, and so on. The right to vote and contest elections as a transgender person is legally possible, but very hard to execute in actual practice.

Therefore, transgendered individuals are faced with not only a denial of their fundamental rights under Articles 14 and 21 of the Constitution but also a denial of fundamental rights under Articles 15 (prohibition of discrimination on grounds of religion, race, caste, sex or place of birth) and 16 (equality of opportunity in matters of public employment) of the Constitution.

Effectively, transgendered people are not entitled, as a matter of right, to equal treatment as men and women only because of their circumstances. This has resulted in the disempowerment of the transgender community and led to them being a deprived section of society. To right this social wrong seems to be the reason NALSA has addressed the issues confronted by transgender people in general.

While the concern of NALSA is certainly worthy of emulation, what was the material before it to come to a prima facie conclusion that transgender persons needed its umbrella protection? NALSA had a few historical events to back up its claims for the intervention by the Supreme Court. It appears that transgender persons could be registered as voters in the category of 'hijras' by the Election Commission of India; from 1994, they could vote as males or females but still not as transgendered people.

For the first time in 1999, a transgender person named Kamala Jaan broke the glass ceiling, as it were, and contested an election, though as a male. She was elected as the mayor of Katni in Madhya Pradesh. But her election was set aside in 2003 by the Madhya Pradesh High Court on the grounds that the seat was reserved for a woman candidate, while Kamala Jaan was registered as a male, although she referred to herself as a female.[3]

Soon after, in 2000, a transgendered person named Shabnam Mousi contested an election as a female. She was elected to the State Assembly in a by-election from Suhagpur in Madhya Pradesh.[4,5] However, her entry into and participation in the State Assembly was anything but comfortable. It is said that one Radha Krishna Malviya sarcastically asked for her gender, and she responded by asking him 'Tu bata, tu Radha haiki Krishan hai?' (Tell me, are you Radha or Krishna?). A biopic called *Shabnam Mausi* was produced on her life in 2007.

A similar ignominy awaited two other transgender individuals – Asha Devi and Kamala Kinnar. Asha Devi was elected as a mayor in Gorakhpur, Uttar Pradesh, but was ousted in 2003 as the post was reserved for a woman.[6] Kamala Kinnar was elected as a mayor in 2009 in Sagar, Madhya Pradesh, but was unseated in 2011 as the seat was reserved for a woman belonging to the Scheduled Caste category.[7] When the 'third gender' was eventually recognized as a result of the decision of the Supreme Court in 2014 on the petition filed by NALSA, yet another transgender, Madhu Kinnar, was elected as the mayor of Raigarh (Chhattisgarh) in early 2015[8] in the sex category of 'other'.[9]

In addition, NALSA had well-researched documentation for establishing that transgendered people were discriminated against, and had occasion to suffer social ignominy. Some of these articles were personal experiences. Included in the materials placed before the Court was an Issue Brief of December 2010 by the United Nations Development Programme (UNDP) titled 'Hijras/Transgender Women in India: HIV, Human Rights and Social Exclusion'.

Amid the gloomy scenario facing the transgender community, NALSA had available with it some positive steps taken by Tamil Nadu and Karnataka for the benefit of transgendered people. For example, Tamil Nadu has formulated welfare schemes for them, including free sex reassignment surgery. A database of transgendered people was created to assist in the management of their requirements such as housing, ration cards, voter identity cards and health facilities.

In fact, a welfare board was constituted for transgendered people, with official and non-official members. One of the functions of the board is to 'formulate and implement welfare programme for providing social security and status to the Transgender in the State of Tamil Nadu'. In Karnataka, transgender individuals were eligible to avail of reservation in government and public sector employment and, in fact, insurance companies provided employment to some as recovery agents. Even the Karnataka High Court employed a transgender in a Group D post commensurate with her qualifications.

NALSA also had with it legislation from the United Kingdom, Australia, the European Union, United States and South Africa. Case law from the United States and the European Union was also available. In other words, enough material was ready with NALSA to approach the Court to grant relief to the transgender community, equal protection and basic rights as are or have been made available to male and female citizens of other countries, and to recognize transgender people as a third category for all practical purposes, including for education and employment.

Armed with substantial relevant material for making out a case for relief to the transgender community, NALSA preferred a Writ Petition in the Supreme Court under Article 32 of the Constitution.[10] The Writ Petition was admitted for hearing on 1 October 2012.

Public Interest Litigation (PIL) in India is not treated as adversarial, primarily since it is entertained in public interest. This has been the view of the Supreme Court at least since *Bandhua Mukti Morcha v. Union of India*[11] wherein it was held in the context of the prohibition of bonded labour:

> There is a considerable body of juristic opinion in our country also which believes that strict adherence to the adversarial procedure can sometimes lead to injustice, particularly where the parties are not evenly balanced in social or economic strength... Therefore, when the poor come before the Court, particularly for enforcement of their fundamental rights, *it is necessary to depart from the adversarial procedure and to evolve a new procedure* [emphasis mine] which will make it possible for the poor and the weak to bring the necessary material before the Court for the purpose of securing enforcement of their fundamental rights.

Proceeding on this basis, the state governments filed affidavits in response to NALSA's Writ Petition. In brief, the views expressed in the affidavits were to the effect that: (i) There is recognition of the problems faced by transgender people; (ii) The grievances of and problems faced by transgender people need to be redressed; and (iii) Remedial steps would be taken (in future) for improving the living conditions of transgender people.

The views expressed in the various affidavits on the record of the Court, therefore, reveal a rather apathetic attitude of the state governments. It is important to mention this because a PIL often does not evoke a positive response from the governments in terms of actual remedial action – the usual response focuses on what will be done in future rather than what is being done in the present.

This was also the general tenor of the response to the Writ Petition filed by NALSA. If there was serious and meaningful concern for the rights of the transgender community, the state governments could and should have taken remedial steps even during the pendency of the proceedings in the Supreme Court rather than wait for the judgement to be delivered on the subject.

* * *

Be that as it may, the PIL resulted in some positive interventions from a transgender person named Laxmi Narayan Tripathy who, incidentally, represented the Asia Pacific region in the United Nations in 2008 where she spoke on the plight of sexual minorities. Another positive that came out of the litigation was the submission of the Government of India to the effect that the Ministry of Social Justice and Empowerment had constituted an expert committee on issues relating to transgender people. The judgement in the petition was delivered on 15 April 2014 and dealt with a variety of issues, including the development of the law.[12]

Historically, the Criminal Tribes Act, 1871 was the first and perhaps the only legislation to provide for the registration, surveillance and control of 'certain criminal tribes' and eunuchs. The statute was divided in two parts, the first dealing with 'criminal tribes' and the second with eunuchs, who were defined as 'all persons of the male sex who admit themselves, or on medical inspection clearly appear, to be impotent.' The law provided for the local government to maintain a register of the names and residences of all eunuchs 'who are reasonably suspected of kidnapping or castrating children, or of committing offences under section three hundred and seventy-seven of the Indian Penal Code, or of abetting the commission of any of the said offences.'[13]

A penalty could also be imposed on a registered eunuch who appeared 'dressed or ornamented like a woman, in a public street or place, or in any other place, with the intention of being seen from a public street or place...or who dances or plays music, or takes part in any public exhibition, in a public street or place or for hire in a private house.'[14] The significance of this statute is that for the purposes of criminal law, the sex or gender of a eunuch was irrelevant and there was a pronounced bias in the assumption of their possible criminality. Fortunately, this law was repealed in 1949, though the motivating reason appeared to be for decriminalizing the so-called 'criminal tribes' rather than for benefiting eunuchs.

As far as the development of the law through court decisions is concerned, the Supreme Court noted two strands of thought. The first strand arises from a decision of a divorce court in England in *Corbett v. Corbett (Otherwise Ashley)*.[15] In this case, Arthur Cameron Corbett sought a declaration that his marriage with April Ashley, a transwoman, was null and void since she was a person of the male sex. It had come on record that the respondent was born a male, but had undergone a sex change operation. The respondent legally changed her name to April Ashley and was considered a female for insurance purposes. However, she was unable to persuade the concerned official to change her birth certificate. It was held that the biological sexual constitution of a person is decided and fixed at birth. This cannot be changed through medical or surgical intervention. Consequently, it was held that the marriage between a man (Arthur) and a male-to-female transsexual (April) was void *ab initio*.

The second strand of thought arises from decisions rendered in New Zealand in *Attorney-General v. Otahuhu Family Court*[16] and in Australia in *Attorney General for the Commonwealth v. 'Kevin and Jennifer' & Human Rights and Equal Opportunity Commission*.[17] The decision rendered by the New Zealand Court did not agree with *Corbett* and noted that the law in New

Zealand has shifted away from sexual activity to emphasis on the psychological and social aspects of sex, which are sometimes referred to as gender issues. It was also observed that 'There is no social advantage in the law not recognizing the validity of the marriage of a transsexual in the sex of reassignment. It would merely confirm the factual reality.'

It was, therefore, held that there is no legal impediment in a person marrying as a person of a different sex pursuant to a post-operative sex reassignment. The Australian case was also one of post-operative sex reassignment. Kevin (a pseudonym) was born a female but underwent sex reassignment as a male through hormonal treatment and irreversible surgery. On the question of the validity of the marriage between Kevin and Jennifer, the trial judge took the view that 'man' included a post-operative transsexual (female to male) and the marriage between them was valid.

In a detailed decision, the view expressed by the trial judge was upheld on merits, and it was also observed that the finding was consistent with international law and humanity. A contrary view would result in injustice to transsexuals and their children, for no apparent purpose. The issue of a pre-operative transsexual was not discussed by the Court.

The Indian Supreme Court referred to some decisions from other jurisdictions, including the European Court of Human Rights, and concluded that 'transsexuals, who, whilst belonging physically to one sex, feel convinced that they belong to the other, seek to achieve a more integrated unambiguous identity by undergoing medical and surgical operations to adapt their physical characteristic to their psychological nature. When we examine the rights of transsexual persons, who have undergone *SRS* [sex reassignment surgery], the test to be applied is not the "biological test" but the "psychological test", because psychological factor and thinking of transsexual has to be given primacy [rather] than binary notion of gender of that person.'

What is the gender to be assigned to those transgender

individuals who have not undergone surgery or cannot do so due to some constraint, including financial constraints and absence of medical expertise? What about people whose sex cannot be specified at birth? There are persons in India who fall in one or more of these categories. The Supreme Court considered their plight from the international law perspective, the fundamental and human rights perspective and the humanitarian perspective.

Legislations enacted by some countries were discussed by the Court with a view to appreciate how some jurisdictions have tackled the legal posers. Provisions of treaties and conventions such as the Universal Declaration of Human Rights, the International Covenant on Civil and Political Rights and the Yogyakarta Principles were considered by the Court. The Court took the view, relying on a series of earlier decisions that those recognized principles not inconsistent but in harmony with the various fundamental rights must be recognized and followed.

Following up on this, the Court then examined several fundamental rights including the right to equal treatment under law (Article 14), prohibition on grounds, inter alia, of sex (Article 15), equality of opportunity in matters of public employment (Article 16), freedom of speech and expression (Article 19 (1) (a)) and the protection of life and personal liberty (Article 21), which should be interpreted and correctly appreciated to benefit transgender persons. It was noted that the law in India only recognizes 'the paradigm of binary genders of male and female, based on one's biological sex.'[18] But the Constitution of India does not make any such distinction and indeed the Fundamental Rights chapter refers to 'persons', that is, human beings, and the term is gender neutral.

On a reading of the Fundamental Rights chapter, the Court rejected the biological test laid down in *Corbett* and instead said that 'we prefer to follow the psyche of the person in determining sex and gender and prefer the "psychological test" instead of "biological test"'.[19] A different view would deprive transgender individuals of the benefit of welfare schemes and legislations as well as deny them equal treatment and protection of the law.

On this basis, an insightful conclusion was arrived at, namely that the constitutional provisions are not limited to the male or female gender and that 'gender identity as already indicated forms the core of one's personal self, based on self-identification, not on surgical or medical procedure. Gender identity, in our view, is an integral part of sex and no citizen can be discriminated on the ground of gender identity, including those who identify as third gender'.[20]

In this manner, the Supreme Court recognized the rights of transgender persons generally, regardless of whether anyone had undergone any surgical procedure or not. Quite obviously, the Court managed to skirt a difficult 'moral' question, and accept a profound reality.

In 'defining' a transgender, the Supreme Court unwittingly accepted the opinion of the Intersex Society of North America, which takes the view that a transgender person is a female in a male body or a male in a female body. Transgender people therefore have a gender identity that does not fit the standard gender binary assigned at birth, where the physiological and psychological genders correspond. This view is also in line with the understanding in the Yogyakarta Principles[21] (2006), which state in the Preamble:

> Understanding 'gender identity' to refer to each person's deeply felt internal and individual experience of gender, which may or may not correspond with the sex assigned at birth, including the personal sense of the body (which may involve, if freely chosen, modification of bodily appearance or function by medical, surgical or other means) and other expressions of gender, including dress, speech and mannerisms...

However, this does not appear to be a universally accepted view. The European Court of Human Rights is believed to have noted in 2017 that 22 countries under its jurisdiction required sterilization as a part of legal gender change. These countries were ordered to stop that practice.[22] A non-profit organization, the World Professional Association for Transgender Health (WPATH), had written to the Minister for Justice and the Minister for Health in Japan in 2019[23] to amend the legislation known as the 'Act on Special Cases in Handling Gender Status for Persons with Gender Identity Disorder'. The law provides, inter alia, for a diagnosis of 'Gender Identity Disorder' before a transgender person can apply for legal recognition of the appropriate gender.

Some of the objections appear to be that 'Gender Identity Disorder' is considered a mental health issue and a change of gender must be accompanied by a sterilization requirement. The Supreme Court of Japan in a decision rendered in January 2019 in the case of Takakito Usui held that the sterilization requirement is constitutionally valid.[24] WPATH uses 'the term "transgender" as an adjective to describe all those who identify as a gender other than the one that matches the sex they were assigned at birth.'

* * *

What have been the gains from the decision of the Supreme Court in the NALSA case? As expected, there are some positives, such as awareness and recognition of transgender rights. It is this that prompted the state of Kerala to be the first to frame the State Policy for Transgenders in Kerala, 2015. The policy employs the expansive definition of 'transgender' and therefore includes female to male transgendered individuals, male-to-female transgendered individuals, and intersex persons.

The policy was framed by the social justice department of the state of Kerala after understanding the issues faced by transgender people through a state-wide survey, which covered basic details, awareness about one's body, self-esteem, civil rights, access to health services, and the ability to live with dignity and with freedom from violence. The survey included a section on understanding the aspirations, needs and priorities of transgendered people. The goals and objectives of the policy are stated to be the attainment of:[25]

> A just society where men, women, and TGs [transgender people] have equal rights to access development opportunities, resources and benefits;
> The right to live with dignity and enjoy a life free from all forms of violence;
> The right to freedom of expression in all matters that affects them;
> Right to equal voice and participation in key development decisions that shape their lives, communities, and the state.

In keeping with this policy, the Kochi Metro Rail Limited recruited 23 transgender persons, and gave them the necessary training and suitable postings.[26] Karnataka framed in 2018 the State Policy on Transgenders with the objectives of enforcing the constitutional guarantees of dignity, non-discrimination, equal access and redress; identifying the responsible state institutions and departments for implementation; and defining accountability measures. The policy document notes that these require measures (which have been detailed) for empowerment, remedy and sustainability, and mechanisms for implementation and accountability.

Sometime in 2008, Tamil Nadu constituted the Tamil Nadu Transgender Welfare Board for the purpose of formulating and implementing welfare programmes for providing social security and status to transgender persons in the state. Subsequent to the decision of the Supreme Court, Maharashtra followed the lead taken by Tamil Nadu and constituted the Transgender Welfare Board in 2019 after a public consultation in 2013 supported by the UNDP.

The welfare board is tasked with providing formal education and employment opportunities, conducting health programmes and providing free legal assistance to transgendered people. Similarly, the state of Gujarat also constituted a Transgender Welfare Board in 2019 to increase access to essential services for transgender people, which included health care, housing, education and employment.

Institutionally as well, some positive steps have been taken. Again, by way of example, a Transgender Resource Centre was established by Delhi University in 2018 to provide educational counselling for transgendered persons, although the third gender category was introduced in 2015. Since then, the university has received about a hundred applications for admission, but it is not clear how many transgender individuals were actually granted admission.

In 2018, the Transgender Resource Centre saw between 10 and 15 transgender individuals reaching out for admission-related information. However, no one enrolled in the regular courses of the university. The preference is for long-distance education programmes because, as one transgender person put it, they have to work for financial support, and this makes it difficult to attend regular classes.

In 2019, the Centre had plans to introduce an outreach programme and target a thousand transgender persons. The Centre proposed introducing an online registration process for admissions.[27] The 2019 outreach has resulted in one transgender applying for admission to a regular course in Delhi University.[28] But how these programmes eventually work remains to be seen.

As far as political rights are concerned, in the recent general elections, thanks to the Election Commission of India, some transgender persons in Delhi were rather excited about being able to vote for the first time as members of a 'third gender', while earlier they were required to cast their vote either as male or female.[29] According to the Chief Electoral Officer, a total of

660 transgendered persons were eligible to cast their vote. How many actually voted is not known.

In Maharashtra, a transgender called 'Sneha' Nivrutti Kale contested the elections as an independent candidate and quite a few voted in her favour (759). In the entire state of Maharashtra, 1,168 voters were registered as transgender or 'others', including 142 first-time voters in the age group of 18–22 years.

Interestingly, the Election Commission of India noted this development and appointed Gauri Sawant, a transgender activist, as its brand ambassador for the state.[30] Apsara (earlier Ajay) Reddy had completed her higher studies in Australia and England, and worked as a journalist. She has been associated with a few political parties and was appointed an office bearer of a national political party in 2018 (perhaps the first one to be so appointed).[31]

There are several instances of transgender individuals having succeeded in different fields, but it is not possible to document all the 'success stories'. A few of them may be mentioned by way of examples. Life changed for the better for a transwoman, Gauri Sawant, after she 'adopted' Gayatri, a young girl. Unfortunately, her efforts to legally adopt Gayatri have not borne fruit despite the decision of the Supreme Court.[32] She believes that life for transgender people has not changed for the better even after the decision of the Court.[33]

Ratikanta Pradhan of Kandhamal district joined the Odisha State Civil Service in 2010 as a male – and was perhaps the first transgender person to become a civil servant. The decision of the Supreme Court enabled her to declare her transgender status (which was recognized as a special gazette notification of the Odisha government in 2017), and change her name to Aishwarya Rutuparna Pradhan.[34] In August 2014, a transgender person called Padmini Prakash, who was disowned by her family when she was only 13 and had also tried to commit suicide, became the first anchor for a daily television news programme.[35]

Padmini's name was suggested for the assignment by another transgender woman, Rose (earlier Ramesh) Venkatesan, who was educated in the United States, was a web designer, and had a master's in biomedical engineering. Rose was the first transgender to host a talk show called *Ippadikku Rose* (Yours, Rose) in Tamil Nadu, way back in 2008.[36]

Nartaki Nataraj was thrown out of her home when she was only 11 years old. She became an accomplished Bharatanatyam dancer and a guru for many others, and was awarded the Padma Shri in 2019, the third-highest civilian honour in the country.[37]

* * *

Where do we go from here? There is sufficient work done by the National AIDS Control Organization (NACO) and UNDP to lay out a road map for the next steps. 'Good Practices Post the Supreme Court Judgement' is a compendium intended primarily to provide action points for introducing initiatives similar to those taken in the states of Chhattisgarh, Kerala, Maharashtra, Rajasthan and Tamil Nadu, that 'directly address the vulnerabilities of Transgender and thus makes them avail social welfare measures'. The compendium is informative and exhaustive and provides:

1. An overview of the current activities being taken up by various state governments to address vulnerabilities;
2. An overview of the process of institutionalizing participation of transgender people, especially the evolution, functioning of the transgender welfare boards in states;
3. An overview of the policies framed or in process to mainstream transgender [people] in the states.

'Skilling for Livelihood Opportunities for Transgenders in India' is a publication that makes some very useful and pragmatic recommendations such as:

1. Effective and functional institutional mechanisms for the welfare of the transgender community.
2. Transgender community-specific education and employment services coordinated through welfare mechanisms (point 1).
3. Policy changes at national and state level to deal with transgender identity- and address-proof issues.
4. Demand-based modifications of mainstream education and skill development schemes for the transgender community.
5. Facilitation of employment for transgender persons.

'Uptake of Social Protection Schemes by Transgender Population in India' is yet another publication that makes worthwhile recommendations similar to the ones in the publication mentioned just above.

'The Report of the Expert Committee on the Issues Relating to Transgender Persons' was finalized on 27 January 2014 but for some reason, it was not made available to the Supreme Court before the judgement was delivered on 15 April 2014. Be that as it may, the report is an exhaustive document, and Chapter 13 thereof contains a summary of conclusions and recommendations. These are placed under the topics relating to the definition of transgender people, the issues facing the community, as well as possible approaches to resolving the issues relating to employment, health, and so on.

Quite clearly, considerable effort has been put in by NACO and UNDP in addressing the issues faced by transgender persons, and finding solutions to those problems. The report of the expert committee is also an extremely important document and its recommendations, if implemented, can bring about a huge societal change in mainstreaming and integrating transgender persons.

As far as legislative changes are concerned, the betterment of the transgender community has been pending with Parliament for quite a few years. Initially, a private member's bill called The Rights of Transgender Persons Bill, 2014 was introduced in the Rajya Sabha on 12 December 2014 and passed on 24 April 2015. Nothing seems to have come out of this bill.

Instead, the Government of India then introduced The Transgender Persons (Protection of Rights) Bill, 2016 in the Lok Sabha on 2 August 2016. The Statement of Objects and Reasons for the Bill stated:

STATEMENT OF OBJECTS AND REASONS

1. Transgender community is one of the most marginalized communities in the country because they do not fit into the general categories of gender of 'male' or 'female'. Consequently, they face problems ranging from social exclusion to discrimination, lack of education facilities, unemployment, lack of medical facilities, and so on.
2. Though Article 14 of the Constitution of India guarantees to all persons equality before law, clauses (1) and (2) of Article 15 and clause (2) of Article 16, inter alia, prohibit in express terms discrimination on the ground only of sex, and sub-clause (a) of clause (1) of Article 19 ensures freedom of speech and expression to all citizens, yet the discrimination and atrocities against transgender persons continue to take place.
3. The Hon'ble Supreme Court, vide its order dated 15 April, 2014, passed in the case of *National Legal Services Authority v. Union of India*, inter alia, directed the Central Government and State Governments to take various steps for the welfare of the transgender community and to treat them as a third gender for the purpose of safeguarding their rights under Part III of the Constitution and other laws made by the Parliament and the State Legislature.
4. The Transgender Persons (Protection of Rights) Bill, 2016 seeks [to]:
   a) Define a transgender person;
   b) Prohibit discrimination against a transgender person;
   c) Confer the right upon a transgender person to be

recognized as such, and a right to self-perceived gender identity;

d) Issue of certificate of identity to transgender persons;

f) Provide that no establishment shall discriminate against transgender persons in matters relating to employment, recruitment, promotion and other related issues. [There does not seem to be any clause (e)]

g) Provide for grievance redressal mechanisms in each establishment;

h) Establishment of a National Council for transgender people;

i) Punishment for contraventions of the provisions of the bill.

5. The Bill seeks to achieve the above objects.

The Bill was referred to a select committee, which gave its report on 19 July 2017. The committee examined several parties including NGOs, stakeholders and experts. It also examined a large number of documents, including written submissions made by individuals, organizations, stakeholders and NGOs, as well as the decision of the Supreme Court. On an overall consideration of the issues and material before it, the select committee made the following recommendations that 'will have a direct bearing on the welfare of transgender persons':

1. In NALSA, the Supreme Court directed the Central Government and the state Governments to take steps to treat transgender persons as socially and educationally backward classes of citizens and extend all kinds of reservation for admission in educational institutions and for public appointments. The Bill is silent on granting reservations to transgender persons under the category of socially and educationally backward classes of citizens.
2. The Bill does not refer to important civil rights like marriage and divorce, adoption, etc., which are critical

to transgender persons' lives and realities, wherein many are engaged in marriage-like relations, without any legal recognition from the State.

3. There should be separate HIV Sero-surveillance centres operated by the Centre and state governments since hijras/transgenders face several sexual health issues.
4. There should be a provision to provide the transgender persons separate public toilets and other such facilities.
5. There should be counselling services provided to the transgender persons to cope up with trauma and violence on the model of Rape and Crisis Intervention Centres.
6. Helping for career guidance and online placement support should be established.
7. At the end of clause 2(i) in Chapter-I of the Bill, definition of 'persons with intersex variations' should be given as 'Persons who at birth show variations in their primary sexual characteristics, external genitalia, chromosomes, hormones from the normative standard of female or male body are referred to as persons with intersex variations'.
8. A provision providing penal action against abortions of intersex foetuses and forced surgical assignment of sex of intersex infants should be there in the Bill.
9. A provision for separate frisking zones of transgender persons at public places such as airport, government and private office complex, etc. should be there. For this purpose, transgender persons should be appointed.
10. Transgender persons remain at risk of criminalization under Section 377. The Bill must at the very least recognize the rights of transgender persons to partnership and marriage.
11. The Bill must recognize transgender persons' right to marriage, partnership, divorce and adoption, as governed by their personal laws or other relevant legislation.
12. A census for transgender persons is a separate exercise from the drafting of guidelines for self-registration. The Census can be proceeded with independently.[38]

However, with the dissolution of the Lok Sabha, the Bill lapsed. Now, another act of 2019 has been passed by Parliament and has been notified into law on 5 December 2019. The Act of 2019 has some improvements over the Bill of 2016, but requires many more.

There are at least two serious problems with the Act of 2019. Firstly, section 4 provides that a transgender person shall have a right to be recognized as such, and a person recognized as transgender shall have a right to self-perceived gender identity.

However, section 6 virtually nullifies this by prescribing that upon receiving an application for a certificate of identity as a transgender person, the District Magistrate 'shall issue... a certificate of identity as transgender person after following such procedure and in such form and manner, within such time, as may be prescribed indicating the gender of such person as transgender.'

The form and procedure are still not known and could possibly be a method of introducing a 'screening committee', thereby violating the principle of self-identification recognized in section 4, and also violating the decision of the Supreme Court. In effect, the determination of one's gender, something intensely private, will be outsourced to the bureaucracy.

Secondly, the punishment provided for physical or sexual abuse against transgender persons is much less than that provided for comparative offences against women. What is the reason for this? The constitutionality of the Act has been challenged in the Supreme Court by India's first transgender judge, Swati Bidhan Baruah.[39] As on the date of writing this essay, the Supreme Court has issued notice on the petition and will hopefully deliver a verdict on its constitutionality soon.

While it is not the scope of this essay to critique the bills tabled in Parliament at different points of time, an organization called PRS Legislative Research has provided a comparative statement in the form of a tabulated chart.[40] The exercise carried out is definitely a pointer to the need for far greater engagement on the issues that confront transgender people, and the solutions to the problems they face. Serious issues have been raised by the expert committee and the select committee, and they need to be addressed.

There are some imponderables in a dynamic society that also need to be visualized, as has recently been evidenced by a decision of the Madras High Court in *Arun Kumar and another v. The Inspector General of Registration and others*.[41] In this decision, the first petitioner and the second petitioner (a transgender) were married according to Hindu rites and customs and, according to them, it was a valid marriage under the Hindu Marriage Act, 1955. However, the concerned authority under the Tamil Nadu Registration of Marriages Rules declined to register the marriage and an appeal against the decision of that concerned authority was rejected.

One of the reasons for declining to register the marriage was that the second petitioner was not a 'bride' within the meaning of section 5 of the Hindu Marriage Act, 1955. The petitioners then approached the High Court for quashing the orders passed by the registering authorities and for a direction to them to register their marriage. While allowing the petition, the High Court noted the distinction between sex and gender, and relied upon the decision of the Supreme Court, which took the view that Article 14 of the Indian Constitution provides that equality shall not be denied to 'any person' and this mandate would therefore apply to transgender persons too. The High Court held as follows:

> Sex and gender are not one and the same. A person's sex is biologically determined at the time of birth. Not so in the case of gender. That is why after making an exhaustive reference to the human rights jurisprudence worldwide in this regard, the Hon'ble Supreme Court held that Article 14 of the Constitution of India which affirms that the State shall not deny to 'any person' equality before the law or the equal protection of the laws within the territory of India

> would apply to transgenders also. Transgender persons who are neither male/female fall within the expression 'person' and hence entitled to legal protection of laws in all spheres of State activity as enjoyed by any other citizen of this country.

Following up on this, the High Court took the view that the word 'bride' in section 5 of the Hindu Marriage Act, 1955 will have to include within its meaning not only a woman but also a transwoman as well as an intersex person/transgender who identifies and perceives herself as a woman.

News has now filtered in of a traditional Bengali wedding recently performed in Kolkata where both people underwent sex reassignment. They were surrounded by family and friends. The times, they are a-changing!

* * *

At the end of the day, it can safely be said that the struggle for recognition of the rights of the transgender community and an acknowledgement of their gender identity is on the front page. But awareness alone is not enough. There are recognized minorities, but the implementation of civil and human rights for them has made little or no progress.

Women's rights, child rights and tribal rights are all well recognized and accepted, but constitutional equality for them is still a distant dream. The rights of transgender people have, in comparison, only taken baby steps, and progress is slow but sure. The optimism of the Beatles who sang 'The long and winding road that leads to your door will never disappear' will remain.

From the Margins to the Mainstream

ZAINAB PATEL

He woke this morning
Another night of her dreams

He glanced into the mirror
She's not real it seems

Society unknowingly accepts
The image presented
Unaware of the damage
Being self-inflicted

He hides her for fear of rejection
She battles for her reflection.[1]

Transgender people have been present in India for centuries, as reflected in descriptions in the *Kama Sutra*, the well-known ancient Sanskrit text from over 1,500 years ago. A chapter in the *Kama Sutra* describes 'tritiya prakriti' (third nature), which may be interpreted to mean any gender outside the binary male/female gender framework, and includes descriptions of 'males' who have long hair and wear dresses, and who provide sexual services to men.[2]

Descriptions of transgender men and women are also found in the major Sanskrit epics of India, in the oldest surviving epic poems on earth. Images of transgender people are depicted in many ancient Indian temple carvings as well. In the 16th and 17th centuries, when the Mughal Empire controlled most of the Indian subcontinent, transgender people attained special status in the emperor's court as political advisors, administrators and generals, as well as serving as the guardians of women in the harems. Thus, the concepts of a third gender – that some male-born and female-born persons desire to identify with a gender that is different from those assigned at birth, and that transwomen may engage in sex work – were relatively well known in India for centuries. From this perspective, transgender people in India have a longer documented history than most nations on earth.

Traditionally, hijras have been described as individuals born with male genitalia, who are 'neither man nor woman'.[3] However, hijras belong to a complex and heterogeneous group that includes male-to-female transgender persons who may want to live sometimes or all the time as women, and both those who desire a sex change operation and those who don't want such an operation.

Recently, the term 'third gender' has been used in the mainstream media to denote transgender people, although some transgender activists oppose this term for a variety of reasons. First, not all transgender people wish to be recognized as the 'third gender', as some may aspire to be recognized as a man or woman. Second, some gender-queer-identified people feel that this term merely reinforces the mutually exclusive categories of gender, going from binary gender to three genders. Third, it is only assumed that both trans men and women wish to be combined under the single category of the 'third gender'. Fourth, and relatedly, 'third gender' is equated with visible transwomen/

hijras, not with transmen. Finally, there is a hierarchy and devaluation implicit in the term 'third gender': first gender being man, second being woman, and then, last, 'third gender'.

Although the term 'hijras' is known to most transpeople throughout India, there are several other indigenous terms by which transpeople, especially transwomen, self-identify. These terms vary by region in India: Kinnars, Thirunangai (or Aravanis) in Tamil Nadu, Mangalmuki in Karnataka, Shiv Shakti in Andhra Pradesh, Jogappa or Jogta in parts of Karnataka and Maharashtra.[4]

* * *

'No one would "choose" to be transgender! No one would choose to have this be the life they live!' I've heard it said over and over again. To be fair, I've probably said it myself. I know the rhetorical function it serves: It lets the world know that transgender people face serious and complex discrimination, and a wide variety of barriers to access of different kinds; it tells people that being transgender is hard; it says that being transgender is not a choice.

Society has always been intrigued to know about transgender people: Who are they? What are their bodies like? Why do they dress in a particular manner? Why do they have certain mannerisms? This is apparent in the many news stories and articles on 'hijras', and yet so much is unknown, so much remains hidden and left to the imagination.

Let me share my own story with you briefly. I was born in 1981 on a cold winter morning in Mumbai, 10 years after my eldest sister and eight years after my middle sister were born. My Roman Catholic parents were elated when the doctor announced the baby born was a male. My mother, a homemaker from Mangalore, was a devout Catholic. Deeply religious and a doting parent, she made sure we learnt the important lessons of life and integrated them into our daily living.

I was a sickly baby, unlike my older sisters. Due to this, I was perhaps spared the trauma of studying in a boarding school, while my sisters were not so fortunate and were sent off to a Christian all-girls boarding school to learn Catholic values and a disciplined life.

I had a very sheltered life growing up in the by-lanes of Parel, a lower-middle-class locality in central Mumbai, typically characterized by its textile mills at that time.

As a young 'feminized' male studying in an all-boys school, I was bullied and harassed all through my school years. I absolutely dreaded going to school; each day was an absolute torture. I was verbally, sexually and physically abused for being me, and even my school teachers and supervisors normalized these events. My parents then decided that I need to firm up as a person and, more importantly, as a man. Someone came up with the ingenious suggestion of sending me to a Catholic seminary school so my vocation for priesthood could develop. It was all right if I didn't marry; I could just be a priest!

And I was packed off to Lonavala to study at a boarding school. The damp weather and incessant rains made me physically sick and led to frequent hospitalizations. The daily gym drills, badminton matches and football training took me to the absolute edge. Finally, my parents bought me back to Mumbai.

After losing that school year, I attempted suicide about eight times, and then landed up in the OPD of KEM Hospital, Mumbai, on Christmas Eve. As a result of my injuries, I lost control of my peripheral nerves and had to undergo physiotherapy to recuperate.

I passed school and college, where I began to experiment with my sexuality. I liked men but as a woman within, not as a man. I started meeting gay men and transgender people socially, and realized that there was nothing wrong with me.

Coming from a conservative Catholic family, it was difficult to come out to my parents and my siblings. But I mustered up enough courage and spoke to my mother about it. She just smiled and said she had always known about me, as well as about my lovers. We never had a conversation after that; it was a contract of silence.

I was a young college student in 2001, and had a wild rebellious streak in me. I wanted to see meaningful work done for the LGBTQ community. I joined an LGBT organization in Mumbai – the Humsafar Trust. This is my alma mater – it nourished me, strengthened me, made me what I am today. Ashok Row Kavi and Vivek Anand, the founders of the Trust, showed immense faith in me, and allowed me to grow both as a person and as a professional.

It was around this time that we heard in the print and television news that the police had arrested NGO staff working on MSM ('men who have sex with men') and HIV issues in Lucknow. The police raided the offices of the Bharosa Trust and the Naz Foundation International as they carried out their duties of educating the community on AIDS awareness and HIV prevention. Accused of running a 'gay sex racket', four staff members were arrested allegedly for obscenity, conspiracy and for aiding and abetting an offence under Section 377, IPC. They were detained for 47 days, sometimes without access to potable water, clean food and sanitation facilities.

This act of police brutality was in a way India's Stonewall Riots moment. The resulting community mobilization and strategic litigation contributed to what eventually took place in July 2009 – the reading down of Section 377. This 2009 judgement, however, was overturned in 2013 by the Supreme Court, which then also dismissed a review plea. It took till 2018 for the Supreme Court to overturn this judgement and decriminalize same-sex behaviour.

From the Humsafar Trust, I joined organization 'A', a trilateral aid organization working in Maharashtra on HIV prevention and care, though we were mandated to work on social issues and amongst the most vulnerable people – women in sex work, homosexual men, drug users and migrants.

While working with this institution, which was supposedly delivering on public health and had a human-rights-based approach, I've personally encountered and witnessed some of the worst homo- and transphobia. There was an extremely callous approach towards civil society groups and community leaders coming from the LGBTQ community; there was insensitivity around partnerships with these groups; and there was blatant mockery of people from the LGBTQ community towards other LGBTQ people (based on real or perceived sexual orientation and gender identities of persons).

Finally, I got an extremely lucky break to join the United Nations Development Programme (UNDP India) in August 2009. For a person like me who had never travelled out of Mumbai, I migrated to the city of djinns – Indraprastha – Delhi in 2009.

To move to a different city and a bureaucratic organization was a life-changing decision for me. And I met the most amazing boss, Alka Narang, who helped me grow from a small-time consultant to the National Programme Officer. I even got a chance to serve as the Regional Policy Analyst on Human Rights at the UNDP, Bangkok. In fact, I am the only out and open transgender hire in the UN system in India.

In 2012, I realized that it was time to start my transition. I fought against all odds and started the slow, painful process of finding the real me. It started with finding a name for myself. I experimented with 'Anna' and 'Meera' but then sensed that my life's calling, my identity, would also come from a name. I was also drawn to Shia Islam and came across the name 'Zainab' – a fragrant flower, and the best orator in modern-day Islam. So Zainab it was.

2019 was the seventh anniversary of my medical and societal transformation from a body that was born male to the woman, and related gender markers, that I am legally known as today.

The last 10 years have been a rollercoaster ride for me, from navigating a known space as an effeminate male to a transgender woman with her own identity and opinions. Not that I didn't encounter resistance or challenges. It was extremely challenging to transition at the workplace, to find gender-neutral washrooms, navigate same-sex partner benefits, medical insurance, and so on.

Getting my name and gender right was especially difficult for my colleagues, for they had got comfortable with my deadname.[5] Also, I was stereotyped in a different manner – a higher degree of passing off as a women, being articulate, holding a decent job and having a social presence made my colleagues, friends and others start making comparisons between other transgender persons they met, and me. They used to tell me that if I could be so successful as a transgender person, so could others.

I had set the bar higher for myself. And the result was that people around me expected other transgender persons to be like *me*. But no one realized that by putting me on a pedestal and expecting other transgender people to be like me, they had unknowingly widened the gap in diversity and inclusion. While this thought may sound good, it is not feasible or even possible.

The kind of life I've already led as a transgender person is not the norm. I've been far more fortunate than my less-privileged transgender brothers and sisters. I have met with ministers, presidents, bureaucrats, human rights officials and politicians, and found it easy to deal with them. I can waltz into meeting rooms or into public spaces and claim those spaces with confidence. I can be who I am, but it is not easy, and it is not something every transgender person can necessarily manage as they come from varying socio-economic circumstances. And everyone is a unique and different individual at the end of the day.

I am privileged to be born in India, where the sociocultural learning system has put special emphasis on the value of gurus in our lives.

Om agyana timiandhasya gyananjana shalakya
chaksur unmalitam yena tasmay sri guruve namah

(I offer my obeisance to my guru, my master who with the collyrium[6] of knowledge has opened my eyes blinded by the darkness of ignorance.)

Apart from my biological mother, Montin, two amazing hijras changed my life. My hijra guru, Laxmi Narayan Tripathi, and my hijra mother, Gauri Sawant, have had a profound influence on my life. These women have fiercely protected me, chided me, egged me on to become who I am today. From Ernest to Zainab, from a feeble person to a voice, these women were the alchemists in my life, who turned my base metal into gold, helping me go through my trials in the furnace of hardships. These three women have taught me the most profound lessons in life – to follow your truth, to pursue your happiness, and to have an appreciation for everyone.

I have been very privileged to transition quickly and safely in such a supporting community relative to other communities. Knowing that things could have gone much worse for me, I am very grateful for the way my life has evolved. And I want to be able to give back, to become an advocate when necessary. What can I, what can each of us do to use whatever privileges we may individually have to stop the violence that is rife in the Indian LGBTQ community? What can we do about the fact that maybe daily young transgender persons are kicked out of their home and have to rely on sex work and begging to stay alive, vulnerable to being targeted by the police?

A large part of our transgender existence goes into being forced onto the streets to survive, thanks to society considering us to be impossible to understand, unemployable, unfit for the values of that society, unhuman. Being constantly harassed and assaulted on the streets or in jails is traumatic, especially when trans feminine individuals are thrown into men's jails. Hospital workers often refuse to provide any care, much less adequate care, and the lack of medical care is an issue that especially impacts transgender persons.

I have met and made many relationships, families of 'choice', brothers and sisters, daughters and 'chelas'. Our Indian society, just like others in the world, has coerced many of them into working in occupations and participating in activities that society has deemed illegal in order to survive. Only a third of my sisters are with me today; most have succumbed to AIDS, and some have died in a way that confirms society's uncaring attitude: shot multiple times, stabbed, mutilated, burned, drowned, left to bleed to death, and ultimately dumped like trash, the ultimate and unfortunate metaphor of a society that considers transgender people, especially those on the trans feminine spectrum, to be nothing but garbage.

These injustices also persist because of the images of transgender people that pervade the media. Jokes and slurs are made with trans feminine individuals as the punchline. India, while celebrating the largest global festival of democracy in the 2019 General Elections, had at least 10 elected representatives and political persons calling Opposition persons 'hijras' and other such slurs to drive in the point that being a hijra is a sin, an abomination that continues in life and death. In fact, even relatives refuse to bury them after their passing as they feel these individuals bring shame to the family even in death.

All these realities pushed some of us transgender persons to approach the judicial system to secure our rights. After all, the right of equality before law and equal protection of the law *is guaranteed under Article 14 of the Indian Constitution* to each and every citizen of the country.

In April 2014, the Supreme Court of India ruled in *NALSA v. Union of India* that the rights and freedoms of transgender people in India were protected under the Constitution. I was one of the petitioners in this case.

The judgement was immediately considered a landmark, both in terms of its expansive reading of constitutional rights to empower transgender individuals, and its wide-ranging directions that promised to provide equal citizenship to a historically marginalized group. In its decision, the Court affirmed that the transgender community was deprived of a range of fundamental rights. It held that not recognizing gender identity violates the right to equality (Article 14) and the State has to act to ensure that the promise of equal protection of the laws applies to transgender persons as well.

The Court also concluded that discrimination on the grounds of sex includes 'gender identity'. It explained that the prohibition of discrimination on account of 'sex' was included in these articles to prevent the different treatment of people simply because they do not behave in the way that is expected of their gender.

The Court went on to say that the right to freedom of speech and expression (under Article 19 (1)(a)) includes the right to expression of one's self-identified gender. Since self-identified gender can be expressed through dress, words, action or behaviour or any other form, a transgender person's personality could be expressed by the individual's behaviour and presentation. The State thus cannot prohibit, restrict or interfere with a transgender person's expression of their personality, subject of course to the 'reasonable restrictions' on the grounds specified in Article 19 (2), i.e. public order, decency and morality.

Furthermore, the Court stated that gender is a very important part of a person's identity and that recognition of self-defined gender identity is part of the fundamental right to dignity, which is part of Article 21. The Court had in the past noted that dignity included the right to express one's self in different ways. Given that gender constituted the core of one's sense of being as well as an integral part of one's identity, the recognition of an individual's gender identity would lie at the heart of the right of dignity.

Coming to its order, the Court directed the Centre and the State Governments to legally recognize gender identity, whether it is the third gender, or whether it is to do with persons changing their gender from male to female or from female to male. With respect to the former, the Court recognized that fundamental rights are available to the third gender in the same way as they are available to males and females. For recognizing gender change from male to female or from female to male, the Court said a 'psychological test' should be followed instead of a 'biological test'. They also ruled that insisting on 'Sex Reassignment Surgery (SRS)' as a condition for changing one's gender was illegal.

Finally, with respect to stigma and public awareness, the Central and State Governments were asked to take steps to create public awareness so that transgender persons would feel that they were also part and parcel of the social fabric; they were also asked to take measures so transgender people could regain their respect and place in society. Further, they needed to seriously address problems such as fear, shame, gender dysphoria, social pressure, depression, suicidal tendencies and social stigma faced by transgender people.

However, five years after this historic ruling, I see that various Indian states are still struggling with how to recognize the self-identified gender of transgender people.

As mentioned earlier, the Court's declarations are to be read in conjunction with an Expert Committee Report on Transgender Persons constituted by the Ministry of Social Justice and Empowerment. Since the report is quite broad, these already broad declarations can be seen side by side to push the Government to do things that are not specifically mentioned in the judgement but are mentioned in the report. For example, recommendations in the report like setting up of crisis centres, and gender sensitization in institutional settings, can easily be seen as part of the NALSA judgement's broad declarations.

In August 2019, the Government of India introduced and passed the Transgender Rights Bill 2019 in the Lok Sabha. The Bill was passed by the Rajya Sabha as well, and was enacted into law by a Presidential notification of December 2019. It has now become an Act. This Act was based on a private member's bill that had previously been passed unanimously in the Rajya Sabha. The Act is supposed to correct infirmities (potential loopholes) and improve upon the Rajya Sabha Bill.

However, this Act has received widespread criticism from transgender representatives, activists and legal scholars alike – the consensus suggesting that it was fully open to the exploitation of loopholes and misinterpretation, with several activists noting that the Rajya Sabha Bill passed earlier, though not ideal by itself, was better and preferable to this one.

Simply put, the Act continues to dwell on unresolved issues:

1. A person still needs authorization from the State Government to choose their preferred gender;
2. The Act doesn't recognize non-biological families – it does not accept the choices that transgender persons make to form either guru–chela relationships or other family bonds.
3. The Act *reduces* the criminal penalties for sexual assault on transgender persons (6 months to 2 years) compared to cis-gendered women.
4. The Act remains silent on reservation for transgender persons, making this Bill purely tokenistic.

* * *

To return to a personal note, I want to share that in 2012, I met my love and life. He swept into my existence, and a fairy-tale romance started. 'Prince', as I fondly call him, proposed one day, and we got married in South Africa. We are still fighting for the recognition of our marriage in India and In Sha Allah one day this will also be a reality. There are many issues that we will continue to battle in the long fight for the recognition of ourselves, our civil, political and cultural rights.

Here's what I have learnt, and what I love about my transgender life:

1. After so many years of being uneasy in my own skin, I love the fact that these days I look in the mirror and I recognize myself.
2. I love that I know who my real friends are. The people in my life love me for 'me' and they are committed to my well-being.
3. I treasure the fierce hijra community I am a part of.
4. I love the way that being transgender has made me cognizant of my own privilege in other areas and how to work with that privilege.
5. I am thankful that my own struggles with finding access to safe spaces (like bathrooms, dressing rooms, etc.) has made me aware of broader issues of accessibility both as a transgender person and as that of a minority religious group.
6. I am thankful that my experiences with feeling marginalized have taught me to read various holy books such as the Bible, the Quran and the Bhagavad Gita, from that perspective which has, in turn, opened up a world of new interpretation for me.

So, as a transwoman from India who was one of the original petitioners in the NALSA case, I have seen how far we have come. I am now working for an international management agency and am one of the first transgender directors of human resources in the Asia Pacific region.

I have been lucky in my journey, but I can also see how much remains to be done if the civil rights of transgender people in India are to be protected. We have the absolute and inalienable right to define ourselves, in our own terms and in our own languages. We have the right to express ourselves and our identities without fear of violence or retribution. We are human beings, holders of human rights, and we need to be recognized as such within the societies we live in. In order to bring a meaningful change to the lives of this persistently marginalized population, what I have learnt from my experience in India is that the Legislature must walk in tandem with the Supreme Court judgement. As an eminent psychiatrist once said, 'What is not brought to consciousness comes to us as fate.'[7]

With all of the struggles I have had finding a place in the world because of my identity, I don't think I would trade it for anything else. This life has taught me so much, introduced me to amazing people, deepened my faith in ways I couldn't have imagined, and helped me to find peace.

Let me end on a high note; let me end with some Urdu shayari, which sums up my entire existence:

Manzil toh mil hi jayegi, bhatak kar hi sahi,
Gumraah toh woh hai, joh ghar se nikale hi nahi.

Sex and the Community

Love and Marriage

SAURABH KIRPAL

If dignity and autonomy are the pillars of the constitution, there is no possibly no greater manifestation of that autonomy than the right to choose a sexual partner. And nothing is a greater expression of that choice than marriage. It seems apparent that both the right to choose a partner and the right to marry are intensely personal choices over which the State and the community really ought to have no control.

However, this view ignores the reality that these choices have rarely been free – both historically and in contemporary times. The right to choose a partner is often pitted against caste, community and religious claims. The right to marry is even more enmeshed in the claims of the community as a state-sanctioned institution, which gives valuable rights while according social recognition to a relationship.

There is thus an innate tension between personal autonomy and dignity, and the rights of the community. In 2019, the Supreme Court ruled in favour of the individual in two cases. Both these cases will be examined in this essay to attempt to understand the nature of the individual choices the Court is willing to protect. But while the Court may protect the existing right of an individual to choose and marry a partner, will it also be as willing to extend that right to persons of alternative sexuality?

AUTONOMY AND THE RIGHT TO CHOOSE A PARTNER

The Constitution envisages the individual as the primary agent through which the State engages. The word 'family' did not even appear in the chapter relating to fundamental rights.[1] Of course, the right to family life has been read into the Constitution as being part of the right to life. However, it is important to note that the right to a family life rests in an *individual* so as to enable her to live her life with dignity and autonomy. The collective family does not have any corresponding rights against the individual. This individualistic theme in the Constitution has given rise to many cases where the autonomy and dignity of the individual have clashed with the demands of the community.

Amongst the first cases to mention rights to a family and marriage was the fundamental rights case of *H.H. Kesavanada Bharti v. Union of India.*[2] That judgement only had a stray observation by one judge in a bench of 13 judges that 'a man cannot exist, cannot make good his right to marriage or found his family unless he is entitled to ownership through acquisition of property'. This early case shows that, initially, family rights were seen through the lens of property (a fact that does not seem to have changed all that much over the years).

As society changed and developed, so did the jurisprudence of the Supreme Court. There were periods when the Constitution's focus on the individual gave way to the rights of the collective. However, there has recently been a strong resurgence of the individual's right to dignity and autonomy. The most famous of these cases is the privacy judgement,[3] which was the precursor to the Aadhaar judgement.

The privacy judgement recognized that an individual does not lose her identity/character as a separate person merely because she lives in society. While it is true that to live in society one must surrender certain freedoms so as to be able to peacefully co-exist, there remains in an individual a fundamental right to dignity, liberty and autonomy. The individual was the core of constitutional focus, and the preambular ideals of justice, liberty, equality and fraternity were the animators to secure a dignified existence to an individual.[4] One fundamental feature of the right to privacy was the ability to make a choice about one's life for oneself. The role of the State was merely that of a facilitator or enabler, intervening so as to protect the ability of a person to make choices for herself.

The privacy judgement recognized that life and liberty, being inalienable rights, were not creations of the Constitution; instead, these rights were an intrinsic and inherent part of the human condition. Privacy was a facet of this right – being both a value in itself as well as a means to achieving other rights guaranteed by the Constitution. Specifically, the Court also held that 'privacy includes at its core the preservation of personal intimacies, the sanctity of family life, marriage, procreation, the home and sexual orientation. Privacy also connotes a right to be left alone. Privacy safeguards individual autonomy and recognizes the ability of the individual to control vital aspects of his or her life.

'Personal choices governing a way of life are intrinsic to privacy. Privacy protects heterogeneity and recognizes the plurality and diversity of our culture. While the legitimate expectation of privacy may vary from the intimate zone to the private zone and from the private to the public arenas, it is important to underscore that privacy is not lost or surrendered merely because the individual is in a public place. Privacy attaches to the person since it is an essential facet of the dignity of the human being.' (Primary judgement, paragraph 323).

Thus, the Supreme Court has recognized that the right to choose a partner is fundamental to the human condition. This freedom should seem obvious, but we know the reality in India to be different. There are two cases in the recent times where this choice has been put under severe strain. Both cases reflect the fault lines along which Indian society is divided.

The first case is that of Hadiya, a young woman who married outside her religion, and was loudly proclaimed to be the victim of 'love jihad'. The other case is that of khap panchayats, seeking to regulate marriage between castes and gotras.

Hadiya née Akhila's case

Hadiya, or Akhila as she was called before she changed her name, was the only child of Ashokan and Ponamma. She started a course in homeopathy in Salem, Tamil Nadu, where she shared a room with two Muslim students, Jaseena and Faseena. At some point, Ashokan alleged that Jaseena and Faseena, and their father, Aboobacker, had forcibly converted Akhila to Islam. This led to Aboobacker being arrested under charges of promoting enmity between different religious groups.

However, when Ashokan filed a case in the Kerala High Court, Hadiya appeared and said that she had converted to Islam of her own free will and wished to live away from her parents. Noting this fact, the High Court allowed her to continue her studies and live as she wished.[5]

This should have been the end of the matter, but was not to be. Undeterred by the High Court order and his own daughter's statement of her wishes, Ashokan moved the Court again, stating that his daughter was about to be whisked off to Syria.

This time the Court took a different approach. An immediate interim order was passed restraining Hadiya from travelling abroad. However, when she appeared before the Court and reiterated her wish to stay away from her parents, the Court demurred and allowed her to do so. This reprieve was short-lived.

When she appeared before the Court later in the proceedings, the Court directed that she move to the college hostel to complete her studies. This order was ostensibly passed to ensure that Hadiya got her professional degree.[6] Her agency, however, was not fully denied at this stage – she was not compelled to act as per the dictates of her parents or forced to live with them.

That stripping away of Hadiya's choice happened next. When she appeared in Court after being admitted to the college hostel, she came with a man who she claimed was her legally wedded husband. She produced a marriage certificate, which also recorded that she had changed her name to Hadiya. This enraged the High Court. Even though Hadiya was present in Court, the Division Bench refused to interact with her to ascertain her wishes or enquire about the authenticity of her marriage. An order was passed directing that she be held almost incognito[7] in a shelter home while her husband was to be thoroughly investigated.

The fact of the marriage seemed to have irked the Court. The Court recorded the reason for its order thus:

> It is necessary to bear in mind the fact that the detenue who is a female in her twenties is at a vulnerable age. As per Indian tradition, the custody of an unmarried daughter is with the parents, until she is properly married. We consider it the duty of this Court to ensure that a person under such a vulnerable state is not exposed to further danger, especially in the circumstances noticed above where even her marriage is stated to have been performed with another person, in accordance with Islamic religious rites.

The Kerala High Court ultimately ruled against Hadiya and her husband, and their marriage was deemed to be a nullity. Even though she was 'an ordinary girl with moderate intellectual capacity', she was deemed to be gullible to have first converted to Islam, and then to have ostensibly married a Muslim man. The custody of the unmarried daughter belonged to the parents – in other words, her body and mind were virtually owned by her parents.

Hadiya's situation raises a crucial issue in Indian society. Does an adult woman not have agency over herself and her life?

The Court noted that there were other cases pending before it where women had been 'forcibly' converted to Islam, allegedly through the fear of going to hell in case she did not convert. The Court held that Hadiya's was not a normal case of a man and a woman belonging to different religions falling in love and marrying, which it was 'familiar' with; this was a case of an arranged marriage. After her conversion to Islam, Hadiya's name had been put on a website[8] and her husband had come forward with a proposal. The High Court ruled that it was this that set the case apart from a normal case of inter-religious marriage.

Oddly enough, the Court seemed to be saying that if a marriage was arranged by a girl's parents, it was perfectly acceptable, but a marriage arranged by anyone else was not. As a parting shot the Court held that 'Ms. Akhila is the only child of her parents. There are no other persons in this world, who would consider the welfare and wellbeing of their daughter to be of paramount importance than her parents. The nature provides numerous examples of even animals taking care of and protecting their progeny sacrificing their very lives for the purpose. The Homo sapien is no exception... A girl aged 24 years is weak and vulnerable, capable of being exploited in many ways... A Single Bench of this Court has...taken note of the functioning of radical organizations pursuing activities of converting young girls of Hindu religion to Islam on the pretext of love. The fact remains that such activities are going on around us in our society. Therefore, it is only appropriate that the petitioner and his wife, who are the parents, are given custody of Ms. Akhila.'

The upshot of the above ruling is that the issue was not merely one of religious conversion; nor was it about the right to get married outside one's religion. The Court seemed to worry that the right of the parents to choose a husband for their daughter had been usurped by persons of a different religion. The strands of patriarchy, religious difference and paternalism (both of the parents and the Court) had created the perfect storm.

The matter was carried to the Supreme Court, which set

aside the judgement of the High Court annulling the marriage and directing Hadiya to remain in the custody of her parents. Two separate judgements were delivered in the case. A majority judgement was delivered on behalf of Chief Justice Dipak Misra and Justice Ajay Manikrao Khanwilkar. There was a separate concurring judgement by Justice Dhanjay Yashwantrao Chandrachud. The majority judgement is an impressive analysis of the writ of habeas corpus – literally a writ to 'produce the body' in court.

The Supreme Court held that the duty of any court was to ensure that no person was kept in wrongful confinement, that is, without the authority of law. If a person freely made a choice to live with someone else, there was no illegal detention and the enquiry of the Court would end. The judgement of the High Court was roundly criticized as being based upon some 'social phenomena that was frescoed around it'.

The Supreme Court held that the right to choose one's faith was central to the idea of individual autonomy. Equally, the right to choose a partner was also a freedom vested in every adult with mental capacity. The judgement seemed to consider the right to choose a partner almost axiomatic. No precedent was quoted to specify that choice.

Justice Chandrachud held that the choice of a partner 'whether within or outside marriage' lay within the exclusive domain of the individual. This choice of words set up a future right to choose a partner regardless of marriage as an aspect of autonomy and dignity.[9] Most importantly, the judgement admonished the Kerala High Court by stating that it demonstrated paternalism by straying into a private space reserved for men and women in which neither the law nor the judges have the right to intrude.

Hadiya's case is a rather sordid saga of the abuse of the legal process. While the Supreme Court ultimately ruled in her favour, it cannot be forgotten that the Kerala High Court had ruled that she was incapable of taking decisions on her own, denying her the capacity to lead a life due to every adult citizen of the country.

Most young and vulnerable women in our country can barely afford to go to the police, much less the High Court or the Supreme Court. In such a social setting, judgements such as the Supreme Court's verdict in Hadiya's case often remain pious promises on paper.

If religion is a great divider in our country, arguably caste is an even greater cause of divisions in society. While inter-religious marriages do encounter social opprobrium, historically, inter-caste marriages are met with great violence. This is not to say that inter-religious marriages are easier or are not met with violence. It is just that inter-caste marriages are potentially more common since Hindus are the majority religion in India.

In spite of this, the data is extraordinary. As per a study conducted by the National Council for Applied Economic Research in 2012,[10] only 5 per cent of marriages were inter-caste. In states like Madhya Pradesh, Himachal Pradesh and Chhattisgarh, 98 per cent of the people married within their caste. Shockingly, only a quarter of the people even knew someone who had married outside their caste. This last statistic shows that even if an inter-caste marriage happens, it quickly goes underground, out of the public glare. This may be through social ostracization. Often, unfortunately, this happens through honour killings.

In this context, the issue of khap panchayats is rather telling. The fragmentation of Hindu society in India is not merely on the basis of caste but also, in the case of khap panchayats, the gotra.

GOTRA, HONOUR AND THE KHAP PANCHAYAT

Inter-caste marriages were generally frowned upon in Hindu texts. Curiously, one aspect of same caste marriage – intra-gotra marriage – was allegedly equally sinful.

The 'gotra' is a slippery concept. In his *History of Dharmasastra,* Pandurang Kane states that the general conception about gotra is that it denotes all persons who trace an unbroken male line from a common ancestor. The same text, however, while discussing Medhatithi's commentary on Manu, says that the gotra is 'anadi' – not derived from a common ancestor but from time immemorial.[11] However, there is no definitive conception of what a gotra means, leading the learned author to exclaim in despair that 'the mass of material on gotra and pravara in the sutras, the puranas and digests is so vast and so full of contradictions that it is almost an impossible task to reduce it to order and coherence'.[12]

Even though there is no certainty as to the exact meaning and origin of the gotra, it did not stop people from sowing divisions in its name. There was claimed to be a rule that people from the same gotra had common ancestry and, accordingly, marrying someone from the same gotra was like marrying someone within the family. This was seen as a form of incest and was hence taboo.

While the rule against intra-gotra marriage (sagotra) marriage claimed to have ancient vintage, disputes relating to its correctness also have respectable legal antecedents. As far back as 1945, a case came before the Bombay High Court about the validity of sagotra marriages. Two sons sued their father, claiming that the father's second marriage to a woman of the same gotra was invalid. They wanted the exclusion of their father and the step-mother from their thread ceremony.

A strong bench of the High Court comprising of Justices Sir Harilal Jekisundas Kania and Pralhad Balacharya Gajendragadkar (both of whom went on to become Chief Justices of India) held that there was no injunction against sagotra marriages in the scriptures. To the extent there were some verses or commentators that had held to the contrary, the same were discounted. In a remarkably modern passage, the court held

> Since the said commentaries were written, several centuries have passed by and during this long period the Hindu mode of life has not remained still or static. Notions of good

> social behaviour and the general ideology of the Hindu society have been changing; with the growth of modern sciences and as a result of the impact of new ideas based on a strictly rational outlook of life, Hindu customs and usages have changed. The custom as to marriages between persons of the same *gotra* which I have held proved in this case is an eloquent instance in point... In such a case it is obviously the duty of the legislature to intervene and to amend the material provisions of Hindu law so as to make them consistent with the custom and usage prevailing in society and thus help to place the Hindu law of marriage on a more rational basis.[13]

The Legislature did in fact step in, and enacted the Hindu Marriage Removal of Difficulties Act, 1946.[14] This was followed by the Hindu Marriage Act, 1955, which prohibited only sapinda marriages[15] and did not prohibit sagotra marriages. But it seems that the news of the change in the law did not reach the north. Caste or khap panchayats still sought to rigorously enforce prohibitions against sagotra marriages.

Khap panchayats are informal groups (not necessarily recognized as panchayats under the 73rd Constitutional Amendment) of elders (almost always men) of the same gotra. In areas where access to formalized justice is difficult, the writ of the khap panchayats runs free. While the khaps may not be able to enforce their orders by the coercive use of their law, they can impose social and economic boycotts which are strictly enforced.

There have been several instances of khap panchayats issuing rulings against women. However, it was the rulings against marriages of young men and women from the same gotra which caught the public imagination.[16] A particularly horrific case was that of Ved Pal and Sonia.

Ved Pal was a resident of Mator village in the Jind district of Haryana. He worked as a medical practitioner running a clinic in Singhwal village, also Haryana. He fell in love with a girl called

Sonia, who used to live near the clinic. They both belonged to the same caste but, unfortunately for them, also the same gotra. They wished to get married, but this was opposed by Sonia's family.

Valuing love over tradition, they eloped and got married in a temple. The khap panchayat in Sonia's village declared this to be a capital offence. A decree was passed directing that the couple be found and killed. For reasons that are not fully clear, the couple were soon forcibly separated.[17] Ved Pal approached the Punjab and Haryana High Court seeking police protection to enable him to go to his wife's house to bring her back. The Court duly ordered police protection.

In the evening of 23 July 2009, Balwant Singh, the SHO of Narwana Sadar, and Suraj Bhan, a warrant officer of the High Court, arrived along with a police party at Ved Pal's residence in Mator village. They promised to escort Ved Pal to Singhwala, where his wife Sonia was forcibly confined in her parents' house, in order to get her back. As soon as he reached Singhwala, Ved Pal was attacked. He was dragged to the terrace in Sonia's house and stripped. His face and torso were beaten with sticks and his neck and shoulders were cut open with sickles and scythes. As Suraj Bhan was pushed from the terrace, the 15 policemen fled.[18] The perpetrators were ultimately convicted and awarded a life sentence.

These instances led to an NGO, Shakti Vahini, to file a Writ Petition before the Supreme Court in 2010. A lengthy and erudite judgement followed in 2018. The judgement made a reference to the report of the Law Commission, which had recommended the framing of a law to ban khap panchayats from passing orders interfering with the free will of any man and woman wishing to get married. The Law Commission had proposed the enactment of a Prohibition of Unlawful Assembly (Interference with Freedom of Matrimonial Alliances) Act.[19] As per the Act, the very holding of a khap panchayat with the intent of deliberating upon a marriage on the ground of honour was to be illegal. Any intimidation, creation of an environment of hostility was also be deemed to be a crime.

However, after noting that the Law Commission had produced such a report, the Union of India gave a rather specious argument as to why it had not accepted the report and enacted a law. The Union said that since the subject matter related to the concurrent list of the Constitution (i.e. where the state and the Centre have concurrent or co-existent jurisdiction over a subject), it was not possible to legislate without consultation with the states. Why the consultation was not complete even five years later was completely glossed over.

The Court did not merely rely on the report of the Law Commission. It ruled that the choice of a partner was a fundamental aspect of dignity and liberty and was constitutionally protected by Articles 19 and 21 of the Constitution. Further, once a right was recognized, it was the duty of the State as well as the Courts to enforce and protect that right.

In his inimitable style, Chief Justice Dipak Misra ruled that 'The concept of liberty has to be weighed and tested on the touchstone of constitutional sensitivity, protection and the values it stands for. It is the obligation of the constitutional courts as the sentinel on qui vive to zealously guard the right to liberty of an individual as the dignified existence of an individual has an inseparable association with liberty… The choice of an individual is an inextricable part of dignity, for dignity cannot be thought of where there is erosion of choice… When two adults marry out of their volition, they choose their path; they consummate their relationship; they feel that it is their goal and they have the right to do so.

'And it can unequivocally be stated that they have the right and any infringement of the said right is a constitutional violation. The majority in the name of class or elevated honour of clan cannot call for their presence or force their appearance as if they are the monarchs of some indescribable era…'[20]

Recognizing the need to protect the freedom of choice, the

Court laid down a series of guidelines. They were preventive, remedial and punitive in nature. A duty was cast on the police to attempt to stop the holding of a khap panchayat in the case of an inter-caste or sagotra marriage. In case such prevention was not possible, the police and state authorities were required to both provide security to the married couple as well as file FIRs against the persons who held the khap panchayat and intimidated the couple. Finally, failure to prevent the panchayats would also result in punitive action against the erring police and state officials.

The judgement thus upheld the right of an individual to choose a partner. It was one more in a long series of cases to do so. The novel feature of the judgement was that it went on to hold that khap panchayats, as extra-judicial coercive machineries, were invalid. The Court held that 'the consent of the family or the community or the clan is not necessary once the two adult individuals agree to enter into a wedlock. Their consent has to be piously given primacy…[the law] does not recognize any space for informal institutions for delivery of justice. It is so since a polity governed by "Rule of Law" only accepts determination of rights and violation thereof by the formal institutions set up for dealing with such situations.'[21]

This judgement rightly implies that if power is vested in non-state actors, the same is likely to be misused.[22] The very concept of the Rule of Law necessitates concentration of coercive power in institutions operated by and under the control of the State.[23] In a democracy, such institutions are answerable to the people as well as to a constitution.

Khap panchayats are extra-constitutional and feel little need to respect the values espoused in the Constitution. Individuals who are at the receiving end of adverse rulings thus have limited scope to rely on the fundamental rights guaranteed under the Constitution. This is because the vast majority of the rights are guarantees against state excesses, not private abuses of power.

This ruling thus brings into sharp focus another deeply

troublesome feature in the subjugation of women, that is, the public–private divide. Typically, a woman is likely to be subjected to oppression from within the family. Manu, in the *Manusmriti*, states that a young girl must be under the control of her father during childhood, her husband during her marriage and her sons after her husband's death.[24]

More tellingly, he goes on to declare that a husband must be constantly worshipped as a god by a faithful wife even though he may be 'destitute of virtue, or seeking pleasure (elsewhere), or devoid of good qualities'.[25] This diktat is still taken rather seriously and literally across vast swathes of the country. Men have economic, social and physical power over women and don't hesitate to use it. Most of this repression happens within the family home.

Thus, the Law Commission's report on khap panchayats has been criticized for ignoring the fact that the violence against women is largely inflicted upon them by members of their own family.[26] By restricting the sanctions of the law to khap panchayats, the patriarchal assumptions of the Commission (and presumably by extension the Court) have been allegedly demonstrated.

However, this criticism does seem a bit excessive. The public–private divide does exist with different problems and issues; consequently, it demands different and more nuanced solutions. It seems difficult to imagine what equivalent law the critics of the Law Commission report would suggest in case of familial resistance to inter-caste or inter-religious matters. Any broad-based legislation might be held to be unconstitutional as it will impinge upon the privacy rights of individuals. The better course in cases of private abuse is probably through the use of the agency of the Courts to enforce the regular criminal law.

The cases of Hadiya and the khap panchayat tell an interesting tale of difference and commonality. While it is true that religion and caste are both dividing features of society, the reason to oppose unions between religions and castes are slightly different. Opposition to inter-religious marriage may stem from simple prejudice and is of a more recent vintage. Injunctions against inter-caste marriage have an ancient lineage stemming from diktats of the Hindu religious texts.[27]

These differences nevertheless cannot hide the commonality between the two cases. The ability of a person to choose her partner has been negated and hence their autonomy is diminished. But what is it about marriage that needs this complete societal domination and control, and why has it not changed yet?

MARRIAGE AND THE LAW

Marriage is an ancient institution that has existed in virtually every society. Therefore, it seems almost an innate feature of the social structure, an aspect of the human condition. But this statement hides the wide variations in the concept of marriage, both in its form and in its content as well as in its rationale. The song made famous in Frank Sinatra's words would have us believe that love and marriage are two sides of the same coin – like a horse and carriage. Apparently, you cannot have one without the other!

Charming as this picture is, it is hardly true. Historically, marriage has been more about property rights and getting the right in-laws.[28] Love was neither a necessary nor a sufficient reason to get married. Alliances were fixed between families without any intervention on the part of the couple. In India, in the context of the arranged marriage, this still holds true.

Prakasa[29] states that arranged marriages serve six functions in the Indian community: '(1) It helps to maintain the social stratification system in the society; (2) gives parents control over family members; (3) enhances the chances to preserve and to continue with the ancestral lineage; (4) provides an opportunity to strengthen the kinship group; (5) allows the consolidation and extension of family property; (6) enables the elders to preserve the principle of endogamy.'

Nevertheless, the institution of marriage has changed undeniably. Once women became freer and more able to assert themselves, they also ventured out to choose their own partner. Particularly, there has been a weakening in many of the six functions of the arranged marriage noted by Prakasa. Greater inter-caste marriage weakens reasons (1), (3) and (6); focus on economic well-being over religious and other considerations weakens (2) and (4); and increase in the number of nuclear families and greater migration and urbanization affects (5).[30]

Marriage lies at the intersection of society and the law. Societal traditions are crystallized into the rules relating to marriage by law. The law is however a dynamic concept. Inevitably the nature of marriage would change if there is a change in society. Consequently, the law would have to be amended to keep pace with this societal change. This is exactly what has happened in the case of laws relating to separation and divorce.[31]

However, one cannot ignore that the supreme source of the law is the Constitution, and hence the egalitarian and liberating spirit of the Constitution must necessarily interact with social rules. Even if society does not change, the principles of the Constitution must nevertheless apply. The principles of dignity and autonomy underlying the cases of inter-caste and inter-religion marriages actually are foundational principles and ought to apply in all cases. These values have been applied in just such cases, although indirectly.

The recent judgement decriminalizing unnatural sex was based to a large extent on the autonomous right of an individual to choose her own partner, regardless of sex.[32] In an interesting passage, Chief Justice Dipak Misra speaking for himself and Justice Khanwilkar said that 'There can be no doubt that an individual also has a right to a union under Article 21 of the Constitution. When we say union, we do not mean the union of marriage, though marriage is a union. As a concept, union also means companionship in every sense of the word, be it physical, mental, sexual or emotional. The LGBT community is seeking realisation of its basic right to companionship, so long as such a companionship is consensual, free from the vice of deceit, force, coercion and does not result in violation of the fundamental rights of others.'[33]

The line 'When we say union, we do not mean the union of marriage, though marriage is a union' is particularly interesting. At first blush, the Chief Justice seems to suggest that Article 21 does not confer a right to gay marriage, just a union. But if union includes marriage, how can the right to marriage possibly be excluded from the fundamental right to life? The Chief Justice noted that 'even marriage was not equated to procreation' and hence, non-procreative sex could not be against the order of nature. That, of course, begs the question, if procreation is not the purpose of marriage, why deny that right that extends to heterosexual couples to gay couples?

Justice Chandrachud, who was party to the Navtej Johar judgement, had also authored a judgement in the privacy case. The privacy case in fact could reasonably be said to be the foundation of the Navtej Johar judgement. In several passages, he laid the groundwork not merely for the eventual overruling of the Suresh Kumar Koushal judgement[34] but also for the recognition of gay marriage. Justice Chandrachud held that 'family, marriage, procreation and sexual orientation are all integral to the dignity of the individual. Above all, the privacy of the individual recognizes an inviolable right to determine how freedom shall be exercised'.[35]

Justice Sanjay Kishen Kaul held that 'It is an individual's choice as to who enters his house, how he lives and in what relationship. The privacy of the home must protect the family, marriage, procreation and sexual orientation which are all important aspects of dignity.'[36] Thus a majority of at least five of the nine judges who were party to the judgement held that people of alternate sexuality had a right to family life, which included marriage.

Since the issue did not directly arise in that case, the Court probably held back in ruling finally on the issue. Of course, how the courts rule once the matter comes before them is uncertain. Even the Union of India, though it did not oppose the petition in the Navtej Johar case, filed an affidavit stating that in case the Court was going to address the issue of gay marriage, it would have taken a different stand.

The cases of young couples seeking the protection of the Court when they get married contrary to the wishes of the community show that the institution of marriage is strong. Even if individual marriages are easier to break up through liberalizing divorce laws, more people, at least in India, seem to be looking to get married. But why is love not enough? Why do people seek to get married?

The answer is not far to look. Marriage has real social and economic consequences. When two individuals get married, there is a state and a social sanction to the relationship. There are also mutual rights that the parties to the marriage have. For instance, one partner cannot simply walk away and marry someone else. There are clear pecuniary effects too. The laws of inheritance recognize a married spouse and give him or her a right in the property of the other spouse. There are insurance and tax benefits, which unmarried couples do not have.

Marriage is thus both an instrumental as well as an intrinsic good. As an instrumental good, it enables couples to accomplish social and economic goals. As an intrinsic good, it enables persons to declare their love to one another and hence enhance and preserve their dignity.

These benefits, both instrumental and intrinsic, which extend to all married couples do not currently extend to same-sex partners.

Therefore, there has to be marriage equality to fulfil the Constitution makers' promise to all Indians. Not only because all individuals are deserving of a right to choose their partner, but also because all women (and men) are equal.

The Constitution demands liberty, justice and fraternity for an individual. It also promises equality. As seen above, the love jihad and the khap panchayat cases reflect the constitutional values of autonomy and dignity. But same-sex marriage shows another facet of the Constitution – that of equality. It would appear that autonomy and equality, while they are different concepts, have a lot in common. Rather like love and marriage, in the case of equality and dignity too, you cannot have one without the other. It is tough to imagine leading a dignified life with any sense of self-worth if you are treated as a second-class citizen.

That is precisely the point in the case of gay marriages. The inability to get married to your same-sex partner is an effective undermining of your right to choose your partner. It is also a violation of your right to equality when you see your heterosexual friend get married.

The Court has intervened in the case of inter-caste and inter-religious marriages to protect the choices of those who wish to get married so as to protect their right to dignity. The Courts have generally upheld their role as the sentinel on the qui vive – jealous and zealous guardians of constitutional liberties. But in the case of the latest battleground of marriage – same-sex marriages – the issue is open. The Constitution is ready for gay marriage. The question is whether the society and the courts are ready.

From Adultery to Sexual Autonomy

The Constitutional Potential of *Joseph Shine*

MENAKA GURUSWAMY and ARUNDHATI KATJU

2018 was a dramatic year for Indian constitutionalism. This was the year the Indian Supreme Court embraced sexuality as an integral part of citizenship. In *Navtej Singh Johar v. Union of India,*[1] the Court finally recognized the constitutional rights of equality, dignity, expression, life and liberty of LGBTQ Indians. In *Indian Young Lawyers Association v. State of Kerala,*[2] better known as the Sabarimala decision, the Supreme Court found that it was constitutionally obligated to allow Hindu women of faith of a menstruating age to access the Sabarimala temple in Kerala, from which they had hitherto been excluded. Finally, in *Joseph Shine v. Union of India,*[3] the Court struck down Section 497 of the Indian Penal Code, 1860, which enabled a husband to file a criminal complaint of adultery against his wife's male lover, because it was unconstitutional.

This was also the year that the Supreme Court celebrated constitutional morality. The underlying logic of each of these decisions was that constitutional morality leads the Court to strike down laws that may be justified in the name of social convention, but social morality must bend before constitutional values of equality and dignity. In *Johar*, constitutional morality led the Court to strike down the sodomy law; in *Sabarimala*, it held that religious sentiment could not trump women's right to equality; in *Shine*, the Court held that constitutional morality would also govern marriage.

Is marriage a private relationship or a public one? Marriage may be the most delicate and intimate of relationships, but it also enjoys social, political and economic functions. Any entry that the law may make into the matrimonial bond has been heavily contested. Recall B.R. Ambedkar's resignation over opposition to the Hindu Code Bill, the continuing debate over the validity of the cruelty provisions under Section 498A of the Indian Penal Code, 1860[4] and what might be thought of as the failure of the dowry prohibition law.

Marital rape is an area of both matrimonial and criminal law that has remained stubbornly resistant to reform. Exception 1 to Section 376 of the Indian Penal Code, 1860 ('the marital rape exception') provides that non-consensual sexual intercourse by a man upon his wife, when she is above the age of 15, is not a criminal offence. In this paper, we argue that by extending the doctrine of constitutional morality to the marital relationship, *Joseph Shine* is a crucial stepping stone to striking down the marital rape exception.

THE CRIMINAL OFFENCE OF ADULTERY IN INDIA

The *Joseph Shine* petition challenged the constitutionality of the criminalization of adultery. The five-judge panel that heard this case comprised the then Chief Justice Dipak Misra, along with Justices Khanwilkar, Rohinton Nariman, D.Y. Chandrachud and Indu Malhotra. The Chief Justice and Justice Khanwilkar wrote the majority decision, with the other three judges writing separate concurring judgements.

The Indian Penal Code, 1860 criminalized adultery under Section 497. More specifically, the offence fell within Chapter XX of the Penal Code, which pertains to 'Offences Relating to Marriage'. Therefore, the Penal Code conceived of this offence as one of many relating to the institution of marriage – having sexual intercourse with a woman by deceitfully inducing a belief of lawful marriage (Section 493), bigamy (Section 494), and enticing or taking away or detaining with criminal intent a married woman (Section 498), amongst others.

Section 497 IPC did not criminalize adultery because it damaged the marriage of two persons, for if this were the law's intention, then extramarital sexual relations by either spouse should have been penalized. Not that we agree with the criminalization of extramarital sex, but let us assume that this was the apparent aim of the law, and that this aim had merit. But a reading of Section 497 makes it clear that this was not the law's intention:

> **Adultery** – Whoever has sexual intercourse with a person who is and whom he knows or has reason to believe to be the *wife of another man, without the consent or connivance of that man* [emphasis supplied], such sexual intercourse not amounting to the offence of rape, is guilty of the offence of adultery, and shall be punished with imprisonment of either description for a term which may extend to five years or with fine, or with both. In such case the wife shall not be punishable as an abettor.

Section 497 had four facets: first, a man had sexual intercourse with a woman whom he knew or had reason to believe was married to another man; second, such sexual intercourse was without the consent of the woman's husband; third, the sexual activity was consensual; fourth, only the man could be punished, not the woman.

Section 497 has colonial origins, with roots in the Victorian morality of 1850s' and 1860s' England – but that is true for almost the entire Indian Penal Code. Section 497 had been challenged at regular intervals, for it most obviously distinguished between adulterous husbands and adulterous wives while providing a criminal remedy only to the hurt husband and not the hurt wife. (By 'hurt' we mean the party to the marriage who was cheated on.) A hurt husband could file a criminal complaint against the man who had sexual intercourse with his wife, but a hurt wife had no criminal recourse against a woman who had sexual intercourse with her husband.

Clearly the penal provision envisioned a husband's sexuality and autonomy differently from that of a wife. This in itself is unremarkable: Section 497, like the sodomy law under Section 377, made assumptions about consent, sexuality and the role of the State based on the morality of 19th-century England. What is remarkable, however, is that despite the fact that the adultery offence was challenged at regular intervals, it was upheld by the Supreme Court on multiple occasions.

The Penal Code did not stop at punishing a man who had sexual relations with the wife of another. It went a step further, criminalizing anyone who might enable a married woman to have sexual relations outside of her marriage. Section 498 of the Indian Penal Code, 1860 provides that:

> **Enticing or taking away or detaining with criminal intent a married woman** – Whoever takes or entices away any woman who is and whom he knows or has reason to believe to be the wife of any other man, with intent that she may have illicit intercourse with any person, or conceals or detains with that intent any such woman, shall be punished with imprisonment of either description for a term that may extend to two years, or with fine, or with both.

Section 498 has three facets: First; that a third party (not the two involved in the sexual relationship) takes or entices a married woman; second, he or she knows that the woman is married to someone else; and finally, such 'enticing or taking' is done to enable her to have sexual relations outside of marriage with another person. For lack of better language, such an 'enabler' may be punished with a prison term that may extend to two years.

Such a provision would likely penalize 'enticement' or enabling by a friend or family member or anyone who may even socialize with such a couple, or even a friend who goes along with a married woman to meet her lover. It was clearly intended not only to punish the male lover of the married woman, but even any friend of either party involved with this extramarital sexual encounter. Therefore, this law took very seriously the rights of the husband to control the sexuality of his wife, to the extent of punishing any other party or anyone who may be seen to entice this wife to seek sexual relations outside of marriage.

The question remains as to how someone can actually entice a woman, married or otherwise, to have sex with anyone. But, apart from the ridiculous nature of the offence, there also remains the question of how to demonstrate this in a court of law – is a third person who accompanies his/her friend to the lover's home an accused? Or a person who goes to a movie with the two lovers, who then head to a hotel room to have sex?

Outside of speculating how one would demonstrate the criminality of 'enticement', what the provision does demonstrate is the lack of any understanding of the law of a woman's sexuality: A woman does not need to be enticed or cannot be enticed to have sexual relations with another person. She would only do so on her own volition, and her autonomy includes independent desire.

Be that as it may, it took Indian courts a long time to appreciate all the glaring flaws in the adultery provisions; the inability to appreciate a woman's independent sexual autonomy; the lack of a constitutional awareness of the demands of equality between spouses; and a continued misunderstanding of the nature of marriage.

How did Indian courts treat the criminalization of adultery through the decades after the adoption of the Constitution? Colonial-era courts could justify the adultery provision as being in tune with the moral code of the day, applying the Victorian moral standards that led to the formulation and then application of such laws.

But, after 1950, Indian constitutional courts had the benefit of the Constitution and its values of equality between genders as well as prohibition of discrimination on grounds of sex. Constitutional courts were required to judge all laws against the benchmark of the Constitution; pre-constitutional laws carried no presumption of constitutionality. So, how did the courts of independent India interpret this obviously discriminatory provision in the face of constitutional values?

THE HISTORY OF THE ADULTERY CHALLENGES

There were three significant challenges to the adultery law, spread over the decades, after the Constitution was adopted. These three unsuccessful challenges formed the backdrop to the necessity of a five-judge panel to examine the constitutionality of the prosecution by the husband of the male paramour who has an adulterous relationship with his wife.

Preceding the challenge in *Shine* were cases like *Yusuf Abdul Aziz v. State of Bombay.*[5] Aziz was being prosecuted for adultery, but we know little about the details of his case. The legendary Justice Vivian Bose, after hearing arguments by the then Attorney General M.C. Setalwad, decided that Section 497 did not violate the equality guarantee under Article 14, since Article 15 (3) of the Constitution allowed the state to make special provisions for women. Presumably Justice Bose thought that the penal provision that allowed for the prosecution of a man for adultery and not the woman was a special provision in favour of women. Decades later, this assessment was set aside by the Chief Justice Misra and Justice Khanwilkar in *Shine*.

This is the appropriate time to briefly examine Articles 14 and 15 of the Constitution to make the discussion of the past and present equality challenges against the adultery law easier to follow. India's equality doctrine has its foundations in Articles 14 and 15 of the Constitution. For the purposes of our conversation, the most critical tenets of India's equality doctrine are captured in these three textual provisions:

1. Article 14 states that 'the State shall not deny to any person equality before the law or equal protection of the laws within the territory of India.'
2. Article 15 (1) prohibits the State from discriminating against 'any citizen on grounds only of religion, race, caste, sex, place of birth or any of them.'
3. Article 15 (3) states that 'nothing in this article shall prevent the State from making any special provision for women and children.'

Between these three textual provisions of the Constitution, it's made clear that equality before the law between men and women is mandated, and that the State is prohibited from discriminating against any citizen on grounds of sex.

The State may also make 'special provisions' for women in the form of affirmative action or remedial measures to help mitigate or address historical disadvantages suffered by this group. Such special measures could take the shape of different criteria for the length of service in rural areas with regard to male and female doctors,[6] or in allowing employers to consider sex in making employment decisions when it is done in a properly or legally chartered affirmative action plan.[7] This is how Justice Vivian Bose in *Yusuf Abdul Aziz* justifies the exclusion of the female erring spouse or female lover of the husband from any prosecution under the adultery law. Such exclusion was protective legislation in favour of women.

In 1985, the Court would have the opportunity to re-examine the assumptions it made about the adultery law. And yet again, it would fail to look to constitutional values. In *Sowmithri Vishnu v. Union of India*,[8] the Supreme Court, through a three-judge bench comprising Chief Justice Y.V. Chandrachud and Justices R.S. Pathak and Amarendra Nath Sen, was confronted with an acrimonious divorce that included the husband filing a complaint under Section 497 IPC against his about-to-be-divorced wife's lover, who went by the name of Dharma Ebenezer.

Chief Justice Chandrachud, who wrote the judgement, found that Section 497 did not violate Articles 14, 15 and 21 (the constitutional guarantees of equality, non-discrimination, and life and liberty). In a twist, he opined that the argument that the section discriminates since it only enables a husband to prosecute the 'adulterer', and does not confer any similar right on a wife whose husband indulges in such actions, spoke 'to the policy of the law and not to its constitutionality unless while implementing the policy any provision of the Constitution is infringed.'[9]

Such reasoning is rather surprising. Any law that patently treats men and women differently, or a situation where the 'equality' and 'non-discrimination' tenets of the Constitution are violated, forces the tests of constitutionality to be applied. If anything, the adultery provision is a simple exposition of how such constitutional demands of equality are violated. The judicial review of statutes against the fundamental rights guaranteed by the Constitution is a fundamental role and duty of any constitutional court. Such adjudicatory obligations and expectations cannot be passed on to the legislature, which applies the standard of social acceptability and social morality – which may be at odds with the Constitution.

Such a bypassing of the obligations of a constitutional court to

applying the Constitution to a penal provision that discrim
reminds us of the final few lines from the infamous *Sures*
Koushal v. Naz Foundation,[10] where Justice Singhvi con
judgement upholding the constitutionality of Sectio
which criminalized LGBTQ Indians by failing to
the section and leaving it to Parliament to decide to
reform Section 377.

Chief Justice Chandrachud further termed
advanced on behalf of the petitioner that the
inclusive as being 'a crusade by a woman ag
Eventually, he rejects all lines of challenges
section is constitutional since it enables at
of adulterous relationships as being punis
of marriage is not an ideal to be scorned

The third time the Supreme Cou
to Section 497 was a few years late
V. Revathi v. Union of India.[13] In this
grounded their challenge in the leg
barring her from prosecuting the
challenge was similar to *Sowmith*
their case from *Vishnu*, the pe
two lawyers Geeta Ramasesha
to focus their efforts on contest
Criminal Procedure, 1972 (henceforth
section goes hand in hand with Section 497
enables prosecution of the penal law.

Section 198 (2) CrPC provides for:

Prosecution of offences against marriages – (1) No Court shall take any cognisance of an offence punishable under Chapter XX of the Indian Penal Code (45 of 1860) except upon a complaint made by some person aggrieved by the offence;

(2) For the purposes of sub-section (1) no person other than the husband of the woman shall be deemed to be

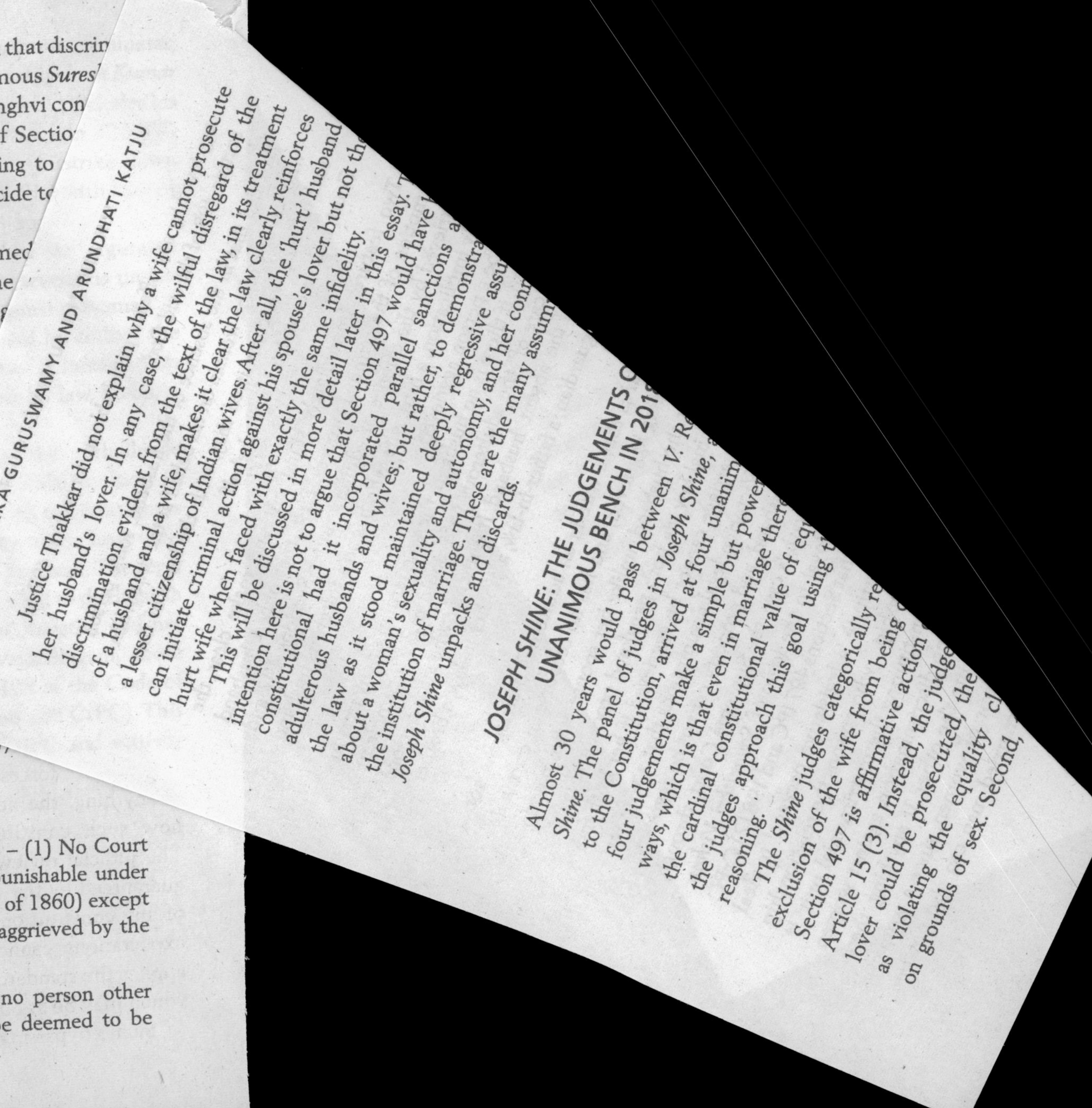

Justice Thakkar did not explain why a wife cannot prosecute her husband's lover. In any case, the wilful disregard of the discrimination evident from the text of the law, in its treatment of a husband and a wife, makes it clear the law clearly reinforces a lesser citizenship of Indian wives. After all, the 'hurt' husband can initiate criminal action against his spouse's lover but not the hurt wife when faced with exactly the same infidelity.

This will be discussed in more detail later in this essay. T
intention here is not to argue that Section 497 would have
constitutional had it incorporated parallel sanctions a
adulterous husbands and wives; but rather, to demonstra
the law as it stood maintained deeply regressive assu
about a woman's sexuality and autonomy, and her con
the institution of marriage. These are the many assum
Joseph Shine unpacks and discards.

JOSEPH SHINE: THE JUDGEMENTS O
UNANIMOUS BENCH IN 201

Almost 30 years would pass between V. R
Shine. The panel of judges in *Joseph Shine*, a
to the Constitution, arrived at four unanim
four judgements make a simple but powe
ways, which is that even in marriage ther
the cardinal constitutional value of eq
the judges approach this goal using t
reasoning.

The *Shine* judges categorically re
exclusion of the wife from being
Section 497 is affirmative action
Article 15 (3). Instead, the judge
lover could be prosecuted, the
as violating the equality cl
on grounds of sex. Second,

violates equality and non-discrimination on grounds of sex by envisaging the husband as being the owner of the wife's sexual agency. Finally, the Court shows that its own appreciation of the institution of marriage has evolved. The bases of the Court's judgement were as follows:

(i) The adultery law does not make special provision for women as mandated by Article 15 (3).

In all three cases that upheld the constitutional validity of Section 497 and 498, *Yusuf Abdul Aziz*, *Sowmithri Vishnu* and *V. Revathi*, the Court found that the provision that exempted the women lovers from prosecution was about being protective, or specially providing for women as given in Article 15 (3) of the Constitution. This line of reasoning is important to appreciate since it is this paternalistic protectiveness that invariably disempowers and debilitates women. Such reasoning was also recognized in cases like the Bombay Bar girls.[16]

In *Shine*, Chief Justice Misra, Justice Chandrachud and Justice Malhotra discuss Article 15 (3) elaborately in their individual opinions. The Chief Justice and Justice Khanwilkar make it clear that affirmative action cannot discriminate against women. Justice Nariman also disagreed with the interpretation of Article 15 (3) that the Court adopted in *Yusuf Abdul Aziz*. He writes that in 'treating women as chattel', Section 497 discriminates against women on grounds of sex only and is in violation of Article 15 (1) and not protected by Article 15 (3).[17]

Justice Chandrachud held that 'Articles 14 to 18 are constituents of a single code of equality' and that 'discrimination which is grounded in paternalistic and patriarchal notions cannot claim the protection of Article 15 (3)'.[18] He explains further that the 'protection afforded to women under Section 497 highlights the lack of sexual agency that the section imputes to a woman.'[19] Further, women are saved from penalty under Section

497, not to protect them but because the law presumes they are chattel. The Court clarifies that 'the constitutional guarantee in Article 15 (3) cannot be employed in a manner that entrenches paternalistic notions of protection.'[20]

In her opinion, Justice Malhotra found that Section 497 IPC could not be a legislation beneficial for women because of the inequality between men's and women's abilities to prosecute adultery. She also reasoned that, under Article 15 (3), the 'true purpose of affirmative action is to uplift women and empower them in socio-economic spheres. A legislation which takes away the rights of women to prosecute cannot be termed as beneficial legislation.'[21]

(ii) A husband cannot own his wife's sexuality: The foundation for marital rape

All four judgements spoke firmly in favour of recognizing the integrity and autonomy of female sexuality. The Chief Justice along with Justice Khanwilkar held that the 'section treats women as chattel and the property of the man'.[22] Justice Nariman also supported this interpretation of the section assuming that women are 'chattel'.[23] Justice Chandrachud argued that Section 497 treats a married woman as her husband's property: 'women occupy a liminal space in the law; they cannot be prosecuted for committing adultery, nor can they be aggrieved by it, by virtue of their status as their husband's property.'

Justice Chandrachud explains further that 'Section 497 is premised upon sexual stereotypes that view women as being passive and devoid of sexual agency. The notion that women are victims of adultery and therefore require the beneficial exemption under the section.'[24]

Amongst the most important observations by the Court are those pertaining to women being considered the property of men. This is significant not only from the perspective of the constitutionality of adultery, but also going forward from the perspective of the recognition of women's sexuality in general.

(iii) Recognition of Women's Sexuality

There are two threads within the judgement that we would like to explore further, for the foundational role they will play in future litigation with regards to women's sexuality, and also the conception of marriage itself. First, the foundational premise of Section 497 is that women were the property or chattel of men. Therefore, in the words of Justice Chandrachud, 'when there was connivance or consent of the man, there is no offence.'[25] Hence, it is not the sanctity of marriage that is being protected by the penal provision. For if sanctity of the institution as a general value that warranted criminalization of adultery, then extramarital sex on the part of either the husband or the wife would be penalized uniformly.

However, per Section 497, a wife cannot initiate a criminal complaint, and nor can a woman who has sexual relations with a married man be prosecuted under it. What the section does is that it only enables the husband to initiate the criminal process against his wife's male lover. Such assumptions of subordination of women immediately place the penal provision in the zone of unconstitutionality. As the Court recognizes, a 'woman has the right to love according to her choice and also an absolute right to reject.'[26]

Second, as Justice Chandrachud says, there is the explicit recognition that 'marriage is a constitutional regime founded on the equality of and between spouses. Each of them is entitled to the same liberty which Part III guarantees.' He goes on to say that 'Section 497 is inconsistent with the Constitution, since it treats a woman as but a possession of her spouse… The essential values on which the Constitution is founded – liberty, dignity and equality – cannot allow such a view of marriage.'[27]

JOSEPH SHINE: CONSEQUENCES FOR MARITAL RAPE IN INDIA

In *Joseph Shine*, the Court sought to ensure that marriage enters the domain of the application of constitutional dignity of each citizen, including those of wives. Many years ago, Menaka Guruswamy argued elsewhere that men and women alike possess equal citizenship rights under the Indian Constitution, and that 'the ability to withhold consent in the context of sex is a crucial ingredient of the constitutional self.' [28] The article details how India was an outlier when it came to the recognition of marital rape as a crime, and that countries as close as Nepal and Bhutan, along with 102 other countries from the global South and the global North, had criminalized marital rape.

The Penal Code regulates marriage through a number of provisions, including the marital rape exception. Section 376, the rape law provision, excludes marital rape. It says 'sexual intercourse by a man with his own wife, the wife not being under 15 years of age, is not rape.' Amendments to the Penal Code in 2013 made it an offence for a man to have non-consensual intercourse with his wife if they were legally separated (Section 376A IPC), but the marital rape exception under Section 375 IPC was left untouched.

In *Joseph Shine*, the Supreme Court makes a preliminary case for the recognition of marital rape, 'implicit in the seeking to privilege the fidelity of women in a marriage, is the assumption that a woman contracts away her sexual agency when entering a marriage… Curtailing the sexual autonomy of a woman or presuming lack of consent once she enters marriage is antithetical to constitutional values.'[29] Since the Court had decided *Navtej Singh Johar* before *Shine*, it could look at its own jurisprudence on sexual autonomy and consent from *Johar*, and rely on it.

Deleting the marital rape exception outright has found few takers. The Law Commission of India dealt with the marital rape exception its 84th and 172nd Reports, issued 20 years apart in 1980 and 2000, respectively. In the 84th Report, the Law Commission recommended raising the age of the wife to 18 years rather than abolishing the exception outright.[30] Since the Child Marriage Restraint Act, 1929 prohibited girls younger than 18 years old from marrying, the Law Commission recommended that the minimum age of consent should be a uniform 18 years across the board, whether for statutory rape or for the marital rape exception.

The Law Commission took up the issue again in 2000, in its 172nd Report. It argued again in favour of retaining the marital rape exception, this time recommending that the age of the wife be placed at 16 rather than 18 years. Deleting the exception for women above 16 would amount to 'excessive interference with the marital relationship.'[31]

The sexual assault law under the Indian Penal Code, 1860 was amended extensively in 2013 following the 16 December 2012 gang rape of a young woman in the nation's capital. However, the Criminal Law (Amendment) Act, 2013 left the marital rape exception untouched. The J.S. Verma Committee, tasked with making recommendations for the overhaul of the sexual assault law after the 16 December rape case, had recommended withdrawing the exception.[32] Many of its recommendations were incorporated into the Criminal Law (Amendment) Act, 2013, but not this one about marital rape.

The J.S. Verma Committee reasoned that the marital rape exception was based on an outdated notion of marriage. Women were no longer regarded as the property of their husbands, and the exception had been withdrawn in many jurisdictions such as England and Wales, Canada, South Africa and Australia. The European Commission of Human Rights had endorsed a conviction for marital rape in *CR v. United Kingdom*, leading to amendments being passed in the Criminal Justice and Public Order Act, 1994.[33]

When the issue arose in the Indian Parliament, the department-related Standing Committee on Home Affairs rejected the

Verma Committee's recommendations regarding marital rape in its 167th Report on the Criminal Law (Amendment) Bill, 2012. The Standing Committee had called for suggestions from the public and from State and Union Territory governments. With respect to marital rape, the Committee received the suggestion that marital rape could be included in the proposed Section 376A of the Indian Penal Code (which penalized non-consensual sexual intercourse by a man with his wife during a legal separation), making rape by a husband during the subsistence of the marriage punishable at par with the general rape law.[34] This suggestion was also rejected.

Instead, during the Committee's final deliberations it was noted that

> several Members felt that the marital rape has the potential of destroying the institution of marriage. The Committee felt that if a woman is aggrieved by the acts of her husband, there are other means of approaching the court. In India, for ages, the family system has evolved and it is moving forward. Family is able to resolve the problems and there is also a provision under the law for cruelty against women. It was, therefore, felt that if the marital rape is brought under the law, the entire family system will be under great stress and the Committee may perhaps be doing more injustice. Some Members also suggested that the age mentioned in the exception to the Section may be raised to 18 years from 16 years. The exception provides that sexual intercourse or sexual acts by a man with his own wife, the wife not being under 16 years of age, is not sexual assault. The Home Secretary, responding to this suggestion, stated that by doing so by one stroke, the marriages in thousands in different States would be outlawed. One Member again suggested that for the words 'with or without the other person's consent, the words 'with or without the complainant's consent' may be used. The Committee, however, felt that by using complainant, a proper message will not go and existing formulation may continue.[35]

D. Raja and Prasanta Chatterjee, members, Rajya Sabha (both from the Communist Party of India) had submitted a note of dissent objecting to the retention of the marital rape exception. They argued that the marital rape exception 'is contrary to the provisions of the Indian Constitution which considers all women as equal human beings who have a right to live with dignity and free from violence within and outside marriage.'

In *Independent Thought v. Union of India*,[36] a Division Bench of the Supreme Court consisting of Justices Madan Lokur and Deepak Gupta examined whether the marital rape exception would hold where the wife was between 15 and 18 years old. Even though the petition before it had challenged the marital rape exception itself,[37] the larger question was not pressed, and the Court limited the issues before it to cases of marital rape where the wife was aged between 15 and 18 years. This allowed the Court to frame the issue in terms of child sexual abuse and child marriage rather than as one involving the sexuality of adult women within the institution of marriage.

The principal opinion, authored by Justice Madan Lokur, relied on the National Family Health Survey-3, which found that 46 per cent of Indian women between the ages 18 and 29 years were married before they turned 18; the NFHS also estimated that there were 23 million child brides in the country. It turned to reports by the UN on violence against women, and by the Government of India on child sexual abuse, and also considered the Government of India's National Charter for Children, 2003, and the National Plan of Action for Children, 2016.

The Court noted that the Prohibition of Child Marriage Act, 2006 criminalized child marriage but no corresponding changes were made to the rape law, and also looked into the criminalization of child sexual abuse under the Protection of Children from Sexual Offences Act, 2012, as per which the offence of penetrative assault was enhanced to aggravated penetrative assault if the perpetrator was related to the survivor; this relationship could also be through marriage.

The Court noted the anomalies between the statutory rape provision, which criminalizes sexual intercourse with a girl below 18 years, irrespective of consent; it also noted that husbands could be convicted of the sodomy offence (Section 377, which was still on the books) and for outraging the modesty of their wives (under Section 354 IPC). The Protection of Women from Domestic Violence Act, 2005 allowed a wife to get a protection order from a court if her husband had committed acts of sexual abuse against her; the Prohibition of Child Marriage Act, 2006 makes a child marriage voidable but punished people who performed or permitted a child marriage.

In striking down the marital rape exception as it applied to girls aged between 15 and 18, the Court invoked Article 15 (3) of the Constitution, and also the right to bodily integrity and reproductive choice. It found a conflict between the IPC and the Protection of Children from Sexual Offences Act, 2012 (POCSO), and relied on the doctrine that the special law overrides the general law. It also held that there was no rationale to distinguish between the age of consent in cases of statutory rape and marital rape. The age of consent was 18 years across the board, and a woman younger than 18 was a child under all provisions of law.

During arguments, the Government opposed raising the age limit in the exception from 15 to 18 years, reasoning that sexual activity between a husband and wife should not be criminalized looking at the 'social realities of the nation':

> Economic and education development in the country is still uneven and child marriages are still taking place... As per National Family Health Survey-III, 46% women between the ages 18–29 years in India were married before the age of 18. It is also estimated that there are 23 million child brides in the country. Hence, criminalizing the consummation of a marriage union with a serious offence such as rape would not be appropriate and practical... Providing punishment for child marriage with consent does not appear to be

> appropriate in view of the socio-economic conditions of the country... Exception 2 of Section 375 IPC envisages that if the marriage is solemnized at the age of 15 due to traditions, it should not be a reason to book the husband in case of offence of rape under IPC... It is also necessary that the provisions of law should be in such a manner that it cannot affect a particular class of society. Retaining the age of 15 years in Exception 2 of Section 375 IPC has been provided considering the social realities of the nation.[38]

During oral submissions, the Government argued that the law was justified as (1) by getting married, the girl consented to sexual intercourse with her husband, (2) child marriage is a tradition in different parts of the country, and (3) the 167th Report of the Parliamentary Standing Committee, noted above, opined that criminalizing marital rape had the potential of destroying the institution of marriage.[39]

In short, the Government's response was located in social morality: the practice of child marriage is socially acceptable, and so it ought not to be criminalized. And some of these arguments could well be made for marital rape per se (that marriage amounts to blanket consent to sex, that criminalizing marital rape would destroy the institution). While the Court rejected these justifications in *Independent Thought*, it did so on the ground that the law did not penalize a form of child rape merely because the child was married. In his concurring opinion, Justice Deepak Gupta observed that 'merely because something is going on for a long time is no ground to legitimize and legalize an activity which is per se illegal and a criminal offence.'[40]

This is not to dispute that *Independent Thought* makes a significant advance in enhancing the age of consent for married women. The judgement protects girls married underage, who can now – at least in law – refuse to consent to sexual intercourse with their husbands. Legal change can provide the impetus for social change; and these legal protections do result in changes on the ground.

Yet *Independent Thought* will have limited application to challenge the marital rape exception per se. And indeed, the Court concluded by reiterating that it was not 'deal[ing] with the larger issue of marital rape of adult women since that issue was not raised before us by the petitioner or the intervenor.'[41]

The question of the marital rape exception also arose before a single judge of the Gujarat High Court, in *Nimeshbhai Bharatbhai Desai v. State of Gujarat*[42] (2018). The single judge, after noting the judgements in *Suresh Kumar Koushal v. Naz Foundation & Ors.*,[43] (which was good law at the time) and *Independent Thought*, found that Sections 354 and 377 were both available in cases of non-consensual sexual intercourse by a husband against a wife. Those offences would apply, the Court reasoned, to acts done in public and in private, and regardless of the wife's age.

The Court observed that retaining the marital rape exception has also led to the curious position where remedies are available against domestic violence, but not for rape. Non-consensual sexual intercourse between spouses can be punished under Section 354 as 'outraging the modesty of a woman' or even as sodomy under Section 377 IPC (since *Johar* only decriminalized consensual relations) but not as rape.

The Court also gave short shrift to the argument that penalizing marital rape would 'become a potent tool or weapon in the hands of an unscrupulous wife to harass her husband and become a phenomenon which may destabilize the institution of marriage.'[44] To the contrary, marital rape was, in the Court's opinion, 'a disgraceful offence that has scarred the trust and confidence in the institution of marriage.'[45] Contrary to the stand adopted by the Government, marriage does not 'give all time consent forever to [have] sex with your spouse.'[46] The argument that a wife filing a complaint of marital rape would effectively end the marriage could be made equally of domestic violence complaints: 'even if the wife initiates proceedings under the provision of the Domestic Violence Act, the marriage could be said to be irrevocably over. Therefore, this logic or analogy, which is sought to be applied by the Government, does not appeal to me in any manner.'[47]

The Court spoke eloquently of the role of the sexual bond in marriage:

> Sexual intimacy brings spouses wholeness and oneness. It is a gift and a participation in the mystery of creation. It is a deep sense of spiritual communion...a husband who feels aggrieved by his indifferent or uninterested wife's absolute refusal to engage in sexual intimacy may legally seek the court's intervention to declare her psychologically incapacitated to fulfil an essential marital obligation. But he cannot and should not demand sexual intimacy from her coercively or violently.[48]

The *Nimeshbhai Bharatbhai Desai* judgement is remarkable for its pointed rejection of the argument that social values require the retention of the marital rape exception. But having been passed before *Joseph Shine*, the High Court did not have the benefit of the doctrine of constitutional morality to strike the exception down outright.

CONCLUSION: THE CONSTITUTIONAL POTENTIAL OF *JOSEPH SHINE*

Shine establishes a firm foundation to recognize marital rape. No doubt the lack thus far of such recognition is a constitutional embarrassment. That a five-judge Bench grounds their reasoning along lines of female sexual autonomy is one of the most dramatic long-term jurisprudential implications of *Joseph Shine*.

The Misra bench that decided *Johar* and *Shine* invoked another common theme, of the role of a constitutional court in unpacking colonial-era laws and the colonial morality that defines them. The *Shine* Bench, like the Bench did in *Johar*, responds to the call of precedent that binds us to colonial morality, with a stern call to look to transformative constitutionalism. It argues that the Victorian morality that inspired this penal provision is antithetical to constitutional guarantees of liberty, dignity and equality. And the Court emphasizes that the criminal law must be in consonance with constitutional morality.[49]

It is constitutional morality that leads to the constitutional court ruling against a 160-year-old sodomy law, or the similarly archaic adultery law or a temple entry ban on women. The rejection of constitutional morality would render the loss of a valuable instrument against social or popular morality or even legislative inaction to reform laws that are constitutionally untenable.

Social morality may call for retention of the marital rape exception. Proponents of social morality seem to argue that allowing rape to happen in marriage preserves an aspect of the marital bond that is essential for our society and culture. They may point to a society that is feudal, poor and backward, where women have a subordinate position within the marital relationship; and argue that changing this dynamic will cause social upheaval and chaos.

The doctrine of constitutional morality challenges this status quo. Constitutional morality requires that, when the law governs intimate relationships, it holds them to the standard of the Constitution – ensuring equality and dignity. The doctrine enjoins the Court to play a counter-majoritarian role, protecting individuals and minorities against majoritarianism. *Joseph Shine* brings the doctrine of constitutional morality to bear in intimate relationships. *Shine* is a crucial step forward in that it holds that intimate relationships, even within the institution of marriage, must be tested against the standard of constitutional and not social morality.

What is the future of marriage in India? Unlike Western Europe, where marriage rates are on the decline, Indian society is a firm believer in marriage. Divorce may be on the rise, but marriage is firmly embedded in the social psyche. As the

Supreme Court noted in *Independent Thought*, in several parts of the country women get married well below the legal age, leading to an increase in population growth. Marriage is not going anywhere.

Law reform has brought forth a number of protective measures for wives, recognizing the imbalance of power in this relationship. Legislation has changed the legal contours of the relationship: Section 498A IPC, the Dowry Prohibition Act, the Prevention of Child Marriage Act, the Protection of Women from Domestic Violence Act, and so on. It's a long list. But the marital rape exception is stubbornly impervious to change.

What is it about sexual intimacy within marriage that makes it an exception? Can we dream of a future where marital intimacy is also thought of within a framework of equality and dignity? The institution of marriage is changing – same-sex couples wish to be embraced in its fold – and *Joseph Shine*'s insistence that intimacies in marriage are governed by constitutional morality, and that women and men have sexual autonomy within marriage, takes us towards that future.

SEX AND THE WORKPLACE

The Beast in Our Midst
How India's MeToo Movement Broke the Silence on Workplace Sexual Harassment

NAMITA BHANDARE

Nobody saw it coming and nobody could have predicted its impact. The complaint itself went back all the way to 2008 when Tanushree Dutta, a former Miss India, complained that the actor Nana Patekar had groped her on the sets of a film *Horn Ok Pleassss,*[1] while she was filming a song.

Patekar, she said, had managed to bully his way into the song and insert an 'intimate' step that wasn't there in the original script. When she protested and tried to leave the sets to go home, her car was stopped by workers from the Maharashtra Navnirman Sena, a parochial party.

There's a video of dozens of screaming, angry men beating down on her car, deflating the tyres and smashing its windshield. You can see Dutta in the back seat, her mobile phone in one hand, the other on her driver's shoulder as if to reassure him – or perhaps herself. Police in uniform stand impassively as one man jumps on the roof of her car. It is terrifying to watch.[2]

Dutta complained to the Cine and Television Artistes' Association (CINTAA). There was no response. The story made no headlines. She eventually got married, moved to America and the story was forgotten.

In September 2018, the Brett Kavanaugh confirmation hearings for the US Supreme Court were broadcast live from Washington. The hearings did not reach a wide television audience in India. Yet, in a global, instantly interconnected world, the accusation by Professor Christine Blasey Ford that Kavanaugh had sexually assaulted her brought forward memories of America's MeToo movement of a year ago, and seemed to have acted as a trigger for some women in India.

It was in the middle of these hearings that the Tanushree Dutta incident resurfaced when she gave an interview to an entertainment channel revisiting the old incident with Patekar.

Just how much had changed in a decade is evident by how quickly Dutta's interview was picked up and how fast it went viral.

CINTAA scrambled to issue a belated apology, saying that its earlier decision was 'not appropriate, as the chief grievance of sexual harassment wasn't even addressed.'

But the real turmoil was taking place on social media.

'Some incidents that take place even a decade ago remain fresh in your memory. What happened with Tanushree Dutta on the sets of 'Horn OK Please' is one such incident – I was there,' began a 13-tweet thread on 26 September by the journalist Janice Sequeira.

Sequeira was bearing witness to what Dutta had been saying all along, hinting at the Indian film industry's dark underbelly – its infamous 'casting couch'. She lamented: 'It could have possibly been the first instance of a Bollywood actress calling out sexual predators, and her voice was silenced by more powerful men who continued to have flourishing careers. Now she's found her voice again. Should we listen?'

It was a rhetorical question because regardless of whether anyone was listening, an unprecedented number of women began speaking up. Silence, for them, was no longer an option.

* * *

How far back do you rewind events to understand India's October 2018 outing – its own MeToo movement?

Those looking for a spark might be tempted to go back no further than a year to the global impact made by *The New York Times* and *New Yorker* investigations into Hollywood film producer Harvey Weinstein, which exposed decades of predatory behaviour and brought his career to an effective end.

Or they might want to look at the publication on social media of 'The List', or to use its acronym LoSHA (List of Sexual Harassers in Academia), by a 24-year-old law student at the University of California, Davis. In October 2017, Raya Sarkar had launched an online campaign to name and shame teachers at Indian universities who were alleged to have sexually harassed or assaulted students.

In a Google document that included 35 names and a Facebook list that had 60, the list named the professors, with locations and, in some cases, details of the assault. In an interview to the news website, *Buzzfeed*, Sarkar said compiling the list was an opportunity to warn students 'to be wary of their professors, because in my opinion, knowing how college administrations function, harassers will continue to hold their positions of power.'[3]

Queer and Dalit, Sarkar was an early disrupter – for her list caused (and still does) outrage amongst some older feminists, including political science professor Nivedita Menon, who wrote an open letter saying that LoSHA ignored due process. 'This manner of naming can delegitimize the long struggle against sexual harassment, and make our task as feminists more difficult,' stated the letter, co-signed by 12 feminists.[4]

A younger generation of feminists disagreed. Due process had failed far too many women in the past and the very long arm of the law was seen as simply too exhausting and too uncertain in its ability to deliver justice. A list, they said, was the only way to out serial predators and warn other women. 'The idea was so basic, and yet so radical,' says journalist Anoo Bhuyan.[5] 'Raya had developed a process that had a method, but not everybody understood it.'

The law asks for us to believe in due process but there are no fixes available, says Bhuyan. 'Due process can be fixed only by people in power – and those people are upper caste men who have no interest in creating a more just society for women.'[6] Bhuyan remarks that the movement has always existed. 'The spectre of sexual harassment and the resistance to it is not anything new.'

Mumbai-based writer and filmmaker Paromita Vohra who runs the excellent website 'Agents of Ishq' agrees: 'People would love to see MeToo as a discrete event. But really what it was, was decades of feminist activism and change.'[7]

And women simply would not be bullied into silence. In July 1988, Rupan Deol Bajaj, an IAS officer, took umbrage when K.P.S. Gill, then the Director General of Police in Punjab confronted her at a dinner party and slapped her posterior in view of the other dinner guests. After getting no satisfactory response to her complaint to the Inspector General of Police, Chandigarh, Bajaj filed a criminal complaint and then, along with her lawyer, Indira Jaising, followed through all the way to the Supreme Court, where she was finally vindicated 17 and a half years later.

With every generation, life is different, Vohra continues. 'I remember hearing one of the first women in the army speaking about how there were no toilets back when she joined but you really didn't complain because you didn't want to admit that you couldn't hack it. Today, we would critique that position. But I get where she's coming from. You're the person who pushed the door open for so many others even though you might have had to use some of the same tools of the structure that you went into.'

Undeniably, one of the milestones on this long journey was when, in 1992, the government of Rajasthan launched a campaign against child marriage, and a 25-year-old woman signed up for it. Bhanwari Devi, from the *kumhar*, potter community in the village of Bhateri, 56 kilometres from Jaipur, had been married off when she had been just a baby. She remains, in her words, an *angootha chaap*, illiterate.[8] As a volunteer, or *saathin*, she received Rs 200 a month for expenses. Her job was to convince parents to postpone the marriages of their minor daughters.

When Bhanwari found out that two children, one just a baby at nine months, were to be married off in her village, she tried to talk the families out of it. The marriages took place anyway. But as revenge for trying to prevent them, the village council announced a social and economic boycott of Bhanwari and her husband, Mohan Lal. Nobody could engage their services or buy the pots they made. The vegetables the couple had grown on a small plot of land for their own consumption were destroyed.

It was an awful price to pay, but not the only one.

On 22 September 1992, five upper caste men caught hold of Bhanwari and Mohan Lal while they were out in the fields. They beat up the husband, and while three of them held her down, two raped her in his presence, she says.

Bhanwari remembers what happened next. When she and her husband went to the Bassi police station to file a complaint, they were told that a medical examination was required as proof of rape. So they went to the local health centre, where the woman doctor was not on duty. Then they took a bus to Jaipur but by the time they reached, the magistrate who was to sign the order clearing the medical exam said it was past his working hours. She would have to wait until the next morning.

Fifty-two hours had passed by the time Bhanwari Devi was medically examined for evidence of rape. When she returned to the Bassi police station to finally file her complaint, the police said she would have to deposit her skirt as evidence. Mohan Lal then removed his turban, unfurled it and gave it to Bhanwari to wrap around herself, she says.

But when judgement was pronounced three years later,

in November 1995, by a judge of the District and Sessions Court, he ruled: 'Since the offenders were upper-caste men and included a Brahmin, the rape could not have taken place.'[9] For the judge, it was unthinkable that upper caste men could have touched a lower caste woman.

In the history of the women's movement, Bhanwari Devi occupies a special place. Women's groups erupted in protest and several non-government organizations working for women's rights came together under the name of Vishaka to file a petition in the Supreme Court asking for a legal framework for women who had been sexually assaulted in the course of their work.

There was, until then, no precedent, law or guideline relating to sexual harassment at the workplace. A three-judge bench headed by the then Chief Justice of India J.S. Verma,[10] Sujata Manohar and B.N. Kirpal had to rely on international treaties such as the Convention on the Elimination of All Forms of Discrimination against Women (CEDAW) to issue a series of 'guidelines' that were to be 'strictly observed in all workplaces'.[11]

The Vishaka Directives served as guidelines for the prevention of the sexual harassment of women at the workplace. These guidelines remained the law until 2013, when the Sexual Harassment of Women at Workplace (Prevention, Prohibition and Redressal) Act was enacted.

The Vishaka judgement remains path-breaking for several reasons. For the first time, India's highest court was defining sexual harassment to include not just physical contact and demands for sexual favours but any unwelcome physical, verbal or non-verbal conduct that was sexual in nature. Moreover, it placed responsibility on employers to prevent or deter sexual harassment and set up processes to resolve, settle or prosecute such cases. It asked employers to create appropriate mechanisms so that complaints could be addressed in a time-bound manner.[12] And it urged Parliament to enact an appropriate law.

'For the first time in our history, sexual harassment was viewed not just in terms of safety but in terms of a violation of women's Constitutional rights to equality,' says Naina Kapur, the lead instructing counsel for the case. 'Going beyond safety, the court was talking about provisions that would enable women to go out to work and make a living.'[13]

The National Commission for Women prepared five draft bills. The 2010 draft was even tabled in Parliament and included additional features to the court guidelines: Monetary penalty for employers and interim relief for complainants.[14] Yet, it took the December 2012 protests against the gang rape and murder of a young medical student for Parliament to finally pass the Sexual Harassment of Women at Workplace (Prevention, Prohibition and Redressal) Act in April 2013.

Twenty-seven years later, Bhanwari Devi says she is thrilled with the Vishaka judgement and the subsequent changes in the law even though she never got justice for her own case where four of the five accused men have died of natural causes.[15]

'I only tried to stop little girls from being married off,' says Bhanwari, who continues to work as a *saathin*. 'I did nothing wrong.'

Bhanwari says she has no regrets and is proud of her role in getting women to speak up. 'MeToo is happening because I broke the silence. Today, women are speaking up because I spoke up nearly 30 years ago. I will get justice some day. And if I don't, then my daughters will get justice. And if they don't, then their daughters will. They will get it because women are no longer prepared to remain silent.'

* * *

If Bhanwari Devi sparked a movement, then Tanushree Dutta certainly lit the October revolution, or what we now in hindsight call India's MeToo movement. It was only the beginning.

Early in October 2018, a Kanpur-based pan masala company sent 1,200 employees, all men, on a cruise to Australia. When *Voyager of the Seas*, a ship operated by Royal Caribbean

International, left Sydney harbour, the men took over the pool deck, bars and buffets, bringing on board burlesque dancers dressed as Playboy bunnies.

'A dream cruise for dozens of Australian families hijacked by more than 1,000 men from an Indian tobacco company on a wild work bender has forced Royal Caribbean International to apologize to distraught passengers and issue mass refunds,' reported 9News, an Australian news outlet.[16]

Many Indians took to social media to express their outrage. Amongst them was a stand-up comedian called Utsav Chakraborty, a part of the now disbanded comedy collective, All India Bakchod (AIB). Founded in 2013, AIB had become one of India's most-viewed comedy channels on YouTube. By October 2018, the group had over 3.4 million subscribers and over 379 million views for its videos.

'Utsav was using his feminist woke cred, when actually he was no better,' Mahima Kukreja, a 28-year-old writer, poet and stand-up comedian, told me. 'The moment I read his tweet, I said, "This is it."'[17]

Kukreja took to Twitter: 'I want everyone to know @Wootsaw [the twitter handle for Utsav Chakraborty] is a piece of shit. He sent me a dick pic, was creepy, then cried saying I'll ruin his career if I tell others. I told two of the most influential men in comedy in India. Nothing happened. Let me tell you what else he has done with others.'

In a series of tweets, Kukreja accused Chakraborty of sexually harassing her and propositioning other women, one of whom was underage at the time. To some women he had sent pictures of his penis. He asked others to send him their nude pictures on Snapchat. 'I have received an avalanche of messages. He has abused and harassed so many. Will only post the ones I'm given permission to post,' tweeted Kukreja as she shared screenshots and messages.

'The first couple of days were insane. It was overwhelming just how many stories were coming up,' says Kukreja. It was, for her, also incredibly traumatic. 'I had three panic attacks on the first day. I was just a complete mess.'[18]

Chakraborty's first reaction on social media was to declare: 'The whole thing is far more complicated than it appears.' It needed, he added, 'an incredible amount of context'.

But at 4.14 p.m. that same afternoon AIB also issued a statement: 'We have been following the allegations made on social media this afternoon by women against Utsav Chakraborty, who has featured in some of our videos. The accusations describe a pattern of behavior that is unacceptable, and we at AIB condemn Utsav's alleged behavior.'

The statement acknowledged that by 'extending safe working spaces and a collaborative environment to people like Utsav, we have contributed towards a toxic environment that can be scary and unsafe for women.' AIB would be 'delisting every single video on our channels that features Utsav.'

Later that same day at 8.24 p.m., Chakraborty conceded: 'To be honest, from all accounts, I've been a piece of shit. And I will try to do everything I can to work past that. There was no excuse.'

That was not the end of it.

Less than 24 hours later, AIB issued a second statement offering clarity on whether members of the collective had known about the accusations against Chakraborty and failed to act on them.

'We messed up,' admitted AIB. It turned out that AIB co-founder Tanmay Bhat – one of the 'two of the most influential men in comedy in India' Kukreja had referred to in her first tweet – had actually received detailed allegations against Chakraborty and had confronted him 'in a personal capacity', he said. This had led to Chakraborty calling up the victim, leading to her further harassment. Yet, the company had continued assigning work to Chakraborty. 'We failed to listen when we should have and for that we are sorry,' the company admitted.

Three days later, AIB's head of human resources confirmed that Tanmay Bhat was 'stepping away from his association with AIB until further notice'. The second of the 'two of the most influential men in comedy in India' in Kukreja's tweet, Gursimran Khamba, was sent on a temporary leave of absence.

It was unprecedented to see big companies owning responsibility and taking action. In the past, the imbalance of power – big-shot male boss, subordinate female employee – meant that complaints of sexual misbehaviour had petered out into inaction and red tape with companies openly siding with the more powerful predatory bosses, and complainants often being forced to leave the organization. The more prudent course for many was just to stay quiet.

A January 2017 survey by the Indian National Bar Association of over 6,000 employees across various sectors found that 70 per cent of women who had experienced sexual harassment at work did not report it.[19] Women said that very often, more than the incident of sexual harassment, dealing with the complaints mechanism was isolating and nerve-wracking. Many were simply unaware of their rights in law. Others just quit and moved on.

Women had been 'waiting for a time and a moment to tell their story', says Kukreja. Now, they were breaking that unspoken rulebook and questioning the silence imposed on them.[20]

* * *

On 6 October 2018, while Mahima Kukreja's tweet storm was still swirling, journalist Ghazala Wahab tweeted: 'I wonder when the floodgates will open about @mjakbar.'

Mobashar Jawed Akbar was the first editor of *Sunday*, a magazine which began as the weekly supplement of the *Hindustan Standard* newspaper published by the Ananda Bazar Patrika group. In 1976, it was launched as a stand-alone magazine. Indira Gandhi's Emergency with its suspension of civil liberties was ongoing but the magazine captured the zeitgeist of the '70s, remaining relevant well into the '90s and well after Akbar had left.[21]

In 1989, Akbar stood for elections on a Congress ticket from Kishanganj in Bihar. He won and was appointed party spokesman by Rajiv Gandhi. In 1991, elections were held again, and it was during this campaign that Rajiv Gandhi was assassinated. The Congress came back to power but with the help of coalition partners. Akbar lost but was, nevertheless, appointed an advisor to the Ministry of Human Resources.

Towards the end of 1992, Akbar announced his return to journalism with the launch of *The Asian Age*, India's first daily newspaper with an international edition. But, by the late '90s, he had diluted his stake in the newspaper and eventually sold off most of it. Between 2000 and 2012, he was an editorial director with the India Today group.

In March 2014, just two months before the general elections, Akbar made the switch back to politics yet again, but this time with the right-wing BJP party because, he said, 'Narendra Modi's leadership is essential for the country.'

The BJP and its allies swept to power with 282 seats. Although he had not contested the elections, Akbar was appointed Junior Minister for External Affairs and brought into Parliament via the Rajya Sabha through a 2015 by-election in Jharkhand.

The complaints of sexual harassment against Akbar go back to the time when he was an editor.

In an article published on 12 October in the news website, *The Wire*, Ghazala Wahab writes about her first introduction to M.J. Akbar, the writer, while she was still a schoolgirl. Reading his books turned a 'desire' to become a journalist into a 'passion'. But joining *The Asian Age* as an intern in 1994 for this small-town girl from Agra soon put all illusions to rest, for 'he screamed, he swore and he drank in the office,' she writes.[22]

'I also frequently heard office gossip about his affairs with sub-editors/reporters or that in every regional office of *The Asian Age* he had a girlfriend. I shrugged all of it off as office culture. I was in the periphery of his attention and remained unaffected.'

But in her third year at the newspaper, she writes, Akbar's eyes fell on her. Her desk was moved to outside his office where, if the door was left ajar, he could watch her. He would send her 'lewd' messages. He would call her in for conversations and shut the door. 'I was the first person in my family to come out of my hometown Agra to study in Delhi and, thereafter, work. In the past three years, I had fought several battles at home to be able to live and work in Delhi. Women in my family only studied but never worked. In small town business families, girls always settled for arranged marriages. I had fought against this patriarchy. I had refused to accept money from my father because I wanted to make it on my own. I wanted to be a successful, respected journalist. I just couldn't quit and go back home as a loser.'

The stories we hear of workplace sexual harassment don't tell us about aspiration, ambition and the million tiny rebellions that women like Ghazala Wahab need to launch just for the right to work.

I could relate to Ghazala's story. When I applied for a master's degree in journalism to the United States in the mid-80s, I did so in the knowledge that what I was escaping was an inevitable arranged marriage to a suitable boy of my mother's choosing. I had other plans.

Back then there was no Internet. I trudged to the US Education Foundation office at Hailey Road in New Delhi, picked up a few brochures, sat down with a bored typist at Shankar Market, wrote out my essays, trekked to the post office to personally mail the packet (to ensure the postage stamps weren't stolen) and then waited 10–15 days or more for a reply.

When I returned from America two years later, I was a different person, having won the right to study and work on my own terms.

For me to ever complain to my parents about workplace sexual harassment was simply out of the question. Women like me knew the inevitable response: *We told you not to work. Now stop this nonsense, come home and get married.*

And so, I never told my parents about my creepy boss. In any event, it was a one-off incident that happened mercifully early at the beginning of my job. I served out my three-month notice at the now defunct *The Independent*, launched by the Times of India group, after working for just a month. The notice period was both a requirement of my employment contract and the needed breathing space for me to find another job, since, as a woman living on my own in Mumbai, I could not afford to be without work for any length of time.

At the height of the MeToo movement I did write an article[23] about the incident, not just the actual sexual assault but the abuse of power when my then editor summoned me to his office and berated me for telling a few people about the episode. It was a humiliating dressing down and I responded by resigning. When the MeToo movement happened in India, my former editor was heading a prestigious literature festival. I wrote to him, received a weak denial, wrote back and never heard from him again.

* * *

Akbar's response to the avalanche of accusations against him – including one alleging rape – was to file a criminal defamation case against one of the early tweeters, journalist Priya Ramani.

Two days after Ghazala Wahab's tweet, Ramani tweeted: 'I began this piece with my M.J. Akbar story. Never named him because he didn't "do" anything. Lots of women have worse stories about this predator – maybe they'll share.'

The 'piece' was an article Ramani had written in the form of an open letter a year earlier in 2017 for *Vogue* soon after the Harvey Weinstein story had broken in American media.[24]

Ramani's article begins with a description of her job interview with an unnamed editor in his hotel room, where the bed was turned down for the night. The editor offered her a drink, which she declined, and then asked her about her marriage plans and taste in music – even singing old Hindi film songs for her. The rest of the article, addressed to the 'Harvey Weinsteins of the world', talks of how entitled, predatory behaviour by such bosses was now on notice.

Within days of Ramani's tweet, as many as 20 women came forward with detailed accounts of being sexually harassed by Akbar. A former intern, the daughter of Akbar's friend, wrote about how he had kissed her on her mouth when she was 18. She says her father confronted him by email. Another woman, a journalist now with National Public Radio in the US, said he had raped her.

Akbar was out of the country when the story broke. Unsurprisingly, it made huge headlines in Indian and foreign media. There were demands for a thorough investigation and for his resignation, made by organizations such as the Indian Women's Press Corps, Press Club of India and South Asian Women in Media. When neither the tweets nor the media coverage showed signs of slowing down, Akbar put in his papers, claiming that he was doing so in order to 'seek justice in a court of law in my personal capacity...and challenge false allegations levied against me.'

To the questions put to him in court by Ramani's lawyer, Rebecca John, Akbar first claimed that he could not remember the interview, then flat out denied that such a meeting had taken place in his hotel room. He also told John that there had been a 'misunderstanding' with the intern but that it had been sorted out. And he confirmed in Court what he had earlier said in a statement to a news agency that he had had a 'consensual' relationship with the journalist who said he had raped her. But he also acknowledged that she was his subordinate.

The heat of the courtroom drama hid the chilling effect of Akbar's defamation suit. He added, in Court, that he reserved the right to issue criminal defamation notices to his other accusers and news outlets that had published their accounts.

At the time of writing this essay, both teams of lawyers have concluded their examination and questioning of witnesses. Akbar's lawyers are to conclude their final arguments and this will be followed by the final arguments put by Ramani's lawyer.

* * *

To understand due process, and the frustration of many women, particularly younger women, with the legal route, you have only to look at two early cases filed under two new laws: the first on rape and the second on workplace sexual harassment.

Tarun Tejpal's *Tehelka* pitched itself as a 'free, fair, fearless' weekly in the pursuit of truth. Politically, it was determinedly left-of-centre – a sting operation exposing corruption in defence deals under the then Atal Behari Vajpayee-led NDA government had nearly cost it its financial survival.

Within the office there seems to have been a general atmosphere of laissez-faire, particularly with regard to relationships between staff. Not all were consensual, and there were complaints by women about a photographer here or a senior editor there. They were often told to not be 'prudish' or even asked, 'Are you getting enough sex?' says a woman journalist who worked there at the time. When a woman reporter complained about her supervisor, she was asked to start reporting to a female boss; no action was taking against the supervisor, she says.

Another woman reporter about to interview a notoriously lecherous lawyer remembers being told that it was OK if the lawyer wanted to stroke her thighs – as long as she got the story. And Tejpal himself had once famously made what seems to have been an off-the-cuff 'joke': 'Now you are in Goa. Drink as much as you want, eat...sleep with whoever you think of, but arrive early at the event.'

That remark was reportedly made at *Tehelka*'s Think festival in 2011 held in Goa. Like many other publications – *India Today, The Economic Times* and the *Hindustan Times* that host leadership conferences – *Tehelka* had branched out into the lucrative, sponsor-rich events space. In 2013, its Think festival, described as 'India's most democratic, most inclusive', was held at Goa's Grand Hyatt hotel with a line-up of 70 speakers including Robert de Niro and Amitabh Bachchan. Of the 32 panels and conversations, not including performances and presentations, held over two days on 8 and 9 November, 20 were moderated by Tejpal's managing editor, Shoma Chaudhury.

The complainant in what came to be known as the Tehelka case had joined the publication in 2009 as a 22-year-old, fresh out of college. 'I believed there was no better place to do journalism,' she says.[25] At the 2013 Think festival, she was detailed to chaperone De Niro and his daughter.

It was at this festival that, according to a written complaint by the journalist to Chaudhury, Tejpal assaulted her twice in the elevator on the nights of 7 and 8 November.

The first assault occurred in the elevator on the night of 7 November when the journalist and Tejpal were returning after escorting De Niro and his daughter to their suite. In her complaint, the journalist says, as soon as Tejpal touched her, she asked him to stop but it was 'like talking to a deaf person'. Until the elevator finally stopped, he continued. 'At that point I did not want to lose my job. And so the next morning, I went about my work determined not to give Mr Tejpal or *Tehelka* a reason to fire me, as I was sure they would do once this story got out,' she says in her complaint.[26] That same night, however, she did tell a few friends at *Tehelka* about what had happened, she says.

The second assault took place the following night, on 8 November, when Tejpal asked the woman journalist to accompany him to 'Bob's [Robert de Niro's] room'. In her complaint, she writes: 'I was scared of getting into the lift with him again, and more terrified that he was going to try and take me into a room this time. By this time he was holding me by the wrist and had taken me into the lift.'[27] Again he sexually molested her; again she said no.

Later that night, she says, she told Tarun's daughter, at the time a friend, what had happened. When Tejpal found out, he was furious. After lashing out at the journalist in person, he texted her later in the night: 'I can't believe u went and mentioned even the smallest thing to her. What an absence of any understanding of a parent–child relationship.'

For the first few days after the festival, the journalist says she did nothing except think, and talk to those she trusted about her next steps. She was getting conflicting advice.

Remain silent.

Speak up.

He's too powerful, he'll finish you.

If you don't speak up, you'll never be able to live with yourself.

If you speak up, your whole life will come under scrutiny. Your career will be finished.

She decided silence was not an option. Tejpal was her boss and she knew she faced the risk of being assaulted again. 'I wanted my job but I knew that he had the power to summon me anywhere at anytime,' she says. 'This made me feel extremely vulnerable.'[28]

At the back of her mind also was the growing indignation of realizing that her boss had believed that it was all right to assault her and that her consent was not required. 'It was the erasure of my agency, my right to existence. The belief that my consent didn't matter even though I very clearly said no that was just galling,' she says.

Back in Delhi, she emailed Chaudhury on 18 November with details of the two assaults. She wanted a written apology. Confronted with these details put to him by Chaudhury, Tejpal apologized 'unconditionally' for a 'shameful lapse of judgement that led me to attempt a sexual liaison with you on two occasions on 7 November and 8 November 2013, despite your clear reluctance that you did not want such attention from me.' [29]

In a separate email to Chaudhury, Tejpal wrote, 'I must do the penance that lacerates me. I am therefore offering to recuse myself from Tehelka, and from the Tehelka office, for the next six months.'[30]

But the journalist wanted this apology to be acknowledged publicly to *Tehelka* staff. She wanted the term 'sexual misconduct' to be included. Chaudhury, she says, told her that she had to 'protect the institution' and in the public acknowledgment, the term is watered down to an 'untoward incident'.

Incredibly, *Tehelka* did not even have an Internal Complaints Committee (ICC) as mandated by the law. Nor was the journalist advised by the management, or anyone else in the organization, of her rights and options under the law, she says. 'Deeply traumatized by the lack of support offered by the organisation', the journalist resigned on 25 November.

Under the new, expanded legal definition of rape by the law passed in the aftermath of the brutal gang rape of a young physiotherapy student in New Delhi on the night of 16 December 2012, rape was now defined to include acts other than forced penile-vaginal penetration. The *Tehelka* journalist's accusation was not an 'untoward incident' or even 'sexual misconduct' but rape – a crime that now carried a minimum of seven years' jail time.

When the story broke, along with leaked emails, the news made instant headlines. Tejpal was among the first high-profile men to be accused under the new rape law. Ironically, he and *Tehelka* had pitched themselves as crusaders fighting for the rights of the oppressed, and pushing for Indian society to break its traditional silence and attitude to sexual violence. One of the sessions that Chaudhury had moderated at the Think festival was with rape survivors called, in ironic hindsight, 'The Beast in Our Midst: Rape Survivors Speak Their Story'.

As it turns out, Manohar Parrikar of the BJP, the Chief Minister of Goa at the time (now deceased) decided to get involved: 'I'm not saying someone is guilty,' he told *The Times of India*.[31] 'But the girl's [sic] email is explicit.'

Two days after the *Tehelka* communication went public, Goa police filed a First Information Report (FIR) on charges of rape and the quaintly named it 'outraging the modesty' of a woman. Tejpal responded by saying he had apologized at the insistence of Chaudhury 'as desired by the journalist' but that his apology did not reflect the 'complete truth'. That, he said, would emerge after police examined security camera footage.

Less than a week later, on 30 November, a Goa Sessions Court rejected Tejpal's anticipatory bail and, that evening, he was arrested and sent to Sada sub-jail in Vasco, Goa.

The charge sheet – the legal document filed by the Goa crime branch that lists the crimes Tejpal was accused of – was filed in February 2014. But it was only on 1 July that the Supreme Court granted him bail, observing that he had already spent six months in jail and did not need to be incarcerated now that the charge sheet had been filed.

In the years since then, the case has moved at glacial pace. In December 2017, the Supreme Court asked the Goa court to begin trial. But even as Tejpal moved the Bombay High Court to quash rape charges and security camera footage of his elevator encounter was illegally leaked to many senior journalists, Tejpal remained a member of the prestigious Editor's Guild – a fact that came to light only when the M.J. Akbar scandal broke in October 2018 and it transpired that as late as December 2018, both editors had managed to remain members.

In August 2019, the Supreme Court directed the Goa trial court to complete its proceedings against Tejpal in six months. The journalist flew to Goa for her cross-examination but the questions put to her by Tejpal's lawyers were so incendiary that she filed a petition in the Goa bench of the Mumbai High Court to ask that no 'irrelevant' questions were put to her. At the time of writing this essay, the case continues to be heard.

Media's entitled and predatory bosses were legendary, an open secret in a trade where not much was secret. When I started out as a reporter in the late '80s, there was no law against workplace sexual harassment. There was, in fact, no term like 'sexual harassment'. What we had was a whisper network of women journalists warning each other to watch out for 'creepy' bosses. It was not an exact or even always effective method. But we had to make do with it.

Now, a new generation of women journalists no longer had to fight for the right to work, no longer had to prove that they belonged in the newsroom and, moreover, had a law that was supposed to protect them. This was not a generation of women that had been brought up to make compromises or, to use that favourite term of many Indian parents, to 'adjust'. They were outspoken, aware of their rights and not about to suffer an injustice in silence. The bosses unfortunately, at least some of them, hadn't changed and remained as blind, as entitled and as 'creepy' as ever.

* * *

The Rajendra Kumar Pachauri case, like the Tejpal case, played out in full public glare and, alarmingly, like the Tejpal case seems to have got lost in a legal maze – until his death on 12 February 2020. The case was significant not because of his status – as Chair of the Inter-Parliamentary Panel on Climate Change, he received a Nobel Peace Prize along with Al Gore in 2007 – but because it was amongst the first to be filed under the Sexual Harassment of Women at Workplace (Prevention, Prohibition and Redressal) Law of 2013.

What should have been a litmus test for the recently enacted workplace sexual harassment law dwindled into a protracted legal battle and, six years after filing her complaint, after being the first to speak up against Pachauri, after waiting for her trial to begin, the researcher will now never receive a verdict.

The woman had joined the research institute in September 2013 when she was 29 and Pachauri 73. In her police complaint, she says, she suffered sustained harassment by Pachauri, which included unwelcome physical contact and a barrage of inappropriate communication. Along with her FIR, she submitted 6,000 SMS, emails and WhatsApp messages from Pachauri.

In February 2015, the researcher approached the head of TERI's ICC with a written complaint. Five days later, she lodged a police complaint.

When the story broke in *The Economic Times*, the impact was immediate. The student-run India Conference at Harvard University said it was 'politely withdrawing' its invitation to Pachauri to attend as a speaker. And in Delhi, lawyers Indira Jaising and Vrinda Grover held a press conference saying that a man charged with such a serious offence should not be allowed to attend the IPCC plenary session, due to begin in a few weeks on 24 February in Nairobi.

Pachauri put in his papers and quit as IPCC chair. In a separate email to TERI staff, he said he was proceeding on leave to remove 'any fears of my influencing the due processes being followed'. He then appointed his own interim successor at TERI. A few days later, on 27 February, he opted out of the PM's Council on Climate Change.

When a trial court agreed to grant him anticipatory bail, it was on condition that Pachauri would not enter TERI's offices or travel abroad without the court's permission.

On 19 May, the ICC submitted its 33-page report, which according to *The Economic Times*,[32] vindicated the researcher and found that Pachauri's conduct amounted to misuse of his position and a violation of TERI's policies against workplace sexual harassment.

For the next 10 days, TERI took no action against Pachauri, as recommended by its own ICC. This gave him the time to approach and obtain a stay from an industrial tribunal on the grounds that the principles of natural justice had not been followed. The stay remains and, over six years later, the ICC report findings have not been made public.

The allegations against Pachauri were drawing considerable outrage in India. Questions were being raised by lawyers and activists about why Pachauri was being allowed the extraordinary benefit of going on leave instead of being sacked. Letters were written to TERI's 10-member Governing Council, which included Naina Lal Kidwai, then the country head of HSBC Holdings and a woman often held up as a leadership role model, reminding it of its responsibility to steer the organization in a 'value-based' direction.

Despite the public hullabaloo, Pachauri got an order from a Delhi court lifting its earlier restrictions on his entry into TERI's office premises – barring the head office and the Gurgaon branch. On 17 July, he strode into TERI's Defence Colony office in New Delhi, where he was greeted like a conquering hero with garlands and flowers.

For some people it was just too much. A dozen TERI employees wrote to the Governing Council asking for Pachauri's removal. In a strongly worded column[33] in *The Times of India* on 22 July, columnist Swaminathan S. Anklesaria Aiyar asked why a man supposedly on leave needed to visit his offices at all. 'Pending his trial, why has he not been suspended by TERI?' he wrote.

The announcement of Pachauri's ouster as Director General came a day later at the Governing Council meeting held in Bangalore, where Pachauri was also present. It was issued by Lexicon, the same PR firm that Pachauri also used, and was as respectfully worded as it could be: His exit was a part of a 'leadership succession process'...the Governing Council was very grateful to the man who had put TERI on the global stage... everyone hoped for a smooth transition and so on.

Only towards the end of the press release is there a fleeting reference to the serious criminal charges against him. But, since the ICC's findings had been stayed by the industrial tribunal, the council had to respect the proceedings and abide by its directions, noted the press release.

It was a pyrrhic victory for the researcher, who told reporters that she welcomed the development but did not know the real reason for it. 'Action should have been taken on the basis of my complaint,' she said.[34]

Pachauri's replacement, Ajay Mathur, was serving out his notice at his current assignment as Director General of the Bureau of Energy Efficiency. Until he joined, Pachauri would continue. A week later, a court permitted him to attend conferences in China and Japan.

The researcher had asked for permission to work from home during the ICC enquiry – a provision allowed to her under the law. In April, she was transferred to another branch and complained that she was being 'shunted out' for speaking up. She went on leave.

By June, she had used up her leave and was told that any additional leave would be without pay. In September, as Pachauri prepared to fly out to attend another conference, this time in Kazakhstan, the head of TERI's ICC probe against him put in her papers and left. No reasons were given and she has, since, maintained a steadfast silence.

It was becoming clear to the researcher that her time at TERI was at an end. Not one person from the organization's senior management had ever reached out to her. She had written to the Governing Council members individually. Not one had bothered with the courtesy of a reply.[35]

Saying that she had been 'treated in the worst possible manner', she finally put in her papers on 2 November. 'TERI failed to uphold my interests as an employee, let alone protecting them,' she wrote in her resignation letter.

Pachauri certainly seemed untouchable. In less than a month, a court noted that since the researcher herself had quit, there was no need to restrict his entry into any of the offices.

By February in the new year, Ajay Mathur was ready to take up his new assignment. Not prepared to let Pachauri go, the Governing Council now created a new post specifically for him – that of Executive Vice Chairman. Pachauri was to continue working out of his imposing fifth-floor offices while Mathur was allocated a room on the second floor. The symbolism was clear.

Then, in February 2016 a second woman spoke up and said she too had been sexually harassed by Pachauri. In a five-page written statement, the former TERI employee said that she would not be filing a police complaint since she had seen what had happened to the first one. However, she was willing to come forward as a 'credible witness'.

The second woman's description of sexual harassment by Pachauri had uncanny parallels with the researcher's complaint. She spoke of how he would call her to the office early in the morning when nobody else was around, of conversations loaded with sexual innuendo, of his use of a sexually suggestive nickname for her, of calls on her mobile to ask personal questions about where her husband was and what she was doing. She spoke about Pachauri's insistence on her presence at conferences where she wasn't required. And of meetings in his office where he would sometimes stand close to her and try and hold her hand.

Once again, Pachauri proceeded on leave.

On 1 March 2016, over a year after the researcher had filed her complaint, Delhi police filed its charge sheet against Pachauri. Running into 1,400 pages and including the testimony of 23 witnesses, many of them TERI employees, the charge sheet accused Pachauri of several transgressions, including assault or criminal force on a woman with intent to 'outrage her modesty', criminal intimidation, sexual harassment and stalking. Judge Shivani Chauhan said there was enough evidence to proceed with the trial.

All this while, Pachauri had insisted that his phone and computer had been hacked. Now, in an article published on 26 March 2016 in the UK-based newspaper *The Guardian*, he added a new claim: The researcher was acting for money and he had been the victim of a sophisticated sting.[36]

'She actively flirted with me and aggressively encouraged a deeper relationship between us,' Pachauri told the newspaper. He said he strongly suspected, but could not prove, a coordinated attempt to destroy him professionally and personally.

A few days after the publication of the *Guardian* article, a third woman spoke up to say that she too had been sexually harassed by Pachauri. She said Pachauri's counter-allegations were 'right in line with his character'.

The woman, a foreign national, said she had been hired by TERI for a year in 2008 when she was just 19. In the first few months, she said, she was subject to relentless sexual harassment that included text messages and emails from Pachauri. In his office, he would put his hands on her waist, hug her for longer than felt comfortable, kiss her on her cheek and question her about her private life. He would call her during non-working hours and on holidays. Once, when she was sick and could not attend office, he landed up at her house with a bouquet of roses. 'This might sound sweet, but at that time I just felt uncomfortable and scared,' she said in her public statement.

The woman asked to be transferred to another division, but Pachauri continued calling her to his office on one pretext or another. When she persisted in making it clear that she did not want to be around him, her year-long contract was terminated after just four months. She was, she said, 'Very relieved that I would not have to face Pachauri's sexual harassment any longer.'

The Governing Council's refusal to act against Pachauri was now turning into a PR nightmare.

Pachauri's term at the Governing Council had ended on 31 March, and in a meeting, the rest of the council decided not to renew it. That effectively brought to an end his role as

Executive Vice Chairman. But he also had an employment contract with TERI that was due to expire only in 2017. The Governing Council finally decided to sever its association with him, agreeing to pay his salary and dues for the rest of his tenure.

To check the veracity of Pachauri's claim of being hacked, the Delhi police had sent his phone and computer to a forensic lab to be tested. Early in November 2016, the Forensic Science Laboratory in Gandhinagar submitted its report: They had not been hacked.

Still, the legal cases plodded along. In September 2018, five years after the researcher had joined Pachauri's office in September 2013, a Delhi court finally ordered the framing of charges against Pachauri. Speaking to reporters outside the court, the researcher said it had not been an easy battle for her. The new development was a 'big leap towards the truth'. But she said she was left feeling utterly exhausted.

* * *

The torrent of India's MeToo stories continued through October 2018 and well into November.

As the days wore on, it became clear that India's MeToo was organic, spontaneous, led by the women themselves and, very often, backed by evidence in the form of screenshots of text messages with lewd propositions.

Women were coming forward to document, to share, to shame, to seek or to hope for justice for what had been done to them. Not every charge had the same stamp of gravity: Some spoke of incidents that fit into the legal definition of rape; others spoke of years of targeted harassment by callous bosses who thought sex with the intern was a perk of the job. Still others spoke about a date gone wrong or just to say that a colleague gave off a 'creepy vibe'.

Not every woman was seeking to make a formal complaint – either the years had passed and they lacked evidence or the legal process seemed far too daunting. Some shared to warn others. Others shared because they were seeking closure. But regardless of the degree of harassment or the expected outcome, women were talking and sharing. It was unstoppable.

'MeToo was such a simple idea,' says Anoo Bhuyan. 'For years women had sat around the table talking about what had been done to them. Now they were telling their stories in public on social media.'

And, for the first time, the media was listening and picking up those stories. Many of the stories cut close to the bone as accusations against editors and star male reporters came tumbling out.

In the entertainment business, filmmaker Vinta Nanda had made a name for herself during satellite television's golden years in the early '90s with *Tara*, the longest-running show on Zee TV that ran from 1992 to 1997. Its star, Alok Nath, was already a well-known actor known for his 'sanskaari', cultured, roles in serials like *Buniyaad* on Doordarshan and films like *Hum Aapke Hain Kaun*. In 1987 he had married Nanda's college friend, Ashu. 'We were all close friends,' says Nanda.

The problem began, when Nath started 'misbehaving' with the actress Navneet Nishan, who played the role of Tara in the serial. 'He would get drunk and become a different person. He started turning up at Navneet's house in the middle of the night, shouting abuses. He would even misbehave on the sets,' Nanda told me when I met her in Mumbai in November 2018. Things came to a head, she explained, when Alok Nath tried to grope Navneet on the sets and she slapped him. 'I decided then to let him go professionally,' she said. Socially, they remained friends, but professionally it was no longer possible for her to work with him.

In 1997, there was a management change at Zee and Nanda was ordered to bring Alok Nath back into the show and drop Navneet Nishan. This made her position untenable and, although she continued as a producer, she stopped writing the episodes and 'washed her hands off the show'. A week later she was called to the Zee office and told that four of her other shows that were running concurrently on the channel were being dropped.[37]

Nanda by then had a full-fledged production house that employed 250 people. Surely, this couldn't be true, she protested. But Zee was not prepared to budge. One of the bosses told her, 'Women like you are not welcome in this country.'

The next few years were a 'nightmare', according to Nanda. Still, she did get a few writing gigs and managed to make a living. Although she had cut ties with him professionally, socially, she continued meeting Alok Nath and his wife. When Nath invited her home for a party while his wife was out of town, she didn't hesitate before accepting. They were friends, after all; moreover, other friends were going to be there. But, recalls Nanda: 'At one point in the night I knew this was not where I wanted to be. I was feeling very funny in my head, so I decided to leave. It was very late and I began walking home when a car pulled up and he [Alok Nath] was driving himself. He said, 'Get in, I'll drop you home.'

She has no recollection of what happened next. She remembers more liquor being poured down her throat. When she woke up next morning, she could not walk. She could not get out of bed. 'He hadn't just raped me. He had brutalized me,' she said. 'It took me days to just get over the violence. It was a shock. I didn't know to what extent I was to blame: I kept asking myself why I drank. Why did I go to that party?'

Her friends told her to keep quiet. She was just about getting back to work. But a week or 10 days later, Alok Nath barged into her house late at night, drunk, and tried to drag her into her bedroom. Fortunately, two girlfriends were present, and intervened.

The next day, Nanda remembers, she and her friends went to his house and told his wife that her husband had raped her.

In those days, there was no law and no ICC. 'Who would I have complained to? Going to the cops back then was not an option,' she said. So she buried it for 19 years, dealing with the post-traumatic stress as best as she could, struggling to find work, to find closure, often finding neither.

Then, Tanushree Dutta's interview in October 2018 went viral and within hours, social media was buzzing with MeToo stories. Nanda remembers her reaction: 'I went "wow". I was really thrilled with the way the media had picked it up, the way it was going viral.'

Nanda spoke to her mother. 'It wasn't planned. I don't know what gripped me. Something in my blood was telling me that this was the right time to speak up. I sat down and wrote about what had happened all those years ago. It took me five minutes to write what he had done to me.'

'I have waited for this moment to come for 19 years. I shout out to each of you who have suffered at the hands of predators to come out and say it aloud. Don't hold yourselves back,' she wrote. 'Speak out. Shout out from the top of the roof.'

Then she went into her mother's room, got into bed with her and went off to sleep.

When she woke up the next morning, the post had gone viral. An unnamed 'sanskaari' actor had been accused of rape.

* * *

As the October outing gathered steam – and this essay by no means includes a complete list – editors, actors, stand-up comics and image consultants were named. The immediate effect was a flurry of mea culpas.

Editor Gautam Adhikari, first accused of molestation by journalist Sandhya Menon and subsequently by a second journalist, Sonora Jha, had retired and was living in Washington DC where he was working for an American think tank, Centre for American Progress. In an email, Adhikari said he did not recall the incidents described but 'would sincerely apologize if I made anyone uncomfortable in my presence'. He then quit his job and announced that he was discontinuing his column for *The Times of India*.

Seven women wrote to *The Times of India* accusing its resident editor, K.R. Sreenivas, of years of unwanted touching and sexual propositions. He was packed off on leave, pending an inquiry. He subsequently quit.

What was unprecedented was not just the breaking of a traditional silence by women but the willingness by companies to acknowledge that they had failed their women employees; that in 2018, workplace sexual harassment could no longer remain an open, unspoken secret; and that they needed to fix the workplace.

Some newspaper managements scrambled to set things right – beyond just the inquiry against accused staff. One newspaper organized a series of sensitization trainings dealing not just with what constituted a legal offence but other sticky areas: What about consensual relationships at work? What if a boss fell in love with his subordinate? Was it OK for colleagues to go on dates? Beyond the legal route, what were other protective measures and options available to women? Could workplaces do more, not just in terms of legal compliance but in terms of making offices less toxic and more accommodating of women and others on the margins – the LGBTQ community, for instance?

'Some of the men really had no clue,' says Paromita Vohra, who conducted these trainings at the newspaper office.[38] At one session, for instance, a woman said that her male supervisor stood too close to her when they were making pages. So, as an exercise, the woman and a male participant stood together to understand what was an acceptable, comfortable physical distance.

Yet, even at its peak, there was a realization that MeToo was leaving out the vast majority of India's working women – some 95 per cent of whom work in the informal sector where protections under law remain on paper. Dalit voices, trans voices, voices from small towns were conspicuous by their absence, and the October outing was entirely seen through the prism of urban, heterosexual, male–female binaries.

Amongst women in the formal sector, there continues to be near-complete silence from doctors, chefs, scientists, bureaucrats, pilots and other professions. The women who were speaking up were upper caste, women of privilege. They had undeniably been abused and had undeniably faced trauma. But they are not the only ones who are subjected to sexual harassment. The stories that received coverage and outrage in the MeToo wave were often those involving high-profile men. One woman who complained against her boss in a small publishing house told me, 'Not one newspaper was prepared to carry my story.'

A year after an anonymous Instagram handle accused artist Subodh Gupta of sexual harassment by unnamed women, Gupta filed a defamation case, seeking damages of Rs 5 crore. In 2019, the Delhi High Court ordered search engine Google to take down 18 news articles on the subject. Google tried to resist the order by saying it would have a 'chilling effect on free speech' but did take down a few. In February 2020, the media reported that Gupta and the handle, whose identity had been revealed only to the court in a sealed cover, had reached a settlement.

* * *

On 19 April 2019, a junior court assistant sent a sworn, signed affidavit to the residences of 22 Supreme Court judges. In it she accused Ranjan Gogoi, the 46th Chief Justice of India, of molesting her and, after she rebuffed him, of persecuting her and her family. The two instances of molestation, she said, dated back to October 2018, just as the October outing was underway and days after Gogoi was sworn in as Chief Justice – the first amongst equals sworn to uphold the law of the land.

'I have been victimized for resisting and refusing the unwanted sexual advances of the CJI [Chief Justice of India] and my entire family has also been victimized and harassed due to that,' stated the woman in a letter accompanying the 28-page, 12,300-word affidavit. She was writing because, she said, the 'victimisation has reached unbearable proportions.' She feared, 'There is imminent danger to my life that I am compelled to speak the whole truth.'

The 35-year-old woman had been working in the Supreme Court since 2014 where she had been posted in the library. In October 2016, one of Gogoi's junior court assistants took leave to get married and she was sent to work in the judge's court. Her annual confidential report for the two years prior to this, she mentioned, were 'good' and 'very good'.

In early August 2018, she says, Gogoi told her that he was going to become the CJI and wanted her to be transferred to his residence office where she was required to come to work at 8 a.m., before any of the other staff.

In earlier interactions, Gogoi had taken a personal interest in her, she says, asking her about her family life and her career plans. She had mentioned to him that her disabled brother-in-law had been unable to find a job.

On 10 October she says, the Chief Justice called her into his office and informed her that her brother-in-law had been appointed a court attendant. It was the first day of Navratri, she writes, so she had worn an orange kurta instead of her usual black-and-white. He told her, 'You are looking pretty good today.' Then, she says in her affidavit, he asked her to come and stand next to him, got up from his chair and asked: 'What can you do for me?' She repeated that she was very grateful, but he 'slid his hand from the back of my head, along my back to my hipline, till my lower back'. When she froze, he pulled her cheeks and said he was like this with his daughter. He asked her to write down what she could do for him.

The next day, she states in her affidavit, the Chief Justice called her again and asked her to show him what she had written. He read her note, in which she had written about how grateful she was to his Lordship, what a blessing he was, how thankful she was and so on. He read the note, got up from his chair and came and stood to her left. She stood up too.

'He then took my hands into his and told me that my hands smell nice, he then pinched my cheeks, he then put his arms around my waist from the front, and said, 'I want this from you.' He was pressing his body against hers, she writes, and when he did not stop 'forcibly hugging me', she pushed him away and he hit his head against a bookshelf.

She left his office in a state of shock. But he called her back into his room in 10–15 minutes and told her she was not to tell anybody about what had happened. That night, back home, a little less dizzy from the day's events, she tried to call him, she told me. But his personal secretary took the call and asked her not to disturb the Chief Justice at night.

From 12 October onwards, she says, the CJI's behaviour towards her changed. When she entered his office, he made sure a peon was present or the door was left ajar. Ten days later, on 22 October, she was transferred out of the residence office and posted to the Centre for Research and Planning (CRP) in the Supreme Court. On 26 October, she says, the Chief Justice called her to his chambers and asked if she wanted to rejoin work in his court. She told him she would continue at CRP.

On 16 November, she was transferred again. The next day, a Saturday, was her daughter's school function and since it got over late, she could not report to work at all that day. She informed her supervisor about the delay.

Two days later she received a memo informing her that she was liable for action under the Court's conduct rules. She replied, explaining the circumstances. On 22 November, she was transferred again – her third transfer in the span of a month.

Within a few days she was told that her explanation was not satisfactory and she was suspended pending an inquiry against her. On 17 December, as she was waiting outside the room of the inquiry office, she had a panic attack, she says, and was rushed unconscious to Ram Manohar Lohia Hospital. The next day she was told that the inquiry had found her guilty and the order noted that the 'delinquent official neither appeared before the Inquiry Officer on 17-12-2018 [nor] she moved any request for adjournment. Therefore, the Inquiry Officer decided to proceed with the inquiry ex parte against her [sic]'. On 21 December she was dismissed from service.

According to her affidavit, the victimization continued. On 27 December, her husband was transferred from the Crime Branch division where he had been working since 2013. The next day, he and his brother were suspended from service. The husband called Gogoi's personal secretary 'as we had by then realized why all these things were being done to us, and why suddenly every member of my family was under attack,' the woman states in her affidavit.

The secretary denied any knowledge of their situation but on 2 January, the husband learnt that a departmental inquiry had been ordered against him for making unsolicited calls to the office of the chief justice. On 10 January, claims the woman, the husband was called to the Tilak Nagar police station and told that if the woman apologized to the Chief Justice, no further action would be taken.

The next day in the presence of the court registrar and a plain-clothes police official, she alleges, she was taken to the Chief Justice's residence where, on the insistence of his wife, she prostrated herself at her feet, rubbed her nose on the ground and said sorry.

For the next two months, the woman says she fell into 'complete depression and would suffer panic attacks'. In March she was in Jhunjhunu, Rajasthan, with her husband at his ancestral home, when the police informed her that someone had lodged a criminal complaint case against her and she would have to report to the Tilak Nagar police station in Delhi.

The complaint had been made by a resident of Haryana who claimed that the woman employee had taken a bribe of Rs 50,000 from him in exchange for a promised job at the Supreme

Court. On the night of 10 March, she was arrested and taken to the Tilak Marg police station, where her feet were shackled to a bench and she was subject to verbal and physical abuse, she writes in her affidavit. She was able to eventually get bail after one day in police custody and one day in judicial custody.

What she wanted now was a special enquiry committee of retired Supreme Court judges to investigate her accusations.

The story, not surprisingly, made the front page of every major newspaper in India as well as international papers like *The New York Times*. A statement given by the court said the allegations were 'completely and absolutely false and scurrilous and are totally denied'. Signed by the Supreme Court Secretary General, the statement also mentioned 'Its is [sic] also very possible that there are mischievous [sic] behind all this, with an intention to malign the institution.'

If the complaint of sexual harassment against a sitting Chief Justice was unprecedented, so was the response.

20 April, the day the story broke, was a Saturday, when the Supreme Court does not work except to hear the most urgent matters. Chief Justice Gogoi called for an emergency hearing along with Justices Arun Mishra and Sanjiv Khanna 'to deal with a matter of great public importance touching upon the independence of judiciary'.[39] Even though he did not think he should 'stoop so low even to deny the allegation', he said, the charges were part of a 'larger conspiracy to destablise the judiciary'. His accuser and her family had criminal antecedents, he said in Court, and he wanted to know how she could have even got a job in the Supreme Court. Moreover, if these were the circumstances in which judges were expected to work then, 'Good people are not going to become judges,' he said. Finally, he mentioned that after 20 years of service, he had a bank balance of Rs 6.8 lakh and this is what he had received for his 'selfless service'.

Never has the imbalance of power appeared to be wider.

Here was the senior-most judge in the highest court of the country calling for an extraordinary hearing at which the attorney general, solicitor general and senior officials of the Central Government were present to hear the accused denounce his accuser in open court and in public. It went against the grain of the most basic legal concept – no person shall be the judge of his or her own case.[40]

The Supreme Court, wrote senior advocate and former Supreme Court Bar Association President Dushyant Dave in *The Indian Express*, is 'a temple of justice, not an instrument to cater injustice'. Please remember, he continued, 'the law so declared binds your Lordships too'.

Within the Supreme Court, there are committees to deal with complaints of sexual harassment by lawyers and court staff. But there is no institutional framework to deal with complaints against judges. Accusations against Justices A.K. Ganguly and Swatanter Kumar had raised this question, but no alternative was ever presented as there were fears that such a mechanism could impact judicial independence and would require a constitutional amendment.

In 2014, a woman judge in the District and Sessions Court of Madhya Pradesh made charges of sexual harassment against High Court judge S.K. Gangele. As many as 58 Rajya Sabha MPs signed a motion seeking Gangele's impeachment but a team of jurists appointed by the then Vice President and Rajya Sabha chairperson, Hamid Ansari, cleared him of charges. The woman judge, meanwhile, quit her job after she was transferred to a remote area.

Now a committee of the Chief Justice's peers, three sitting Supreme Court judges, S.A. Bobde, N.V. Ramana and Indira Banerjee, was about to begin its inquiry into the allegations of sexual harassment made by the junior court assistant. When the woman complainant pointed out that Ramana and Gogoi were close friends, Ramana recused himself and was replaced by Justice Indu Malhotra.

The woman had asked for a special inquiry by retired judges because 'a special inquiry committee would provide a forum for a fair and impartial enquiry and would also protect the independence of the judiciary,' the woman's lawyer, Vrinda Grover, explained.

She had also requested the committee to inform her about the procedure to be followed; she needed the assistance of a lawyer or a support person as she had lost her hearing in one ear and was finding it difficult to follow the proceedings, she said, and she wanted the proceedings to be videotaped.

In the first hearing on April 26, she was told that the proceedings were 'informal'. She was nervous, she said, to appear before three Supreme Court judges, and could not hear what was being recorded of her testimony. On the second hearing on 29 April, she repeated her request to have her lawyer present. Denied. Again.

On the third hearing, 30 April, the woman issued a statement: 'I have not been given a copy of my statement recorded on the earlier two dates of hearing,' she said in a press statement made on that day. 'I told the committee that it would not be possible for me to participate any further if I was not allowed the presence of my lawyer/support person,' she said. She would, as a consequence, no longer participate in the inquiry.

Nonetheless, the 'informal proceedings' continued without the main complainant. On Monday, 6 May, the inquiry panel ruled that there was no substance to the accusations against the Chief Justice of India. The report would not be made public – not even to the woman who had made the complaint.

In January 2020, following Gogoi's retirement a few months earlier in November 2019, the woman staffer was quietly reinstated in the same position and with back pay. With no charges pending against her, she proceeded on maternity leave.

* * *

Classics professor Mary Beard tells the story of Philomena, the teenage girl in Ovid's *Metamorphoses* who is kidnapped by her sister's husband, Tereus, and raped repeatedly by him. Afterwards, Tereus cuts off her tongue so that she is unable to denounce him. When Beard tells the story, it is to illustrate how the culture of silencing women is not new.[41]

'Strong women are always put down,' says Vinta Nanda. 'That is our culture of misogyny. The minute you are bold, refuse to follow the dictates of what women are supposed to be like, you go against the mould, you will face the backlash.'

After Nanda accused Alok Nath of raping her, two other actresses, Himani Shivpuri and Sandhya Mridul, said they too had been molested by Nath. But while hearing Nath's application for anticipatory bail, a Mumbai Sessions Court observed that since Nanda 'did not lodge the report immediately after the alleged incident for her own benefit', the 'possibility cannot be ruled out that the applicant [Alok Nath] has been falsely accused in the crime'.

Nath, it was reported in media, had roles in two upcoming films. The first is *De De Pyaar De* with Ajay Devgn. In response to criticism for continuing to work with Nath, Devgn issued a long statement explaining that shooting the film had been completed before October's MeToo movement and that an attempt to reshoot would entail 'a huge monetary loss for the producers'. Of course, he added, he remained committed to the MeToo movement.

The second film, *Main Bhi*, is based on India's MeToo movement, where Alok Nath, in what can only be ironic oversight, plays the role of a judge who condemns sexual assault.

On 13 June 2019, Mumbai police declared there was no prima facie evidence against Nana Patekar and shut the sexual harassment case filed against him by Tanushree Dutta. She has challenged the Mumbai police's conclusion in a magistrate's court.

'Not every accusation has led to justice or even closure,' says Justice Sujata Manohar, one of the three judges in the Vishaka judgement.[42] But the movement 'shows that now it is at least possible for women to complain of what they could not in the past because of social pressure and stigma. To that extent it is a sign of empowerment.'[43]

Even as the movement was unfolding, questions were being raised. What about false accusations? What if some women were just trying to settle scores? It was clear from some of the anecdotes that some transgressions were not so much workplace sexual harassment, which is an abuse of power and authority over a subordinate, but something else. One woman told Paromita Vohra about the time she had consensual sex with a male boss. Afterwards, he began ignoring her, not taking her calls. 'She felt bad, humiliated,' says Vohra.

Some questions still went unanswered, for example, the situation of a male boss and his female subordinate falling in love or two people at work deciding to have a sexual encounter. Would these instances be against the law? Vohra's own advice: 'If you open yourself to an amorous encounter as a woman in the workplace, you are potentially disempowering yourself, the way that the current gender dynamic plays out in the workplace. Even if you are the boss, you will get undermined. Keeping the professional and the personal separated is not a bad idea, unless one does otherwise with some care.'

All the women I have ever spoken to about workplace sexual harassment have one thing in common: They do not want to lose their jobs or mess up their careers. In some cases, they'd rather quit and look for another job instead of running the risk of being labelled as 'troublemakers'. When they do speak up or complain, it is usually the last step, one that is taken simply because they want the harassment to stop.

When a woman speaks up, particularly to complain about any form of sexual violence, she is placed squarely under the spotlight of public scrutiny. Everything is up for discussion, from her style of dressing to the state of her marriage, from her sex life to her hairstyle. Why did she speak up? Why after so many years? What is her ulterior motive? Has she been bought over by a corporate enemy? Was she, perhaps, passed up for a promotion?

What is clear is that workplace sexual harassment is not new. Shielded by such euphemisms as the 'casting couch', demands for sexual favours in exchange for career advancement – a role, a plum assignment, foreign travel and sometimes just retaining the job – are old hat.

But India's MeToo movement also made it clear that most men are oblivious to the everyday realities of women. The pervasiveness of sexual harassment, not just at work but on the bus, in the metro and on the street as they commute to work, is a daily reality for countless women.

Most men often have no idea about the struggles of women – even women of privilege. The Constitution grants to women the right to work and the right to privacy and autonomy as a citizen. But on the ground, there is a struggle just for a seat at the table. The resistance to claustrophobic arranged marriages as they escape small towns in search of careers and freedom in the big city. The audacity of their ambition, of their dreams.

And the tiny, infinitesimal ways in which women are constantly belittled by male bosses and male colleagues. Forced to smile patiently when a male colleague comments on what she's wearing or the way she looks – because she doesn't want to 'make a scene'. Or learns to grit her teeth as a male boss steals her ideas without so much as a thank you. Underpaid, overlooked for promotions, talked down to – sometimes it's just asking her to order the coffee or take notes in a meeting as if that is a job she is naturally groomed for.

Workplaces are designed by men. More than sexual desire, workplace sexual harassment is an abuse of power by men in positions of authority over subordinate females. In most cases, there is a pattern of behaviour that emerges and abusers are usually guilty of not just one isolated transgression but repeated offences.

Many subsequent 'modern' add-ons in 21st century workplaces – off-sites and 'bonding exercises' over alcohol-fuelled weekend retreats – are also designed by men who often have only to worry about getting to the office on time and not about who's going to put the kids to bed or get dinner on the table. It's a workplace that rarely recognizes a separation between home and the office; a workplace where such role models as Facebook COO Sheryl Sandberg exhort women to 'lean in' – as if workplaces don't need to bend to become more flexible, inclusive and enabling for all employees, including those men who might believe in a life outside the office.

Historically, these male-designed organizations have failed women. TERI is just one instance. It's as if the ecosystem is built by men and designed by them to protect their own.

Paromita Vohra talks about the structure of patriarchal success. 'We say there are these incredibly brilliant men – and somehow they are always men – and put them up on a pedestal, these eccentric geniuses who are mavericks and so counter-cultural and virile. We create this erotic buzz around them. This culture allows these men to behave how they do.'

MeToo sought a course correction by exposing some of these men. In the early days, some were sent packing, but others have fought back through the filing of criminal defamation cases or just simply brazening it out.

'If you don't change the shape of power then different people will come and inhabit that shape,' says Vohra. 'You need to dissociate yourself from the structure of power and change the way things are, and change the qualities we value. You are taking the easy way out by saying, "This man is horrible. Chuck him out".'

Workplace hierarchies have often meant that when it comes to adjudicating between two employees – a powerful boss (usually male) and his subordinate junior (female) – there's an instinctive need to protect the less dispensable employee, the boss. But more worrying is the apparent lack of concern by corporates and organizations to follow the spirit of the law.

To pursue a legal course of action, it's the individual woman who must consider the cost and time of retaining a lawyer. There must be substantial proof of the harassment – something that often takes place behind closed doors. And she must have immense powers of patience and perseverance to navigate India's notoriously tardy legal system.

In a country where the legal process is often a punishment in itself, what does justice look like?

There is no one-size-fits-all. Some, like the TERI complainant, have sought, and will now never receive, a legal pronouncement, and are in a state of legal limbo as they try and get on with their lives.

'My life cannot be what happens between court dates,' says the journalist who complained about Tarun Tejpal. 'I have to pick up the pieces and carry on.' And, yet, what was so radical about what she did? In her words, she simply said no to her boss, and then followed it up with an email to his second-in-command.

Not everyone took the legal route. Others just wanted to state their truth and share with the world what was done to them. Still others could no longer bear the burden of silence and felt compelled and encouraged to speak up at a time when so many others were. And still others just wanted a simple acknowledgement from their harassers admitting that they had been wrong.

But after speaking up, what next?

'You have to figure out a way to give justice where there is real change,' says Mahima Kukreja. 'We need to look at reformative justice and how we can change these men – change the way laws and policy work. Right now the foundation is wrong.'

We need a new design, an improved template. Sexual harassment is against the law and is wrong. There can be no disagreement on that. But more than stamping out sexual harassment, we need an affirmative environment where women can step out and work, contribute ideas, express themselves.

Where they can fulfil the promises and guarantees made to them by the Constitution. Where workplaces understand that there can be no right to work, if there is no right to autonomy first.

The issue is not taking down a few predatory men. If India's MeToo is to succeed, then it must spell out a New Deal at work for all employees, regardless of gender or sexual orientation. It's a New Deal where silence no longer has any space.

Sex and Religion

Triple Talaq

MADHAVI DIVAN

Minutes short of 10.30 a.m. on 22 August 2017, lawyers in black robes jostled for space in Courtroom No. 1 of the Supreme Court of India. A bench of five judges of the court, presided over by Chief Justice J.S. Khehar, was about to assemble to deliver its verdict on a bunch of Writ Petitions, led by a case titled *Shayara Bano* v. *Union of India*.[1]

Hanging in the balance was the fate of the age-old practice of *talaq-e-biddat*, commonly called 'triple talaq', by which a Muslim man could divorce his wife in a flash of a few seconds, by uttering 'talaq' or 'divorce' three times. It was a historic opportunity for the highest court in a country, which is home to more than a tenth of the world's Muslim population, to stamp out a practice that played havoc with the lives of Muslim women.

To strike out triple talaq as incompatible with the Constitution of India needed an enormous leap of faith. Triple talaq was universally acknowledged as deeply egregious, even sinful by the religious orthodoxy. It had long been abolished in most Muslim countries.

Yet, in matters concerning a religious minority, the courts must tread softly. India's relationship with her Muslim minority was stained by the blood and bitterness of Partition. A community abandoned by its privileged elite and unsure of how its future would unfold in partitioned India, found comfort in its religious identity. That identity found security in Shariah-based personal laws, many of which were incompatible with fundamental rights under the Indian Constitution. Those laws underwent reform in Pakistan and Bangladesh, but the slightest attempt in India erupted in angry protestations from the clergy.[2]

Those long years ago, when a newly independent India made a tryst with her own identity, she guaranteed to all her citizens the freedom of religion. But could that guarantee be stretched to an intransigence that drowned out gender freedoms guaranteed by a modern Constitution? The triple talaq case was brought to the Supreme Court by a few courageous Muslim women, determined to be liberated from practices that had been the bane of their lives. Their case was a strong one. But that morning in the Supreme Court, it was hard to tell what the court would do.

The hearing of the case lasted all of seven days in May 2017. That was, relatively speaking, quite a brief hearing for a matter of such importance. Chief Justice Khehar constituted a five-judge bench to hear the case a couple of months before the hearing commenced. To the consternation of many lawyers, the hearing was scheduled in the Court's summer vacation. That was an unusual move in a constitutional case. But the Chief Justice declared that the court vacation, when judges and lawyers are not burdened with routine cases, would afford more time for this sensitive case.

He was publicly criticized for what was perceived as his overenthusiasm. Constitutional lawyer Dr Rajeev Dhavan bitterly criticized the Chief Justice for hearing the case in the summer vacation and attributed motives to his decision, asking whether this was the Chief Justice's 'agenda' or that of the Government.[3]

As the 'master of the roster' (an expression which acquired controversial dimensions during the subsequent chief justiceship of Justice Dipak Misra), the Chief Justice exercises the prerogative of making the choice of judges who comprise a bench.[4] This Bench was a truly motley assortment. The religious diversity of the Supreme Court and, indeed, of multicultural India could not have been on finer display. It was headed by a Sikh Chief Justice. His colleagues on the Bench were Justice Kurian Joseph, a Syrian Christian; Justice Rohinton Fali Nariman, a Parsi Zoroastrian; Justice S. Abdul Nazeer, a Muslim; and Justice U.U. Lalit, a Hindu. The plurality of the composition evoked a great deal of public interest and comment.[5]

But conspicuous by her absence was the most vital representation in a case of the kind – a woman! That made it, what a young colleague of mine described as a '*men*ch', rather than a bench! At the time, in 2017, the Supreme Court of India, which enjoys a sanctioned strength of 31 judges, had only one woman judge, Justice R. Banumathi. She was not on this bench. That might explain why a judgement on a case about gender justice says almost nothing about gender rights. One cannot help wonder whether the composition of the Bench had anything to do with the fact that the issue of triple talaq was examined almost entirely through the prism of personal law rather than from the standpoint of gender justice.

When the Bench assembled that morning of 22 August 2017, there was no advance indication that the Court would speak in more than one voice. When individual judges on a Bench deliver separate opinions (concurring or dissenting), the past practice was to make an advance indication to that effect on the daily cause list of the Supreme Court. But there was no inkling of it this time. So, when Chief Justice Khehar began reading out his judgement at half past ten that morning, one assumed that he was speaking for the Bench. As he read on copiously from a laboriously written judgement, analysing Islamic scriptures, it seemed increasingly clear that he was not inclined to hold in favour of the victims of triple talaq.

In his 272-page judgement, Chief Justice Khehar declared

that the practice of *talaq-e-biddat*, or instantaneous triple talaq, had stood the test of 1,400 years and constituted an *essential* practice of Islam.[6] That was a stunning pronouncement, for not even the most radical and doctrinaire of Muslim groups before the Court had seriously argued this. Many hearts sank, mine own included. Disbelief and dismay rent the courtroom. It was the kind of feeling experienced a few years before, in December 2013, when a two-judge bench of the same court had overturned the Delhi High Court's judgement in the *Naz Foundation* case, making homosexuals criminals once more, on the ground that the law could not be tweaked for the sake of a 'miniscule minority'.[7]

As the gist of the Chief Justice's ruling became clear, a few lawyers rushed out of the courtroom to address the media. Hordes of TV cameras were assembled outside, anxiously waiting for a news byte. The first flashes on television reported that the Supreme Court had upheld the practice of triple talaq and that the petitions had failed.[8]

As Chief Justice Khehar finished reading his judgement and put his signature on it, he announced that Justice Nazeer concurred with him. That was the first inkling that there was at least one more judgement to follow. A glimmer of hope flickered. Justice Kurian Joseph then proceeded to read an extract from his judgement where he declared that the practice of *talaq-e-biddat* was considered 'sinful', and therefore, what is bad in theology must be bad in law.

Justice Nariman followed, declaring *talaq-e-biddat* unconstitutional, but following a very different legal route to get to that conclusion. He held that triple talaq, which was codified into law by virtue of Section 2 of the Muslim Personal Law (Shariat) Application Act, 1937, was 'manifestly arbitrary' and fell foul of the right to equality guaranteed by Article 14 of the Constitution. It was only when Justice Nariman finally declared that the fifth judge on the bench, Justice Lalit, concurred with him, that one could be certain that the practice of *talaq-e-biddat* had been consigned, at least in law, to history. It was a narrow win by 3:2, but nonetheless a win for women, and an epoch-making one.

Having said that, so different were the three opinions of the Court that to decipher the ratio was a challenge. So much so that the All India Muslim Personal Law Board that had strenuously defended triple talaq decided to take its chances, the very next morning after the verdict, mentioning the case before the Chief Justice, and asking rather audaciously, that the Court declare that the majority verdict was actually in its favour![9]

Two days after the verdict, I received birthday greetings from Farzana, my office secretary of 20 years. With her usual greetings was an unusual message. She said: 'Many many happy returns of the day. And congratulations for working hard and struggling for triple talaq case. We all Muslim women have got big relief with the judgement. Thank you for all your efforts.'

I was surprised, only because I knew Farzana to be a woman of few words. Some months before, she had meticulously typed out the written submissions for the case as I dictated them to her. She offered no comment at the time. But the WhatsApp message she sent me that day was the most effusive I had received from her in the two decades of our association. It was also markedly different from the many guarded and qualified, even deeply critical responses of some secular women activists at the time.[10]

THE GOVERNMENT OF INDIA'S STAND ON TRIPLE TALAQ

On a Wednesday evening in September 2016, a little less than a year before the judgement was delivered by the Supreme Court, I received a phone call from the then Attorney General of India, Mukul Rohatgi. He called to ask me to prepare, on behalf of the Government of India, the response to the Writ Petitions challenging the practices of triple talaq, *nikah halala* and polygamy. It was to be turned out on an urgent basis, he said.

I put aside all other work for the next three days to stitch together the response with the help of my young colleague, Nidhi Khanna. At the time, I was a counsel on the panel of the Union of India, marked briefs now and then, in cases sometimes very interesting and sometimes mundane. My own take on this case was that the Government of India should stay clear of being dragged into an interpretation of religious texts on the matter because it is not the business of a secular State to be involved in the nitty-gritty of religion. However, the State *is* concerned with gender justice and the right of women to a life of dignity, and those rights guaranteed by a modern constitution, must trump religious practices as interpreted by some self-serving men seeking to reinforce their patriarchal views through the means of religious orthodoxy.

Women constitute half the population of every community, transcending the barriers of caste and religion. The right to profess, practise and propagate religion under Article 25 of Part III of the Constitution is 'subject to the provisions of this Part'. This is an indication that the freedom of religion must surrender, where necessary, to other fundamental rights under Part III of the Constitution, which include the right to equality, the right against discrimination and the right to life.

'Secular' activities, such as marriage, divorce, adoption and inheritance, associated with particular religious communities, fall outside the protection of Article 25, which is the right to freedom of religion.[11] There was enough indication from the abrogation of triple talaq in an overwhelming majority of Muslim countries that it did not have any legitimate sanction of religion. This was the thrust of my draft on behalf of the government, in effect, supporting the challenge to triple talaq.

Given the importance and sensitivity of the matter, I expected that the draft response would go through many levels of scrutiny in government, and it did. But I was pleasantly surprised to find that not only had it survived mutilation, it had remained intact. I had been a private lawyer for the most part of my career, and it was a given to me that the lawyer must have the final word on both matters of strategy and drafting of pleadings. This time, my client was the Government of India. In a matter of this kind, I had not expected so free a hand.

There should have been nothing unusual about the stand on behalf of the Government. It was a stand that any government ought to have taken. But the chequered history of Muslim Personal Law in India made it very unusual. This was indeed the very first time, in the history of independent India, in a matter relating to Muslim women, that the Government of India had taken a stand in support of women. Indeed, the journey from *Shah Bano* to *Shayara Bano* had been a long and difficult one.

In *Mohd. Ahmed Khan v. Shah Bano Begum,*[12] a case which came up before the Supreme Court in 1985, a divorced Muslim woman from Madhya Pradesh sought maintenance from her husband of 14 years. The Supreme Court granted her maintenance by applying Section 125 of the Code of Criminal Procedure, which makes provision for maintenance of dependants, including a destitute or divorced wife. The question was whether a divorced Muslim woman, who had received her *mahr* or *dower* was entitled to further maintenance under a secular law.[13] The Muslim clergy erupted with angry indignance at the Court's application of a secular law to Muslims, and its foray into the 'no entry zone' of personal law. It did not matter than the Court had granted her a paltry Rs 179.20 per month as maintenance.

In order to placate the Muslim clergy that held sway over the community vote bank, the Rajiv Gandhi Government enacted the Muslim Women (Protection of Rights on Divorce) Act, 1986 to undo the effect of the judgement in *Shah Bano.* This law had the effect of depriving a divorced Muslim woman the right to maintenance from her former husband beyond the period of *iddat.*[14] The constitutional validity of the new law was challenged by Danial Latifi, the lawyer who had argued for Shah Bano in the Supreme Court. The Court upheld the law but only after tweaking it to ensure that a divorced Muslim woman was entitled to maintenance even after the *iddat* period, so long as she was not able to sustain herself.[15]

With that history, the judgement in *Shayara Bano* was path-breaking. Yet, it was no cause for euphoria. The 3:2 verdict meant that the women succeeded by only a hair's whisker. It was deeply disappointing that the Chief Justice of India, along with the sole Muslim judge on the bench, elevated the practice of triple talaq to an 'essential practice' of Islam. Even the most orthodox among the clerics confirmed that triple talaq was 'bad in theology' and 'undesirable', but nonetheless 'good in law'.

The struggle for Muslim women's rights in India has had a long and chequered history. There was a time when Shariat law, which became anachronistic with women's rights under a modern constitution, came to the rescue of Muslim women, liberating them from the constraints of a deeply patriarchal customary law. In the first half of the 19th century, Muslim women in India began to use the Shariat to canvas their claim to property, denied to them under customary law. At the time, Islamic patriarchy was the preferred choice over customary patriarchy.[16]

While in the 1920s, the women's groups, comprising both Hindu and Muslim women, worked unitedly on issues which concerned them for the benefit of all Indian women, later, finding themselves confronted with the orthodox religious clergy, Muslim women began to use the Shariat to reclaim their rights. In matters of inheritance, for example, the Shariat offered better rights than under the prevailing customary law. In Punjab, Muslim women were denied their share in agricultural lands because many Indian Muslims were converts to Islam from Hinduism and continued to cling to customary laws that applied to them pre-conversion.

The Muslim Personal Law (Shariat) Application Act, 1937 that was enacted to ensure the application of Shariat law to all Muslims, in matters of marriage, divorce, inheritance and the like, was opposed by vast sections of Punjabi Muslims who believed that granting women a share in inheritance under Shariat would disrupt the socio-economic structure of rural tribal societies. There was strong criticism against the perceived double standards of Muslim organizations that used the Shariat in matters of marriage and divorce but not in distribution of inheritance and family property. The Begum of Bhopal and other Muslim women reformers of the time campaigned against tribal patriarchy and the Shariat, at the time, actually offered relief from the prevailing state of affairs. The Act was passed in November 1937 and was considered one of the most important strides in the interest of Muslim women.[17]

Even more interesting was a legislative reform that came in 1939 – the Dissolution of Muslim Marriages Act, 1939. Following close on the heels of the Muslim Personal Law (Shariat) Application Act, 1937, the new law was introduced to make it easier for a Muslim woman to obtain divorce. There was no provision in the Hanafi code of Muslim Law enabling a Muslim woman to obtain a divorce from a court if the husband failed to maintain her, mistreated her or deserted her. The Statement of Objects and Reasons for the introduction of this law was that the existing laws had caused 'unspeakable misery to enumerable Muslims women in British India'.

The Act listed the grounds under which a Muslim woman could seek divorce from a court of law for cruelty, desertion, failure to maintain and the like. The grounds enlisted in the Act, which could justify a divorce on the plea of a Muslim woman, are very similar to what later became available as grounds of divorce to Hindus under the Hindu Marriage Act, 1955. Until the Hindu Marriage Act, 1955 was brought into force, there was no concept of divorce under Hindu law, for marriage was regarded as an indissoluble sacred union of husband and wife. The Dissolution of Muslim Marriages Act, 1939 was groundbreaking because a Muslim woman's right to judicial divorce before a secular court on specified grounds preceded that granted to Hindu men and women.

But the real reason behind the introduction of the 1939 Act was to arrest conversion of Muslim women to other faiths. Till that time, a Muslim woman who wanted to opt out of an unworkable marriage had no way out but to convert to another religion to free herself from the marital bond. An irate Ulema issued fatwas against the practice whereby marriages could be dissolved by reason of the wife's conversion and declared that she should be jailed till she returned to Islam.[18] Muslim groups were concerned about the tendency of women trapped in abusive marriages to renounce Islam. Renowned poet and Islamic philosopher Allama Iqbal, who later came to be known as the spiritual father of Pakistan, appealed to Muslim scholars to reform Hanafi law so that the community could be saved from conversions to other faiths.[19]

The supporters of the Bill that preceded the 1939 Act, including religious groups, were propelled not by any desire to improve the status of the Muslim women but rather to put a stop to Muslim women abandoning their faith and hurriedly marrying someone from a different faith so that they could be locked into a new community to prevent return to Islam. Scholar Sabiha Hussain states that conversion was looked upon also from the perspective of the long-term consequences on the numerical strength of the communities which could bring about a demographic disturbance. The change in law, she concludes, was the desire to retain the numerical balance, and not social reform. Thus, preoccupations with community and religious identity overrode issues relating to gender identity and gender rights.

Examining the 1939 Act from a different perspective, it is worth noting that while Muslim women were given a statutory right to approach a court of law for divorce on specified grounds well before Independence, even 80 years later, Muslim men in India continue to enjoy a unilateral right to divorce with no reference to a court of law. Instantaneous triple talaq, or *talaq-e-biddat*, is undoubtedly the most egregious of the different methods of divorce recognized. But even the other two methods, namely *talaq-e-hasan* and *talaq-e-ahsan*, of divorce are desperately one-sided.

Talaq-e-hasan entails three pronouncements of talaq during three successive *tuhrs*, or menstruations, while *talaq-e-ahsan* consists of a single pronouncement of divorce during the period between *tuhrs.*[20] While these two methods of divorce, *hasan* and *ahsan*, allow the man more time for reflection before he takes a final call on the divorce, it is his call at the end of the day. That he must wait three months to take that final call might only be a matter of detail. It is he who calls the shots, and while a woman whose husband resists divorce must approach a court of law, he remains his own master when it comes to liberating himself from the bonds of matrimony.

This state of affairs only tells us that while we may celebrate the abrogation of instantaneous triple talaq, it is only the tip of iceberg when it comes to legal reform in the Muslim community. Seventy years after Independence and working a modern constitution, we have achieved the striking down of only one grossly unfair medieval practice among many.

The *Shayara Bano* judgement, 395 pages long, is surprisingly silent on gender jurisprudence. One probable reason why a judgement on a case about gender justice said very little on the subject appears to be a conscious realization by the court that upholding the equality of status for Muslim women would open up the floodgates of challenge on a range of other aspects of Muslim Personal Law. An unreserved declaration of the equality of status of Muslim women with their male counterparts would mean that the courts would also have to scratch out practices like polygamy and other methods of unilateral divorce. This they were not prepared to do, at least not yet. The judicial reluctance to take the bull by the horns is also apparent from the Bench singling out *talaq-e-biddat* for adjudication even though there were three practices under challenge before it – *talaq-e-biddat, nikah halala* (the practice requiring a divorced woman to marry another man, have sexual intercourse with him and divorce him, before being allowed to remarry her former husband), and polygamy.

In *Shayara Bano,* when the Bench first assembled to hear the case, it took everyone by surprise when it announced that it would limit the hearing to the issue of *talaq-e-biddat,* and the challenges to polygamy and *nikah halala* would be postponed to another time. *Talaq-e-biddat* was the lowest-hanging fruit, and so the court adopted the lowest threshold to strike it down. Justice Nariman speaking for himself and Justice Lalit described the practice as 'whimsical' and 'manifestly arbitrary' because not only was it unilateral but had the effect of snapping the marital cord without any scope for reconciliation. Justice Kurian Joseph, on the other hand, held that among Muslims the practice was regarded as 'sinful' and therefore could not be recognized as valid. It was as if *talaq-e-biddat* was in a class of its own and needed to be dealt with differently. It was clear that the Court did not want to slam the door shut for debate on the other practices.

It is necessary to understand how the hearing came about in the first place. There were two sets of cases being heard before the Supreme Court. One was the *suo moto* petition by this Hon'ble Court in *Prakash v. Phulawati,*[21] listed as in *Re Muslim Women's Quest for Equality,* Suo Moto Writ Petition (Civil) No. 2 of 2015. The second set of petitions were led by *Shayara Bano v. Union of India,* Writ Petition (Civil) No. 118 of 2016.

Prakash v. Phulawati was a case concerning an interpretation of the Hindu Succession Act, 1956.[22] In Part II of the judgement, issues were raised on gender discrimination against Muslim women. Issues of 'arbitrary divorce and second marriage in currency of the first marriage' resulting in denial of dignity and security of Muslim women were raised in the course of the matter.

Shayara Bano and some other women who approached the Supreme Court seeking to have the practice of *talaq-e-biddat* struck down as unconstitutional were themselves victims of triple talaq. But some of these women including Shayara Bano challenged the legality and constitutionality of other practices as well. There were three different practices which were under challenge in these petitions: instantaneous triple talaq (*talaq-e-biddat*), *nikah halala* and polygamy.

The Constitution Bench was constituted in the summer vacation so that there could be a full-fledged hearing on all of these issues which remained unresolved for several decades. So, there was no warrant for confining the hearing to one issue only. This meant a piecemeal adjudication, which was not the object of the *suo moto* reference in *Prakash v. Phulawati*.[23] Merely singling out triple talaq, or *talaq-e-biddat*, could not take the matter very far because all the three practices under challenge are together entangled with the social status of Muslim women in India. Polygamy and *nikah halala* still remain legitimate, as do the other unilateral methods of divorce. But religious sensitivities acquire such enormous proportions when it comes to personal law, that the courts tend to tread very cautiously and conservatively; some would argue, much too cautiously and conservatively.[24]

Triple talaq is linked with *nikah halala* as most instances of *halala* take place because the husband, having issued talaq in an impulse, regrets his decision but cannot have his wife back till she undergoes *halala*. It is not uncommon for *halala* to be accomplished by engaging the services of a *maulvi* for a fee.[25] The original intent behind *halala* might have been to deter a husband from recklessly divorcing his wife (he would have to suffer seeing her married to another before she could be returned to him). But it is horrendously blind to the woman's wishes and treats her as a sexual object that may be passed from one to the other at whim.

All of these practices – triple talaq, polygamy and *nikah halala* – are not isolated, for together, they have a direct bearing on a Muslim woman's social and economic status. They limit her bargaining power in the home and, more generally, her prospects in life. The dread of a husband pronouncing talaq or bringing home another wife hangs like a sword over her, determining her choices through life, both inside and outside the home.

There was little justification for the Bench to have, on the designated date of hearing, singled out only one of the practices in question for determination. In any case, it is not as if this Court had not dealt with triple talaq before. In *Shamim Ara v. State of U.P.*,[26] the court made observations on the arbitrariness of all forms of talaq. Likewise, in *Javed v. State of Haryana*,[27] the Court was critical of the continuance of polygamy. So also in *Sarla Mudgal v. Union of India*.[28] Individual cases had come up over the years. But the purpose of the constitution of a five-judge bench was a once-and-for-all determination of all these issues. Ultimately, however, the Court did not decide all the issues, and limited itself to determining the constitutionality of the instant triple talaq.

It has often been the defence of both Muslim organizations resisting reform and also a number of 'liberal' commentators opposing interference in matters of personal law concerning Muslims, that practices such as triple talaq, polygamy and *nikah halala* have been blown out of proportion and used to 'demonize' Muslim men. Two points need to be made here. That these practices are indeed prevalent and, in fact, fairly rampant is clear from the report of the National Commission for Women by Syeda Saiyidain Hameed, social reformer and former Planning Commission member.[29] The report states that interviews were conducted with Muslim women through public hearings across the length and breadth of the country and these show stories of great suffering by victims of these practices.

The report also shows that income levels are lower in Muslim families than other communities, that Muslim women are educationally backward and participate the least in the work force.[30] There is an obvious nexus between the intra-community social status of Muslim women and the socio-economic status of the community, generally.[31] The irony is that in the early 20th century, relatively speaking, Muslim girls were highly educated and surpassed the national average.[32] But later, perhaps as a fallout of Partition, the exodus of the Muslim elite, the insecurity of those left behind, and the resultant grip of the clergy, the situation declined rapidly. Muslim women were kept back from enjoying what the Constitution offers and the end result is socio-economic disempowerment for the community.

STAND OF THE ALL INDIA MUSLIM PERSONAL LAW BOARD

The main opposition to the slew of petitions by Muslim women came from the All India Muslim Personal Law Board (AIMPLB). The AIMPLB was not a party to the petitions to start with but was joined after it made an intervention claiming to be a necessary party, representing the interests of Muslims in India. The Board enjoys no statutory status and there is no data to indicate how representative it is of the interests of the Muslims in India, much less Muslim women. Yet, for decades it has received disproportionate prominence in matters relating to the Muslim community in India. In recent years, much to the chagrin of the AIMPLB, Muslim women have formed parallel organizations such as All India Muslim Women Personal Law Board (AIMWPLB), Muslim Women Rights Network and the Bharatiya Muslim Mahila Andolan to have their own voices heard.[33]

It might be worthwhile describing in some detail the stand that the AIMPLB took on the petitions filed by Shayara Bano and other women in similar predicaments. In parts, the stand on affidavit is nothing short of shocking. It was somewhat diluted during the very able arguments of senior counsel Kapil Sibal, representing the AIMPLB, but perhaps it was too late in the day. The stand of the AIMPLB helps to explain why practices as horrendous as triple talaq and *nikah halala* must be criminalized. When religious bodies that have dominated the discourse for so long come out to defend medieval practices such as these with such indignation and threatening vehemence, perhaps the only way out is to stamp them out and criminalize them.[34]

To start with, the AIMPLB staunchly resisted any judicial intervention in matters of personal law. It contended, relying upon an old judgement of the Bombay High Court in *State of Bombay v. Narasu Appa Mali*,[35] that 'personal law' does not fall within the expression 'law' in Article 13 of the Constitution and that the framers of the Constitution wanted to leave personal laws outside the ambit of challenge based on any perceived violation of fundamental rights. In other words, any matter of personal law, unlike any other law, could not be tested on the touchstone of fundamental rights. This judgement and its implications are discussed later in this essay.

The AIMPLB claimed that while triple talaq was considered a sin, it was still nonetheless a valid and effective form of divorce. It justified triple talaq on the ground that securing divorce through the court process takes much too long and the delay deters the remarriage prospects of a party. It contended that in cases where serious discord develops between the parties and the husband wants to get rid of the wife, legal compulsions of time-consuming separation proceedings and the high expenses of such a procedure may deter him from adopting such a course, and, in extreme cases, he may resort to illegal criminal ways of getting rid of her by murdering her. Triple talaq is then a better recourse in comparison to these illegal ventures.

The affidavit goes on to say that denying a husband the right to divorce his wife by triple talaq may lead to instances where:

> [H]e may resort to illegal, criminal ways of murdering or burning her alive. Needless to add, a husband who does not fear God may do anything against his wife whom he hates. For only he is with her in the darkness of night. He has more chances of covering up his crime. Often do culprits get the benefit of doubt. This accounts for the rise in the cases of women being murdered and burnt alive.

There were many such astounding arguments justifying the continuance of triple talaq. In all seriousness, the affidavit of the AIMPLB suggested that triple talaq is a convenience for the wife:

> There are innumerable instances where a Muslim wife seeks dissolution of marriage and approaches her husband seeking immediate dissolution by resorting to triple talaq. In fact, many times the Muslim man pronounces triple talaq at the instance of his wife as she does not want to be pressurised by her family members to reconcile with her husband during iddat period and therefore wants instantaneous divorce.

It is not explained, of course, why if it is so often that it is the woman who wants the divorce, she should not be able to declare talaq herself rather than be at the mercy of her husband to say the magic words. The AIMPLB affidavit attempts to explain why the right to grant divorce is given to the man and not the woman:

> Shariah grants the right to divorce husband because men have greater power of decision making. They are more likely to control emotions and not to take a hasty decision.

The AIMPLB justified polygamy as a 'social need' on the grounds that, according to it, the death rate for men is higher because it is 'mostly men who die in accidents'. It also canvassed the 'moral aspect' of polygamy which 'ensures sexual purity and chastity'. It claimed that 'whenever polygamy has been banned, it emerges from history that illicit sex has raised its head.' Polygamy was described, in all seriousness, as 'a blessing not a curse'. It also declared:

> Concern and sympathy for women lie at the core of the provision for polygamy. If a woman is chronically ill or if her husband is [bent] upon taking a second wife because of her barrenness, or any valid or flimsy ground, and if the option of polygamy is not available to him, he will either divorce her which is something reprehensible, or he may

> indulge in illicit polygamy. An unlawful mistress is more harmful for social fabric than a lawful second wife. For the former, blackmails him [sic]. In all the above instances, polygamy is a blessing, not a curse for women. Polygamy is the solution to the problem of divorced women and widows. It is possible only with the second wife's consent. For one cannot take a woman forcibly as his second wife. Women should appreciate this point that if the ratio of women is higher, would they prefer wedlock for fellow women, or let them be illicit mistresses of men, without any of the rights which a wife gets.

PERSONAL LAW AS A NO-ENTRY ZONE: THE GHOST OF *NARASU APPA MALI*

A reference was made earlier in this paper to the judgement of the Bombay High Court in *State of Bombay v. Narasu Appa Mali,*[36] where a Division Bench of the Bombay High Court expressed the view that personal law was beyond the scope of challenge on the test of fundamental rights. *Narasu Appa Mali* was a judgement by a formidable combination of Chief Justice M.C. Chagla and Justice Gajendragadkar, and even a passing observation in the judgement, not germane to the case, ended up having a lasting impact, even on the Supreme Court. That made it deeply problematic.

The case arose out of a Hindu man's challenge to the Bombay Prevention of Hindu Bigamous Marriages Act, 1946. The petitioner, a Hindu man, protested that the law was discriminatory against Hindus as Muslims could continue to have multiple wives. The High Court repelled his challenge, declaring that reform could come to different communities at different points in time and that merely because reform was brought about in the Hindu community beforehand did not make the law discriminatory to Hindus. In a passing and rather unsolicited observation, the Court declared that 'personal laws' were intended by the makers of the Constitution to be left out of challenge before the courts on the ground that they violated fundamental rights:

> [...] Thus it is competent either to the State or the Union Legislature to legislate on topics falling within the purview of the personal law and yet the expression 'personal law' is not used in Art. 13, because, in my opinion, the framers of the Constitution wanted to leave the personal laws outside the ambit of Part III of the Constitution. They must have been aware that these personal laws needed to be reformed in many material particulars and in fact they wanted to abolish these different personal laws and to evolve one common code. Yet they did not wish that the provisions of the personal laws should be challenged by reason of the fundamental rights guaranteed in Part III of the Constitution and so they did not intend to include these personal laws within the definition of the expression 'laws in force'.[37]

This observation, wholly unnecessary in determining the challenge before the Court, became a stumbling block for judicial intervention in matters of personal law. Given the enormous religious sensitivities that surround legal intervention in matters of personal law, particularly those relating to a minority community, there has been legislative reluctance. (That explains why Parliament had to await a judgement on triple talaq to enact a law on the subject.) *Narasu Appa Mali* only made matters worse by immunizing such laws from judicial review, no matter how absurd and out of sync with the times. The result was that personal law was put on a pedestal and became an impregnable fortress where neither the legislature acted nor the judiciary.

The underlying idea behind the preservation of personal laws was the preservation of plurality and diversity among the people of India. However, the preservation of such diverse identities cannot be a pretext for denying to women equal status guaranteed to them under the Constitution as citizens of India. Personal law is necessarily 'law' within the meaning of

Article 13 and any such law which is inconsistent with fundamental rights is void. The *obiter* observation in *Narasu Appa Mali* to the effect that Article 13 of the Constitution does not cover personal law is wrong because the plain language of Article 13 clearly posits that personal law as well as customs and usage are covered within the scope of 'law'. Article 13 reads:

> 13. Laws inconsistent with or in derogation of the fundamental rights
>
> 1. All laws in force in the territory of India immediately before the commencement of this Constitution, in so far as they are inconsistent with the provisions of this Part, shall, to the extent of such inconsistency, be void;
> 2. The State shall not make any law which takes away or abridges the rights conferred by this Part and any law made in contravention of this clause shall, to the extent of the contravention, be void;
> 3. In this article, unless the context otherwise requires law includes any Ordinance, order, bye law, rule, regulation, notification, custom or usages having in the territory of India the force of law; laws in force include laws passed or made by Legislature or other competent authority in the territory of India before the commencement of this Constitution and not previously repealed, notwithstanding that any such law or any part thereof may not be then in operation either at all or in particular areas;
> 4. Nothing in this article shall apply to any amendment of this Constitution made under Article 368.

The meaning of 'law' as defined in sub-articles (2) and (3) of Article 13 is not exhaustive but is an inclusive definition.[38] The Article would therefore include personal law since that also has the force of law and is applicable to the concerned community. Further, under clause (2) of Article 246 of the Constitution, Parliament and State Legislatures have power to make laws also on subject matters enumerated in Entry 5 of Concurrent

List of the Seventh Schedule to the Constitution pertaining to 'marriage and divorce; infants and minors; adoption; wills; intestacy and succession; joint family and partition; all matters in respect of which parties in judicial proceedings were, immediately before the commencement of this Constitution, subject to their personal law'. Since the subject matters of Entry 5 are relatable to personal laws, therefore, 'personal law' is law within the meaning of sub-clause (a) of clause (3) of Article 13 of the Constitution.

The observation in *Narasu Appa Mali* ended up carrying far more weight than it deserved. That might have had to do with the stature of the two judges who authored the judgement. That apart, it lent an easy pretext for the courts to steer clear of wading into the muddy waters of religion. In a string of cases, including *Krishna Singh v. Mathura Ahir*,[39] and *Maharshi Avdhesh v. Union of India*, the Supreme Court took the ostrich-like approach sanctioned by *Narasu* and declined intervention.[40] Yet in other cases, such as *Danial Latifi v. Union of India*,[41] *Mohd. Ahmed Khan v. Shah Bano Begum*,[42] *John Vallamattom v. Union of India*,[43] the Supreme Court actively tested personal laws on the touchstone of fundamental rights. Further, in *Masilamani Mudaliar v. Idol of Sri Swaminathaswami Thirukoil*,[44] which concerned the inheritance rights of Hindu women, a three-judge bench adopted a position contrary to *Narasu Appa Mali*:

> [...] But the right to equality, removing handicaps and discrimination against a Hindu female by reason of operation of existing law should be in conformity with the right to equality enshrined in the Constitution and the personal law also needs to be in conformity with the constitutional goal. Harmonious interpretation, therefore, is required to be adopted in giving effect to the relevant provisions consistent with the constitutional animation to remove gender-based discrimination in matters of marriage, succession etc. [...]
>
> [..] Personal laws are derived not from the Constitution

> but from the religious scriptures. The laws thus derived must be consistent with the Constitution lest they become void under Article 13 if they violate fundamental rights. Right to equality is a fundamental right. Parliament, therefore, has enacted Section 14 to remove pre-existing disabilities fastened on the Hindu female limiting her right to property without full ownership thereof [...][45]

The judgement clearly seems to suggest that personal laws must meet the test of constitutionality. Even so, the position was not quite clear whether in the absence of a codified law recognized under statute, the courts could intervene and examine whether uncodified law (for instance, the Shariah) passed the muster of fundamental rights.

In *Shayara Bano*, the Court was presented with the ideal opportunity to exorcise the ghost of *Narasu Appa Mali* once and for all. Yet, it refrained from doing so. It was obvious that the Court did not want to bell the cat in the triple talaq case. Justice Kurian Joseph and Justice R.F. Nariman found different but interesting ways around *Narasu Appa Mali*. While Justice Kurian Joseph held that since *talaq-e-biddat* was acknowledged as 'sinful', it was not a valid form of divorce at all. On the other hand, Justice Nariman, with whom Justice Lalit concurred, held that this method of divorce, along with other methods of divorce, was codified into statute by virtue of Section 2 of the Muslim Personal Law (Shariat) Application Act, 1937. Therefore, since it had been recognized and integrated into statute, there was no bar against testing it on the touchstone of fundamental rights. He then proceeded to hold that *talaq-e-biddat* was 'manifestly arbitrary' and 'whimsical' because it offered no opportunity for reconciliation and therefore failed the test of reasonableness under Article 14 of the Constitution.

Finally, about a year later in the *Sabarimala case*,[46] Justice D.Y. Chandrachud acknowledged that it was time to do away with *Narasu Appa Mali*. He said:

> Custom, usages and personal law have a significant impact on the civil status of individuals. Those activities that are inherently connected with the civil status of individuals cannot be granted constitutional immunity merely because they may have some associational features which have a religious nature. To immunize them from constitutional scrutiny, is to deny the primacy of the Constitution. Our Constitution marks a vision of social transformation. It marks a break from the past – one characterized by a deeply divided society resting on social prejudices, stereotypes, subordination and discrimination destructive of the dignity of the individual. It speaks to the future of a vision which is truly emancipatory in nature…
>
> The decision in Narasu, in restricting the definition of the term 'laws in force' detracts from the transformative vision of the Constitution. Carving out 'custom or usage' from constitutional scrutiny, denies the constitutional vision of ensuring the primacy of individual dignity. The decision in Narasu, is based on flawed premises. Custom or usage cannot be excluded from 'laws in force'. The decision in Narasu also opined that personal law is immune from constitutional scrutiny. This detracts from the notion that no body of practices can claim supremacy over the Constitution and its vision of ensuring the sanctity of dignity, liberty and equality. This also overlooks the wide ambit that was to be attributed to the term 'laws in force' having regard to its inclusive definition and constitutional history.

DISTINCTION BETWEEN RELIGION AND RELIGIOUS PRACTICES

Over the years, the courts have tried to set the threshold for judicial intervention by attempting to draw a line between religion per se, and religious practices. While 'religion' itself is protected under Article 25 of the Constitution, religious practices that do not constitute the 'core' or the 'essential practice' of the religion are not. What constitutes 'religion' has been explained in a series of judgements. In *A.S. Narayana Deekshitulu v. State of A.P.*,[47] for example, the Court held:

> Though religious practices and performances of acts in pursuance of religious belief are as much a part of religion as faith or belief in a particular doctrine, that by itself is not conclusive or decisive. What are essential parts of religion or religious belief or matters of religion and religious practice is essentially a question of fact to be considered in the context in which the question has arisen and the evidence – factual or legislative or historic – presented in that context is required to be considered and a decision reached.

In *Javed v.* State *of Haryana,*[48] drawing from the Bombay High Court judgement in *State of Bombay v. Narasu Appa Mali,*[49] the Supreme Court held:

> In *State of Bombay v. Narasu Appa Mali* [AIR 1952 Bom 84: 53 Cri LJ 354] the constitutional validity of the Bombay Prevention of Hindu Bigamous Marriages Act (25 of 1946) was challenged on the ground of violation of Articles 14, 15 and 25 of the Constitution. A Division Bench, consisting of Chief Justice Chagla and Justice Gajendragadkar (as His Lordship then was), held (AIR p. 86, para 5):
>
> > A sharp distinction must be drawn between religious faith and belief and religious practices. What the State protects is religious faith and belief. If religious practices run counter to public order, morality or health or a policy of social welfare upon which the State has embarked, then the religious practices must give way before the good of the people of the State as a whole.

Their Lordships quoted from American decisions that the laws are made for the governance of actions, and while they cannot interfere with mere religious beliefs and opinions, they may with practices. Their Lordships found it difficult to accept the proposition that polygamy is an integral part of Hindu religion though Hindu religion recognizes the necessity of a son for religious efficacy and spiritual salvation. However, proceeding on an assumption that polygamy is a recognized institution according to Hindu religious practice, their Lordships stated in no uncertain terms:

> The right of the State to legislate on questions relating to marriage cannot be disputed. Marriage is undoubtedly a social institution an institution in which the State is vitally interested. Although there may not be universal recognition of the fact, still a very large volume of opinion in the world today admits that monogamy is a very desirable and praiseworthy institution. If, therefore, the State of Bombay compels Hindus to become monogamists, it is a measure of social reform, and if it is a measure of social reform then the State is empowered to legislate with regard to social reform under Article 25(2)(b) notwithstanding the fact that it may interfere with the right of a citizen freely to profess, practise and propagate religion.

ESSENTIAL PRACTICE TEST

Taking forward the distinction between religion and religious practices, the Supreme Court evolved the essential practice test. The Constitution accords guarantee of faith and belief to every citizen, but every practice cannot be held to be an integral part of such faith and belief.

In *Commissioner of Police v. Acharya Jagdishwarnanda Avadhuta*,[50] the test was summed up in these words:

> [...] Essential part of a religion means the core beliefs upon which a religion is founded. Essential practice means those practices that are fundamental to follow a religious belief. It is upon the cornerstone of essential parts or practices that the superstructure of a religion is built, without which a religion will be no religion. Test to determine whether a part

> or practice is essential to a religion is to find out whether the nature of the religion will be changed without that part or practice. If the taking away of that part or practice could result in a fundamental change in the character of that religion or in its belief, then such part could be treated as an essential or integral part.

The essential practices test is a problematic one. Our courts are secular courts, not ecclesiastical. Our judges have secular training. They are wading into choppy waters when they attempt to interpret religious texts on which they have little or no expertise. To be able to sift out the 'essential' from the 'inessential' and declare what the 'core' of the religious faith is, is treading on sensitive terrain. The courts must avoid that exercise to the extent possible. They must also steer clear of applying tests of rationality and reason when it comes to places of worship and rituals that accompany religion because faith by its very definition may not be compatible with reason.[51]

At the same time, when laws sanctioned by religion egregiously impact fundamental rights guaranteed by a modern constitution – for instance, practices as horrendous as human sacrifices or sati or those relating to devadasis, religious practices must give way to fundamental rights. That is precisely why the freedom of religion under Article 25 is 'subject to' the other provisions of Part III of the Constitution.

Having said that, the essential practice test is still treated as good law and continues to be applied by the courts. It is interesting in the triple talaq case that the AIMPLB acknowledged on affidavit that the practices of triple talaq and polygamy were 'undesirable' and by no means mandated by religion. This was a clear indication that the practices could never be elevated to the status of an 'essential practice', much less one that forms the substratum or core of the faith. Yet, the minority judgement authored by Chief Justice Khehar held that triple talaq had been in vogue for 1,400 years and enjoyed the status of an essential practice.[52]

INTERNATIONAL PRACTICES AND THE 'IMMUTABILITY' OF SHARIAT

A large number of Muslim countries or countries with an overwhelmingly large Muslim population such as Pakistan, Bangladesh, Afghanistan, Morocco, Tunisia, Turkey, Indonesia, Egypt, Iran and Sri Lanka have undertaken significant reforms in matters of divorce law and polygamy.

Pakistan requires a man to obtain the permission of an Arbitration Council as also of his first wife before contracting a second marriage. A divorcing husband is required to send notice to the Council, and a copy of the said notice to his wife, after which the Council will attempt to broker reconciliation. While practices in Bangladesh are similar to those in Pakistan, in Tunisia and Turkey, polygamy has been criminalized.

Tunisia and Turkey also do not recognize extra-judicial divorce such as the practice of *talaq-e-biddat*. In Afghanistan, while *nikah halala* is an acceptable practice, divorce where three pronouncements are made in one sitting is invalid. In Morocco and Indonesia, polygamy is permitted with the permission of the court and the consent of the first wife. Morocco permits women to include a clause in their marriage contract prohibiting a second marriage. Divorce proceedings take place in a secular court, procedures of mediation and reconciliation are encouraged, and men and women are considered equal in matters of family and divorce.

In Indonesia, divorce is a judicial process, where those marrying under Islamic Law can approach the religious court for a divorce, while the others can approach the District Courts for the same. In Iran and Sri Lanka, divorce can be granted by a Qazi and court respectively, only after reconciliation efforts have failed.[53] Even theocratic states have undergone reform in this area of the law and the irony is that in the secular republic of India, there remains such enormous resistance to reform.

An argument is often made that the Shariah is God-given

and there cannot not be any earthly interference with it. But the fact that Muslim countries have undergone extensive reform belies the case that practices such as triple talaq are part of an immutable religious law. There are many Shariah-based laws which no longer apply. Criminal punishments under Shariah do not apply to Muslims in India. The Indian Penal Code, 1960 applies to all Indians, Muslims included. Secondly, the Dissolution of Muslim Marriages Act, 1939 itself is a significant departure from the Shariah because it recognizes a Muslim woman's right to approach a secular court for a divorce if her husband is unwilling to give it to her.

Interestingly, in the 1950s in Pakistan, there developed a schism between the modernists and the traditionalists over the 'immutability' of the Shariah. While the traditionalists argued that Shariah is God-ordained and immutable, the modernists mooted *ijtihad*, which is the doctrine of interpretative intelligence, to interpret the law according to what social justice demands at a given time. What social justice may have required in the 7th century may not be relevant in the 21st century. For instance, polygamy was encouraged in the 7th century in a war-torn region where there were countless widows and orphans in need of shelter.[54] However, times and social needs have changed, and social justice now demands that polygamy *not* be practised. The Law Commission of Pakistan adopted *ijtihad* and reforms were incorporated in Family Law Ordinance, 1961.[55]

CRIMINALIZATION OF TRIPLE TALAQ

After the Supreme Court struck down triple talaq in *Shayara Bano*, the Government of India mooted a law, criminalizing the practice. The Muslim Women (Protection of Rights on Marriage) Bill, 2018 was passed by the Lok Sabha but suffered some jolts in Rajya Sabha.[56] Eventually, on 30 July 2019, it made it through Rajya Sabha on a third attempt,[57] and finally came into force on 19 September 2019.[58] The law makes the declaration of *talaq-*

e-biddat a cognizable offence attracting imprisonment of up to three years.[59] Opponents of the law argue that since divorce by triple talaq is no longer effective, and the marriage continues to subsist, there is no justification for making a criminal of the husband. So, should triple talaq be criminalized?

What constitutes a criminal offence? There is often an overlap between civil and criminal offences. An act may constitute an actionable civil wrong but may be serious enough to invite punishment as a criminal offence too. The celebrated British jurist Blackstone identified crimes as public wrongs, and torts against the individual as private wrongs. While civil wrongs affect the individual alone, public wrongs impact the community.[60] A private wrong has a civil remedy, usually in the form of compensation, while a public wrong or crime invites punishment because even though the act is, ostensibly, directed at an individual, it is perceived as violating the shared values that define a society.

An example of a criminal offence that concerns marriage is bigamy. In law, the second marriage has no effect. Yet, Section 494 of the Penal Code punishes a spouse who marries again while being married to another with imprisonment of up to seven years. If he conceals from the second spouse that he is already married, he can be punished for up to 10 years.[61]

It may be argued that as in the case of triple talaq, bigamous 'marriage' is no marriage at all so why punish a person for it? There too, a man guilty of bigamy is under an obligation to continue to provide for his first wife and their children and, therefore, a jail sentence may prevent him from doing so. Does punishing a person for bigamy serve no purpose?

Bigamy can afford a good ground for the civil remedy of divorce to a spouse. But the law nonetheless treats bigamy as a criminal offence because it is a social and moral wrong. The object of the law is not so much to imprison a husband for taking another wife as it is to ensure that people know the consequences of such an act and refrain from doing so.

In the challenge to triple talaq in the Supreme Court, the AIMPLB acknowledged that it was a 'sinful' practice,[62] but argued nonetheless that having withstood the test of 1,400 years, such talaq remained 'good in law' and could not be touched by the courts. The vehemence of such an assertion by powerful bodies, defending a practice as abhorrent as triple talaq as part of an immutable personal law, is indicative that merely 'nullifying' such a divorce is not enough. It needs social obliteration, if not through punishment, then at least the prospect of punishment.

It is not only divorced wives who face the brunt of triple talaq, or for that matter any form of talaq, where the man calls the shots and is not answerable to a court of law. All women to whom such laws apply are vulnerable because that spectre haunts them, restricting their choices both within the marriage and outside of it. The very prospect of unilateral divorce where the woman will have no legal recourse draws the *lakshman rekha* for a woman in her home and shackles her choices not only in her marriage but other opportunities for fulfilment.

We have fallen far behind Pakistan and Bangladesh, which comprehensively codified the law on divorce many decades ago and punished even relatively petty omissions on the part of the husband, for example, for failing to give notice to the Arbitration Council prior to divorce. Eventually, more comprehensive reform in Muslim Personal Law is needed. But that debate can resume once the Supreme Court rules on polygamy and *nikah halala*.

Secular India stands at a crossroads today. India has a Muslim population of more than 14 per cent according to the 2011 Census.[63] In actual numbers that means over 172 million people.[64] This number is likely to have swelled since 2011. The Sachar Committee Report, 2006 concluded that Muslims are poorly employed, socio-economically backward and do not have adequate representation in government services.[65] It may not be a mere coincidence that the position of Muslim women has been particularly dismal. It is a truth universally acknowledged that when a woman is empowered, her family reaps the dividends.[66]

Perhaps there is no better example of this than in Bangladesh where the microfinancing of women's projects by Grameen Bank translated into socio-prosperity for their families.[67] Triple talaq is not so much about divorce as it is about the social status of Muslim women. Given the chance, these women may hold the key to transforming the lot of their community. In multicultural India, every citizen must be able to enjoy what a modern, transformative constitution offers. No community ought to be left behind, least of all, women.

Understanding Muslim Law in the Modern Context

JUSTICE B.D. AHMED

We are living in a world flooded with information as well as disinformation. Minds are being altered and mindsets are being manufactured by the media. Because of this, and since people believe what they want to believe, there are a lot of palpably false ideas and concepts that are being embraced by large numbers of people. One such notion, albeit false, is that the Shariah is an arbitrary, rigid and fearful system followed by the Muslims. It is this notion that needs to be examined objectively and specifically in the Indian context. This essay attempts to do that.

Attempts are sometimes made to create a perception that women have been, and are, treated unfairly under Islam. Many have fallen prey to this idea and many people, including Muslims, have aided in furthering this incorrect perception of the Shariah. The whole triple talaq controversy is a case in point.

First of all, triple talaq had already been declared by the Delhi High Court to amount to a single revocable talaq and thus the sting of instantaneous irreversibility of the break in marital ties had been taken out.[1] Secondly, the Supreme Court had, thereafter, held triple talaq to be invalid.[2] Since this was the case, what was the need to legislate and criminalize triple talaq?

Again, the argument for a Uniform Civil Code is couched in terms of gender justice and equal treatment of women across systems of personal laws prevalent in India. The argument is that Islam is 'unfair' to women and hence reform is possible only by abolishing the applicability of the Shariah to Muslims and instead applying a secular version of the personal law – the Uniform Civil Code. Two questions arise here: One, are Muslim women treated unfairly under Muslim law? And two, is the argument for a Uniform Civil Code really based on a concern for Muslims and Muslim women in particular, or is it fuelled by the idea of obliteration of Muslim law in India?

Muslim law is not inherently skewed against women. The perception of Muslim law as being harsh to women has been created due to a lack of understanding, and certain actions, for instance, the instantaneous triple talaq, are perceived as being sanctioned by Islam when such actions are, in fact, in derogation of the spirit of Islam. These perceptions need to change. There are mechanisms within the fold of Islamic jurisprudence such as *takhayyur* – which I shall deal with later in this piece – that can enable a restatement of Muslim law in the modern context while not departing from the basic tenets of Islam.

WHAT IS THE SHARIAH?

The 'Shariah' literally means the path. It is a code of conduct – religious, moral, ethical and legal – for Muslims in particular and the whole of mankind in general.[3]

Fiqh, Islamic jurisprudence, is a part of the Shariah, and has been derived from four roots or sources known as the *usul-al-fiqh*, roots of jurisprudence. These four roots, in order of precedence, are (i) the Quran (ii) the *Hadis* (iii) *Ijma* and (iv)

Qiyas (analogy), or *Aql* (systematic reasoning). If something stated in the Quran needs clarity and specifics, then the *hadis*, *ijma* and *qiyas/aql* may be seen.

The Quran is the primary source for the derivation of any principle or proposition of law. Muslims believe the Quran to be the word of Allah or God, revealed to mankind through Prophet Muhammad, peace be upon him (pbuh). The Quran is immutable and is for all times to come. It contains various verses on subjects which are, in modern times, considered to be part of law. For example, verse 35 of chapter 4, relating to discord between a husband and wife in their marital relationship, prescribes mediation and conciliation as a possible avenue of resolution, which is also the preferred method of resolving such disputes under modern statutes. An English translation of the verse is as follows:[4]

> And if you fear a breach between the two, then appoint an arbiter from his people and an arbiter from her people. If they desire reconciliation, God will bring about agreement between them. Truly God is Knowing, Aware.

Verse 282 of chapter 2 of the Quran is another such example in the field of the modern law of contract. It prescribes that inter-temporal agreements/transactions (agreements and transactions that require actions separated in time; for example, an agreement to buy a house at a future date) are required to be reduced to writing. It is significant that in loan contracts, it is the debtor (and not the creditor, who is almost always in a financially dominant position) who has been ascribed the role of dictating the terms, but he too is commanded to reverence God[5] and 'diminish nothing from it'. This negates the unequal bargaining power of the parties (as is evident in modern-day bank-loan transactions that are heavily loaded in favour of the banks) and ensures that the contract is entered upon with free consent and is a just and lawful contract. A translation[6] of the said verse is shared below:

> O you who believe! When you contract a debt with one another for a term appointed, write it down. And let a scribe write between you justly, and let not any scribe refuse to write as God taught him. So let him write, and let the debtor dictate, and let him reverence God his Lord, and diminish nothing from it. And if the debtor is feeble-minded or is weak, or is unable to dictate himself, then let his guardian dictate justly... Unless it is trade of present goods that you transact between yourselves: then there is no blame upon you not to write it. And take witnesses when you buy and sell between yourselves. And let neither scribe nor witness be harmed. Were you to do that, it would be iniquitous of you. And reverence God. God teaches you, and God is Knower of all things.

The second source relied upon, after the Quran, is the *hadis*[7] (the sayings and acts of the Prophet Muhammad, pbuh). With regard to the authority of the *hadis*, it is revealed in the Quran in verse 113 of chapter 4 that 'God has sent down unto thee the Book and Wisdom, and he has taught thee what thou knewest not...'[8]

Shafi'i[9] in his book *Al-Risala fi usul al-fiqh*[10] explains what is meant by the words 'the Book' and 'Wisdom' as follows:

> So God mentioned His Book – which is the Qur'an – and Wisdom, and I have heard that those who are learned in the Qur'an – whom I approve – hold that Wisdom is the sunna of the Apostle of God. This is like what [God Himself] said; but God knows best! For the Qur'an is mentioned [first], followed by Wisdom; [then] God mentioned His 'favor to mankind by teaching them the Qur'an and Wisdom. So it is not permissible for Wisdom to be called here [anything] save the sunna of the Apostle[11] of God.
>
> The sunna of the Apostle makes evident what God meant [in the text of His Book], indicating His general and particular [commands]. He associated the Wisdom [embodied] in the sunna with his Book, but made it

> subordinate [to the Book]. Never has God done this for any of His creatures save His Apostle.

The explanation makes it clear that the expression 'the Book and Wisdom' appearing in the said verse 113 of chapter 4 refers to the Quran and the precedents (*Sunna*) of the Prophet (pbuh).

Another commandment of God – and there are others of like nature – contained in the Quran in verse 49, chapter 4, makes it clear that Muslims have to obey God and the Messenger. This clearly underlines the importance of *hadis*. Here is the verse:

> O you who believe! Obey God and obey the Messenger and those in authority among you. And if you differ among yourselves concerning any matter, refer it to God and the Messenger, if you believe in God and the Last Day. That is better and fairer in outcome.[12]

The third source is *Ijma* or the consensus of the community (though some sects construe *Ijma* as the consensus of the Imams). The fourth source is *qiyas* or deduction of a principle by analogous reasoning. Some sects substitute *qiyas* with *aql*, which is the same thing as systematic reasoning. At this point, it is pertinent to note that there is some similarity between the third and fourth sources on the one hand and the doctrine of 'justice, equity and good conscience'[13] which is embedded in the law as administered in India since the time of British rule.

Where the legislations do not cover the entire field (similar to where the Quran and the *hadis* are silent on a particular aspect), particularly in the application of personal laws of Hindus and Muslims, the courts are required to decide cases according to 'justice, equity and good conscience'.[14]

Islamic jurisprudence was developed through the process of '*ijtihad*'[15] (intellectual exertion or effort). It is generally agreed by scholars that the authority for conducting *ijtihad* is based on the following *hadis*:

> When Muadh Ibn Jabal was being sent to Yemen, the Prophet (pbuh) asked him as to how he would judge

> when the occasion of deciding a case arises. He replied: 'I shall judge in accordance with Allah's Book'. The Prophet (pbuh) then asked him what he would do if he did not find any guidance in Allah's Book. He replied: 'I will act in accordance with the precedents of the Apostle of Allah'. The Prophet (pbuh) then asked him what he would do if he did not find any guidance in the precedents either. He replied: 'I shall do my best to form an opinion and spare no pains' [i.e., *ijtihad*]. The Prophet was very pleased with the reply.[16]

Thus, through *ijtihad*, jurisprudence or *fiqh* was derived and developed, meticulously and painstakingly, from the '*Usul-Al-Fiqh*'.[17] And this '*ijtihad*' was done by persons known as '*mujtahids*'. They were persons who had a complete knowledge of Arabic, the Quran, the *hadis*, and the rules or legal maxims which were also developing alongside. It is obvious that as there were several *mujtahids* (not necessarily during the same period of time) who, by employing independent reasoning and logic in interpreting the relevant verses of the Quran and as elaborated in the *hadis*, developed principles of law and jurisprudence. This they did by analogical (*qiyas*) or systematic reasoning (*aql*) after recognizing the consensus (*ijma*) on those juristic propositions or principles.

It is but natural that, through this process, different sets of conclusions arose. Each *mujtahid* had his own set of students and disciples, through whom different schools of law developed. For example, the jurisprudence developed by Abu Hanifah and continued by his disciples came to be known as the Hanafi school. The Maliki school owed its origin to Malik b. Anas, the Shafie school to al-Shafi'i, the Hanbali school to Ibn-Hanbal and so on. These are the Sunni schools. Similarly, there are Shia schools such as the Ithna Ashari, Jaffariya and Ismaili schools.

As mentioned above, in the course of the development of Islamic jurisprudence, certain legal maxims or rules emerged such as:[18]

1. *Al tamssuk bil asl*: This rule provides that originally and essentially all beneficial actions are legitimate, and all harmful ones are illegitimate.
2. *Istishaab al haal*: This rule provides that the laws are permanently valid unless there is evidence challenging their beneficial nature.
3. *Al masaalih al mursalah*: Under this rule, the prescription is that a benefit is deemed legitimate if the Shariah is not known to have established or denied it.
4. *Al dharaai*: This rule provides that the legitimacy of that, which is instrumental, is directly affected by the benefit or harm implicit in the final end to which it leads.
5. *Al istiqraa al naaqis*: Under this rule, a universal law may be derived from a particular law through ascending generalization, if no exception is known to challenge the generalization.
6. *Al istihsaan*: This is the rule that a weaker *qiyas* may be preferred to a stronger one if it fulfils the general purposes of the Shariah better.
7. *Al urf wal aadah*: The rule that custom and established practice may be legitimate sources of law (provided they do not contradict the Quran and the *hadis*).

The jurisprudence developed by the above methodology of *ijtihad* and legal principles is not just for academic satisfaction but is a body of law (Muslim law) to be applied to factual situations that arise on a day-to-day basis. Disputes can be settled either privately or through the court system. In matters which can be settled privately, a person need only consult a *mufti* (jurisconsult) of his or her school.[19] The *mufti* gives his *fatwa* or advisory decision based on the law of his school.[20] However, if a matter is carried to the point of litigation and cannot be settled privately then the *qazi* (judge) is required to deliver a *qaza* (judgement) based upon the Shariah.[21]

The difference between a *fatwa* and a *qaza* must be kept in the forefront. A *fatwa* is merely advisory whereas a *qaza* is binding.[22] Both, of course, have to be based on the Shariah and not on private interpretation *de hors* the Shariah.[23] It is necessary to point out that the Supreme Court of India[24] also held that '[a] fatwa is an opinion only an expert is expected to give. It is not a decree, nor binding on the court or the State or the individual.' This is in consonance with the concept of *fatwa* as understood under Islamic jurisprudence. However, it is respectfully submitted, the Supreme Court did not appreciate the clear distinction between a *qazi*, which is the Arabic word for a judge of a court established under the authority of law, and a *mufti*, who is merely an expert on Islamic law, when it observed:

> A **Qazi or Mufti** [emphasis supplied] has no authority or powers to impose his opinion and enforce his fatwa on anyone by any coercive method. In fact, whatever may be the status of fatwa during Mogul or British Rule, it has no place in independent India under our constitutional scheme.

The Qazi does not deliver a *fatwa*; he gives a decision or a judgement in a particular case before him. A *fatwa* is merely an opinion of a *mufti* and is not binding. This has been the clear position under Muslim law, whether under the Mughal period or under British rule. The opinion of an advocate on a point of law is akin to a *fatwa* by a *mufti* on a point concerning the Shariah. On the other hand, the decision of a *Qazi* under Muslim law is similar to a decision by a court of law.

The *Qazi* under Islamic jurisprudence is different from the *qazi* under British Rule in India and the *qazi* in the present-day India. In fact, the judicial functions of the *qazi* as understood in the traditional sense are now being performed, wherever and whenever Muslim law is to be applied, by the judges of courts established under the Indian legal system.[25] Though the Kazis Act, 1880 is still extant, the role of such *qazis* (or *kazis*) is limited to some religious and ceremonial functions only.[26]

The *Qazi*, as traditionally understood, while exercising his judicial functions under the Shariah, was to be guided by the following rules or principles:[27]

1. Rendering justice to those who seek it is both an (Islamic) duty and inevitable.
2. In the court of law all men are equal.
3. The burden of proof falls on the complainant.
4. Any party's request for time to produce the relevant evidence must be granted, within reason. Failure to produce evidence is evidence to the contrary.
5. A judgement proven to be false by evidence ought to be revoked.
6. All adult (Muslims) are legal persons – except those convicted of perjury or of a crime.
7. No human may be charged of his intentions. Only his actions may be so charged and under legal evidence.
8. Where the Quran and Sunnah are silent on any matter, the law may be deduced or extrapolated from a comparable case or principle.
9. That which the Muslims collectively have found good and desirable is so from the standpoint of God.

In modern times, there is a growing feeling amongst the Muslim community and to a greater extent amongst non-Muslims that there is a need for reform within the Shariah. This would be possible using the process of *ijtihad* to bring in, within the fold of the Shariah, the various developments that have occurred in the life of human beings since the so-called 'closure of the gate of the *ijtihad*' around the 10th-century AD.[28] Of course, there is controversy as to whether the gate of *ijtihad* was at all closed and, if so, what were the reasons for it.

The history of Islamic jurisprudence and, indeed, Islamic scholarship over the past millennium has shown a sharp decline in independent reasoning to derive, adapt and adopt principles of law in tune with societal developments. In fact, the doctrine of *taqlid*[29] alone has, by and large, been adopted. *Taqlid* is akin to simply following the conclusion on a point of law as a dogma, without any awareness or knowledge of the reasoning and factual backdrop of such a conclusion. This becomes problematic when there is enhancement of knowledge and changes in circumstances. The original opinion loses its foundation and, therefore, its continued application as a dogma creates complications and altered perceptions about the law.

As such, Islam itself, albeit under misconception, has fallen under severe criticism on account of the perception that its basic principles and rules are out of date. The Quran, as a revealed text and the word of God, cannot be construed as a static document for one time period alone. It is a divine message to mankind for eternity. The *hadis*, as pointed out above, are acts or sayings of Prophet Muhammad (pbuh), pertaining to instances which happened during his lifetime, but they retain their value as precedents to be adopted in similar situations and adapted in newer circumstances. Shariah principles, as I have shared earlier, were derived from the Quran and the *hadis*, through *ijma* (consensus) and ultimately *qiyas*, both of which cannot be frozen in time.

There is a lot of talk that a 'reform' in Islamic law and Islamic thinking is required. At the same time, insofar as Muslims are concerned, there cannot be any change in what is stated in the Quran and, therefore, the word 'reform' cannot at all be used in the context of the Quran. How can a believer even think of changing the word of God? However, this does not mean that there cannot be a *restatement* of the law, in the context of the modern world, though still derived from the Quran and the *hadis*, by *ijma* of the Muslim community and by employing *qiyas*. In effect, this would amount to opening of the 'gate of *ijtihad*' for a fresh look at Islamic jurisprudence.

The question then would be, who would do this exertion, this *ijtihad*? It is obvious that a thorough understanding of

Arabic[30] with all its nuances would be necessary so as to enable the person or persons undertaking the task to fully understand the Quran, the *hadis* and the various commentaries on *ijma, qiyas* and Islamic jurisprudence in general. Apart from that, the person or persons undertaking such a task would have to be knowledgeable in jurisprudential principles and would have to be of high intellect, reasoning and integrity. It is clear that *ijtihad* is not for a lay person who merely has access to a translation of the Quran or translations of a selection of *hadis*.

As is evident from the discussion above, Islamic law has been developed through the interpretation of the Quran in the context of the sayings and acts of Prophet Muhammad (pbuh), the *ijma* of the community and logical reasoning through application of analogy (*qiyas*) by people of great learning (*mujtahids*). To say that there aren't any people of such learning today would be rendering a disservice to mankind. Of course, great effort would be required particularly in arriving at a consensus. But it is not an impossible task. For a start, the principle of *takhayyur* can be adopted, whereby aspects of a school of law, Sunni or Shia, which is beneficial and most closely in sync with modern thinking can be adopted by the other schools of law. This, again, is not an impossibility and, as will be seen later in this article, has even been employed in India.

How and to What Extent Is Muslim Law Applicable in India?

Muslim law, as a part of the Shariah, covers various fields of law such as the law relating to (1) personal status, (2) contracts, (3) torts, (4) criminal law, (5) constitutional law, (6) administrative law, (7) land law, (8) law of trade and commerce, (9) international law, (10) law of war, (11) taxation, (12) public finance, etc. Apart from the arena of law and jurisprudence, the Shariah also covers a much wider field of rituals, forms of worship, as well as ethics and personal conduct.

In India, Muslim law has a very limited application, and that too to Muslims alone. For example, the secular law of crimes in the shape of the Indian Penal Code and the Criminal Procedure Code, etc., govern the law of crimes in India. Similarly, the law of contracts is as per the Indian Contract Act, 1872, though there are many similarities with the Islamic law of contracts. Muslim law in India operates, essentially (apart from the law relating to waqfs), in respect of personal law or family law where the parties are Muslims.[31]

Under British rule in India, several enactments were passed declaring the various laws to be administered in different provinces. For example, for Oudh,[32] the Oudh Laws Act, 1876 provided[33] that in questions regarding succession, special property of females, betrothal, marriage, divorce, dower, adoption, guardianship, minority, bastardy, family relations, wills, legacies, gifts, partitions or any religious usage or institution, the rule of decision was to be (1) any custom applicable to the parties concerned which is not contrary to justice, equity or good conscience, and which had not been, altered or abolished by any enactment and had not been declared void by any competent authority; (2) the 'Muhammadan law' in cases where the parties are Muhammadans, and Hindu law in cases where the parties are Hindus except insofar as such law has been altered or abolished by any enactment[34] or had been modified by any such custom as referred to in (1) above.

It can be immediately noticed that in the field of personal laws, Muslim law was to be applied where the parties were Muslims and Hindu law where the parties were Hindus. But this was subject to any enactment or custom.

Similar provisions declaring the laws to be administered were contained in the Bombay Regulation IV of 1827, the Madras Civil Courts Act, 1873, the Punjab Laws Act, 1875 and the Ajmer Laws Regulation, 1877. In all these enactments, custom was accorded primacy over Muslim law and Hindu law, as the case may be.

The Bengal, Agra and Assam Civil Courts Act, 1887 also applied the Muslim law to Muslims and Hindu law to Hindus, in respect of the specified areas of law, but it did not grant primacy to custom. All these enactments are extant today and they continue to define the laws to be administered by civil courts in various parts of India.

The Muslim Personal Law (Shariat) Application Act, 1937 ('the 1937 Act') was enacted so as to cut out customs and usages which were in derogation to Muslim Personal Law in the fields of intestate succession, special property of females including personal property inherited from parents under contract or gift or any other provision of personal law, marriage, dissolution of marriage including *talaq*, *ila*, *zihar*, *lian*, *khula* and *mubaraat*, maintenance, dower, guardianship, gifts, trusts and trust properties and waqfs.[35]

It is interesting to note that while Muslim law is being mistakenly perceived to be adverse to women, the 1937 Act was enacted to enable Muslim women to enjoy the rights available to them under the Shariah. The 'Statement of Object and Reasons' of the 1937 Act makes it clear that the major objective of introducing the said enactment was to extricate Muslim women from the clutches of certain customs and usages by which they were denied their rights available to them under the Shariah. For example, it had become customary for women to be denied their right of inheritance in the properties left by their parents. This custom, which was prevalent in many parts of India, was contrary to Muslim law and, particularly, to the Quran, where it is explicitly stated [in verse 7 of chapter 4] as under:

> Unto the men a share of what parents and kinsfolk leave, and unto the women a share of what parents and kinsfolk leave, be it little or much – a share ordained.[36]

'In pre-Islamic Arabia only adult men were entitled to inherit. This verse was revealed with regard to the situation of a widow with three daughters left destitute by her husband's male heirs. The verse establishes that both men and women are legally entitled to a fixed and mandatory share of the wealth of their deceased relatives.'[37]

Since Muslim women in India were, by application of customary law,[38] being denied their right to inheritance and were thereby being relegated to the situation which prevailed prior to the revelation of the Quran, the 1937 Act was enacted to do away with such contrary customs and usages and to grant them the rights to which they were entitled under Muslim law. And the provisions in the Bombay Regulation IV of 1827, the Madras Civil Courts Act, 1873, the Oudh Laws Act, 1876, the Punjab Laws Act, 1875 and the Ajmer Laws Regulation, 1877, which gave primacy to customs over Muslim law, were repealed to the extent of the inconsistency with the 1937 Act.

Another interesting legislation that was brought about in pre-Independence India was the Dissolution of the Muslim Marriage Act, 1939 ('the 1939 Act'). There were various grounds under the Maliki school of law, which enabled a Muslim woman to obtain a decree, *qaza*, or judgement, for dissolution of her marriage. Many of those grounds were not available under the laws of other sects, such as Hanafi Law, which is followed by most of the Muslims in India. By virtue of the 1939 Act, the beneficial provisions of Maliki law were adopted for all Muslims in India although they were, by and large, followers of Hanafi law. This is an example of the principle of *takhayyur*. As such, a Muslim woman, Sunni or Shia, not necessarily being an adherent of Maliki school, could, by virtue of the said enactment, approach a court of law for a decree of dissolution of marriage on the grounds specified therein.[39]

The Statement of Objects and Reasons of the 1939 Act explicitly states that certain grounds for divorce are not available to Muslim women who follow the Hanafi school of law, but those grounds are available under Maliki law. It was also stated that Hanafi jurists have laid down that in cases where the application of Hanafi law causes hardship, it is permissible to apply the provisions of Maliki, Shafi'i or Hanbali law, if they alleviate the hardship. This, in effect, is an application of the principle of *takhayyur*. The 1939 Act is a unique example of legislation in India employing *takhayyur*. Its Statement of Objects and Reasons is reproduced below:

> There is no proviso in the Hanafi Code of Muslim Law enabling a married Muslim woman to obtain a decree from the court dissolving her marriage in case the husband neglects to maintain her, makes her life miserable by deserting or persistently maltreating her or absconds leaving her unprovided for and under certain other circumstances. The absence of such a provision has entailed unspeakable misery to innumerable Muslim women in British India. The Hanafi Jurists, however, have clearly laid down that in cases in which the application of Hanafi Law causes hardship, it is permissible to apply the provisions of the – Maliki, Shafi'i or Hambali Law. Acting on this principle the Ulemas have issued fatwas to the effect that in cases enumerated in clause 3, Part A of this Bill (*now see Section 2 of the Act*), a married Muslim woman may obtain a decree dissolving her marriage... As the courts are sure to hesitate to apply the Maliki Law to the case of a Muslim woman, legislation recognizing and enforcing the above-mentioned principle is called for in order to relieve the sufferings of countless Muslim women.

Takhayyur could have been employed in solving the problem of triple talaq (*talaq-e-biddat*). Under the *ithna ashari* school (a Shia school) of law such a talaq is void.[40] The Supreme Court also held[41] *talaq-e-biddat* to be void in respect of all Muslims, but through a different reasoning. What is decried in Muslim law, as also under present-day thinking, is the instant irrevocable nature of *talaq-e-biddat*. This 'sting', as it were, had already been taken out by the decision in Masroor Ahmed's case,[42] where such a talaq was held to be a single revocable talaq.

Now, through legislation, although the Supreme Court had

already nullified the effect of a *talaq-e-biddat* by holding it to be invalid, Parliament has criminalized it. The whole issue which could, in the first place, be solved by employing the principle of *takhayyur*[43] has got unnecessarily complicated by Parliament by enacting a law[44] which converts an invalid civil action into a criminal offence!

CONCLUSION

It is evident from the brief discussion above that Islamic jurisprudence is derived from the two primary sources – the Quran and *hadis*, in that order. It is through independent reasoning and upon recognition of the consensus (be it of the community or the Imams) that jurisprudential principles have been developed.

However, the process of *ijtihad* has remained dormant for close to a thousand years.[45] In this intervening period, civilizations have evolved (though some have also regressed), great scientific achievements have been witnessed and the spread of information has seen a complete revolution. These developments and many more need to be incorporated into Islamic jurisprudence.

Of course, the Quran, being the word of God is immutable and eternal. The *hadis* too serve as guiding stars and invaluable precedents and need to be applied to modern-day situations by analogy. There is a need to have a relook at Islamic jurisprudence through modern eyes but through the traditional method of *ijtihad* and after garnering a consensus. But that may take time and, to plug this gap in time, it would do a world of good if *takhayyur* is applied more freely so that the more beneficial provisions of one school of law are adopted by the others particularly where it concerns the rights of women and children.

An Axis Shift

A Critique of the Sabarimala Case

MUKUL ROHATGI

India is at a crossroads, and we are not mere bystanders.

The Constitution is not a text imposed by colonial powers upon a subjugated race. It was a social contract made between the people of the country who gave unto themselves the Constitution. The phrase 'We the people' does not reflect the democratic voice of only the vocal grouping but also of the silent minorities as well as the silent majority.

Our founding fathers toiled day and night to draft a Constitution that was to accommodate and protect all; that would make this nation great in spite of the myriad and conflicting interests it represents. It was a document for the future envisaged but also for the past that formed our foundation. It was a document so organic that it would mould to and anticipate the needs of an evolving society. It was, however, firm enough as to not lose touch with the original fabric of society.

In this Constitution, there was place for all – the old and the new, the rationalist and the believer, the majority and the minority, the individual and the group. The key to maintain the balance between the rights for all was entrusted to the Supreme Court, as the guardian and the sentinel of these rights.

The case of the Sabarimala temple reflects one such conflict. Prohibiting women between the ages of 10 and 50 entry into the Sabarimala temple pits the rights of women against that of its devotees. The Sabarimala dispute shows that it is one that is likely to be discussed for many years to come. Even after the judgement was pronounced in 2019, the Supreme Court referred the matter to a larger bench to reconsider the position in law.

The Court observed that various practices followed by different religions also get affected by the judgement and as such, the case was required to be sent to a larger bench for reconsideration as the scope of the present judgement has also been widened.

The matter at the time of this essay going to the press is being heard by a larger bench, and the judgement that will be delivered will settle the questions, until they are inevitably raised in another case again.

SABARIMALA AND LORD AYYAPPA

The ancient temple of Sabarimala is dedicated to Lord Ayyappa in his 'naishtik brahmachari' or eternally celibate form. As the lore goes, after Goddess Durga killed the demon king Mahishasur, his sister, Mahishi, set out to avenge him. She carried Lord Brahma's boon that only a child born out of Lord Vishnu and Lord Shiva could slay her. To save the world from annihilation, Lord Ayyappa was born out of the union between Lord Vishnu in his female form (Mohini), and Lord Shiva. It is said that the fiery Parshuram had consecrated the deity in the temple.

Justice Chandrachud specifically explains the historical context of the case. He writes in his judgement that although there are numerous Ayyappa temples in India, the Sabarimala Temple depicts Lord Ayyappa as a 'naishtika brahmacharya', and his powers derive specifically from abstention from sexual activities.[1]

When Lord Ayyappa was born, the divine beings left the boy in a forest near River Pampa. The Pandalam King, Rajasekara, while on a hunting trip in the forest along the banks of the River Pampa, heard the cries of a child. The king reached the banks of the river and found Ayyappa. He took the child to the palace with him, and briefed the queen about the incident. The couple as well as the local people were happy at the arrival of the child.

Lord Ayyappa, also known as 'Manikanta', grew up in the palace and was trained in the martial arts and the Vedas. The guru responsible for Manikanta's education concluded that Manikanta was not an ordinary child but a divine power.

In due course, the queen gave birth to a child they called Raja Rajan. Meanwhile, impressed with Manikanta's talents, King Rajasekara decided to crown him, treating him as the elder child. He ordered his minister to make arrangements for the coronation. However, the minister, desiring the throne for himself, attempted to execute plans to prevent the coronation, all of which failed.

He then approached the queen to persuade her to ensure that her own biological child was crowned king. The minister suggested that the queen pretend that she was suffering from a severe headache, whereupon he told the physician to prescribe the milk of a tigress to cure her. To achieve this, he suggested that Manikanta be sent to the forest.

Manikanta left for the forest, refusing the escort his father wanted him to take along, given the danger of the mission. But the king sent with Manikanta food, and coconuts with three eyes, in the remembrance of Lord Shiva. In the forest, Lord Shiva appeared before Manikanta and told him that though he had done his duty towards the devas, he was left with the task of ensuring the king's comfort. Lord Shiva told Manikanta that he could go back to the palace with Lord Indra in the form of a tiger.

When Manikanta was seated on the tiger, and all the female devatas in the form of tigresses arrived at the palace, the schemers were frightened into confessing their plot. They were convinced of his divine origins and prayed for their own salvation and for the safety of the kingdom. Manikanta disappeared.

The king refused to eat anything till his return. Manikanta finally appeared in the form of a vision before the king. Filled with a mix of emotions – happiness, grief, fear, wonder and devotion – the king stood praying for mercy and the blessings of Manikanta. He repented for not having realized Manikanta's divine power and for treating him merely as his child.

The Lord lovingly embraced the king and granted him moksha. He told the king that he was destined to return to earth. The ruler implored Manikanta to allow him to build a temple and dedicate it to him. The Lord assented. He shot an arrow that fell at the pinnacle of Sabarimala, and told the king that he could construct a temple at Sabarimala, north of the holy River Pampa, and install his deity there. Lord Ayyappa also explained how the Sabarimala pilgrimage should be undertaken, emphasizing the importance of the penance, or 'vratham', and what the devotees can attain by his 'darshan'. However, before the departure of the Lord, the king secured a promise that on Pongal each year, his personal jewellery would adorn the deity at Sabarimala.[2]

The judgement of the Kerala High Court had given the reason for the barring of young women from the temple.[3] The High Court has observed that since the deity is in the form of a naisthik brahmachari, it is believed that young women should not worship at the temple so that their presence does not cause even the slightest deviation from celibacy and austerity observed by the deity.

'Brahmachari' means a student who has to live in the house of his preceptor and study the Vedas, living the life of utmost austerity and discipline. A student who accompanied his guru wherever he goes and learns the Vedas from him is a 'naisthikan'. Four ashrams were prescribed for all persons belonging to the twice-born castes: the student; the married householder; the one who goes to the forest as a recluse; and the ascetic. B.K. Mukherjee, the fourth Chief Justice of India, in his Lordship's Tagore Law Lectures on the Hindu Law of Religious and Charitable Trust, says on page 16 of the second edition thus:

> Ordinarily therefore a man after finishing his period of studentship would marry and become a householder, and compulsory celibacy was never encouraged or sanctioned by the Vedas. A man however who was not inclined to marry might remain what is called a Naisthik Brahmchari or perpetual student and might pursue his studies living the life of a bachelor all his days.

A brahmachari should control his senses. He has to observe certain rules of conduct, which include refraining from indulging in gambling, idle gossip, scandal, falsehood, embracing and casting lustful eyes on females, and causing injury to others. This is given in the *Manusmriti*, Chapter II, shloka 179.[4]

Like many Hindu temples and pilgrimage sites, the journey to the Sabarimala temple is not an easy one and is in many ways symbolic of the path to reach the Almighty. It is said that Lord Ayyappa had set an extensive code for his followers, inclusive of a 41-day 'vratham', which includes a satvik lifestyle and brahmacharya. The terms of the vrath, or fast, include penance in various forms:

1. Abstaining from physical relations with a spouse;
2. Abstention from intoxicating drinks, smoking and tamasic food;
3. Living in isolation from the rest of the family;
4. Refraining from interacting with women in daily life, including those in the family;
5. Cooking one's own food;
6. Maintaining hygiene, including bathing twice a day before prayers;
7. Wearing a black mundu and upper garments;

8. Partaking of one meal a day; and
9. Walking barefoot.[5]

The case of the Sabarimala Temple arose out of a petition filed in public interest by a registered association of young lawyers, challenging the constitutional validity of Rule 3(b) of the Kerala Hindu Places of Public Worship (Authorisation of Entry) Rules, 1965, which restricts the entry of women into the Sabarimala Temple. These Rules were framed under the Kerala Hindu Places of Public Worship (Authorisation of Entry) Act, 1965 and, in effect, codified the pre-existing custom excluding women from the temple.

By the majority judgement 4:1, the Supreme Court held that the temple's practice of excluding women from public places of worship based on a custom was unconstitutional and struck down the rule as being *ultra vires* the 1965 Act and in violation of the fundamental rights to equality, liberty and freedom of religion.

There are various facets of the judgement which, I believe, though called 'reformative', have disturbed the balance so carefully maintained by our founding fathers. The uproar faced by the Government in the implementation of the judgement is but a reflection of the problem this shift in the axis of balance has caused in the existing conflicts of the various interests of the society.

MAINTAINABILITY AND SCOPE OF THE PUBLIC INTEREST LITIGATION REITERATED

In my view, a preliminary and very relevant issue that has not been sufficiently appreciated and only treated as a technicality is that of maintainability. A question arose whether the petitioners who had filed the petition had the locus standi to file it.

The rule of locus standi requires any person who approaches the Court to have some personal interest in the litigation. The courts do not encourage busybodies. In the case of Public Interest Litigation (PIL), the strictness of this rule has been reduced. The Court has acknowledged that in the case of PILs there may be disadvantaged groups who cannot afford to fight their own battles. Hence, even strangers may file cases on their behalf.

The Supreme Court in the case of *S.P. Gupta v. Union of India*[6] held that 'where a legal wrong or a legal injury is caused to a person or to a determinate class of persons by reason of violation of any constitutional or legal right, or any burden is imposed in contravention of any constitutional or legal provision or without authority of law, or any such legal wrong or legal injury or illegal burden is threatened and such person or determinate class of persons is by reason of poverty, helplessness or disability or socially or economically disadvantaged position, unable to approach the Court for relief, any member of the public can maintain an application for an appropriate direction, order or writ in the High Court under Article 226 and in case of breach of any fundamental right of such person or determinate class of persons, in this Court under Article 32 seeking judicial redress for the legal wrong or injury caused to such person or determinate class of persons.'

The fundamental reason in entertaining such petitions would necessarily be that the class of persons is by reason of poverty, helplessness or disability, or due to a socially or economically disadvantaged position, unable to approach the Court. This could hardly be true in the present case of the Sabarimala Temple issue. Yet, this exercise has been brushed aside by the constitutional court as a mere technicality.

Amongst the majority and concurring judgements, this issue was only dealt with by Justice Rohinton Fali Nariman and Justice Chandrachud. Relying on an earlier judgement of the Supreme Court,[7] Justice Nariman held that the Sabarimala case raised issues relating to women, who happen to be between the ages of 10 to 50 generally. Women of those ages were allegedly not allowed entry into the temple at Sabarimala on the ground of a physiological or biological function.

This was thus a feature common to all women between those ages and hence women constituted a group. Also, as the matter raised far-reaching consequences relating to Articles 25 and 26 of the Constitution (the right to freedom of religion and the right to maintain religious institutions), it was found necessary to decide this matter on merits. Consequently, Justice Nariman as well as Justice Chandrachud found that the technical plea cannot stand in the way of a constitutional court applying constitutional principles to the case at hand.

It is only in the dissenting judgement of Justice Indu Malhotra that the issue has been extensively and rightly dealt with. Justice Malhotra specifically records in her judgement that 'the Petitioners do not claim to be devotees of the Sabarimala Temple where Lord Ayyappa is believed to have manifested himself as a Naishtik Brahmachari'. The judgement of Justice Malhotra observed that to determine the validity of long-standing religious customs and usages of a sect, at the instance of an association/ interveners who are 'involved in social developmental activities, especially activities related to upliftment of women and helping them become aware of their rights', would require the Supreme Court to decide religious questions at the behest of persons who do not subscribe to this faith. Justice Malhotra further holds that the right to worship, claimed by the petitioners, has to be predicated on the basis of an affirmation of a belief in the particular manifestation of the deity in this temple.[8]

PILs, particularly those pertaining to religious practices and customs, stand on a different footing as has been noted in the dissenting judgement by Justice Malhotra. I believe that her decision also reflects the consistent philosophy that has been reflected in the various judgements of the Supreme Court itself, which particularly holds that even the test of 'essential practice' is to be determined from the perspective of its adherents.[9]

Justice Malhotra has rightly also held that 'the absence of

this bare minimum requirement must not be viewed as a mere technicality, but an essential requirement to maintain a challenge for impugning practices of any religious sect, or denomination. Permitting PILs in religious matters would open the floodgates to interlopers to question religious beliefs and practices, even if the petitioner is not a believer of a particular religion, or a worshipper of a particular shrine. The perils are even graver for religious minorities if such petitions are entertained.'[10]

It is specifically noted by Justice Malhotra that in the present case, the worshippers of this temple believe in the manifestation of the deity as a naishtik brahmachari. The devotees of this temple have not challenged the practices followed by the temple based on the essential characteristics of the deity. The right to practise one's religion is a fundamental right guaranteed by Part III of the Constitution, without reference to whether religion or the religious practices are rational or not. Religious practices are constitutionally protected under Articles 25 and 26 (b). Courts normally do not delve into issues of religious practices, especially in the absence of an aggrieved person from that particular religious faith or sect.

In a pluralistic society comprising of people with diverse faiths, beliefs and traditions, to entertain PILs challenging religious practices followed by any group, sect or denomination could cause serious damage to the constitutional and secular fabric of this country.

This tilt at the instance of an association/interveners who are 'involved in social developmental activities, especially activities related to upliftment of women and helping them become aware of their rights' against the believers who at no stage have come before the Supreme Court, can open the floodgates particularly with respect to the precious rights of both minorities as well as the majority of faiths.

This will also lead to a peculiar situation, where anyone not having a stake or a say in any religion can challenge the norms without having met the basic need of locus. The Court may take up the exercise without having sufficient assistance in a matter which itself is wrought in a religious thicket. The said position will also substantially dilute the rights of the devotees so preciously protected and guarded by the Constitution.

THE ISSUE OF CONSTITUTIONAL MORALITY AND BALANCING INTERESTS

Article 25 of the Constitution gives to every person right to freedom of religion subject to restraints of public morality. Similarly, Article 26 of the Constitution gives every religious denomination the right to establish and maintain as well as manage the affairs of its religious institutions subject to public morality. Thus, the clearly determining factor in the case is that of public morality. Although the question of constitutional morality was relevant for the scope and magnitude of the rights enjoyed under Articles 25 and 26, this judgement does much more for 'constitutional morality'.

Public morality is a concept which is used to permit restrictions of fundamental rights. Hence, rather than being a concept in furtherance of a specified fundamental right, it is a permissible restriction on the right. Constitutional morality, on the other hand, refers to the underlying ethos of the Constitution, and has been used to expand the content of fundamental rights.

The two concepts – public and constitutional morality – are fundamentally distinct. However, Chief Justice Dipak Misra speaking for himself and Justice Ajay Manikrao Khanwilkar held that the term 'constitutional morality' implies more than public morality and held that a fairly wide amplitude should be given to the definition of morality referred to in Articles 25 and 26. The judges have held that whenever there is a violation of the fundamental rights, the term 'morality' naturally implies constitutional morality, and any view that is ultimately taken by the constitutional courts must be in conformity with the principles and basic tenets of the concept of this constitutional morality that gets support from the Constitution.[11]

As regards public morality, Chief Justice Misra holds that 'the Constitution was not shoved, by any external force, upon the people of this country but was adopted and given by the people of this country to themselves, the term public morality has to be appositely understood as being synonymous with constitutional morality.'[12]

This completely places the concept of constitutional morality on its head. If constitutional morality is to be given an expansive meaning, and is synonymous with public morality, public morality must also be given an expansive meaning. Thus, rather than expanding the scope of the right, the scope of the exception is expanded.

Chief Justice Misra holds that the notions of public order, morality and health cannot be used to restrict the freedom to freely practise religion and discriminate against women of the age group of 10 to 50 years by denying them their legal right to enter and offer their prayers at the Sabarimala Temple for the simple reason that public morality must yield to constitutional morality. Chief Justice Misra, therefore, holds that in case of a conflict between the moralities being public and constitutional, it is the constitutional morality that will prevail.

In my view, this position itself contradicts the stand that public morality is equivalent to constitutional morality. With great respect to Chief Justice Misra, I do not subscribe to the view that 'public morality must yield to Constitutional Morality' (paragraph 111 of the Sabarimala judgement).

Justice Chandrachud also laid great emphasis on constitutional morality for the purpose of deciding the vexed issue. The Learned Judge dwelled on the issue of whether the draftspersons of the Constitution, while defining the content of morality, only engaged with prevailing morality in society or referred to something more fundamental. The Learned Judge then went on to hold that morality for the purposes of Articles

25 and 26 cannot have an ephemeral existence. Popular notions about what is moral and what is not are transient and fleeting. Popular notions about what is or is not moral may in fact be deeply offensive to individual dignity and human rights.

Justice Chandrachud holds that the content of morality is founded on the four precepts that emerge from the Preamble. The first among them is the need to ensure justice in its social, economic and political dimensions. The second is the postulate of individual liberty in matters of thought, expression, belief, faith and worship. The third is equality of status and opportunity amongst all citizens. The fourth is the sense of fraternity amongst all citizens, which assures the dignity of human life.

Added to these four precepts is the fundamental postulate of secularism, which treats all religions on an even platform and allows to each individual the fullest liberty to believe or not to believe. The Learned Judge holds that the founding faith upon which the Constitution is based is the belief that it is in the dignity of each individual that the pursuit of happiness is founded. Individual dignity can be achieved only in a regime that recognizes liberty as inhering in each individual as a natural right.

As per Justice Chandrachud, in public law conversations between religion and morality, it is the overarching sense of constitutional morality that has to prevail. While the Constitution recognizes religious beliefs and faiths, its purpose is to ensure a wider acceptance of human dignity and liberty as the ultimate founding faith of the fundamental text of our governance. Where a conflict arises, the quest for human dignity, liberty and equality must prevail. These, above everything else, are matters on which the Constitution has willed that its values must reign supreme.

It is my belief that laudatory as it sounds, Justice Chandrachud's judgement does the most to tilt the constitutional balance that has so carefully been preserved in favour of individual rights against rights of the group. In my opinion, the reason that revolutionary steps have not been taken in the direction of social reforms in the matter of faith and religion is because a certain sanctity has to be maintained with respect to the faith of the people, and the change has to emanate from within.

I frankly am unable to fully appreciate the new-fangled concept of 'constitutional morality' as referred to in recent judgements by the Supreme Court of India in *Manoj Narula v. Union of India*[13] and *Navtej Singh Johar v. Union of India.*[14] For the first time, the term 'constitutional morality' was used by the Supreme Court in *Kesavananda Bharati Sripadagalvaru v. State of Kerala*[15] by Justice A.N. Ray.

In the said judgement, he has observed that 'Democracy proceeds on the faith and capacity of the people to elect their representatives and faith in the representatives to represent the people. Throughout the history of mankind if any motive power has been more potent than another it is that of faith in themselves. The ideal of faith in ourselves is of the greatest help to us. Grote, the historian of Greece, said that the diffusion of constitutional morality, not merely among the majority of any community but throughout the whole, is the indispensable condition of a government at once free and peaceful. By constitutional morality Grote meant a paramount reverence for the forms of the Constitution, with a perfect confidence in the bosom of every citizen amidst the bitterness of party contest that the forms of the Constitution will not be less sacred in the eyes of opponents than in his own.'

Dr Ambedkar used the phrase 'Constitutional Morality' sparsely in the debates held by the Constituent Assembly during the drafting of the Constitution, and made it to be the alter ego of the 'spirit' and not the 'pillar' of the Constitution. The same was also briefly discussed by this Court in the aforementioned Keshvananda case. The concept 'constitutional morality', if at all, should be equated with the 'underlying spirit of the Constitution' or principles enshrined therein.

For example, power under Article 356 of the Constitution of India[16] can be exercised, but keeping in mind that democracy is a fundamental feature of our Constitution, this power should be used sparingly. Such an interpretation would be in sync with, one may say, the constitutional ethos or, for that matter, the underlying spirit of the Constitution.

That further in my opinion, the concept of constitutional morality has evolved in various recent judgements of the Supreme Court. In *Manoj Narula*,[17] the Supreme Court defined constitutional morality as the requirement to adhere to the norms of the Constitution coupled with an obligation not to act in a manner that would become violative of the rule of law or reflectible of action in an arbitrary manner.

In *Navtej Singh Johar*,[18] the Supreme Court went even further and said that the concept of constitutional morality is said to be not limited to the mere observance of the core principles of constitutionalism. Constitutional morality embraces within itself virtues of a wide magnitude such as that of ushering a pluralistic and inclusive society, while at the same time adhering to the other principles of constitutionalism, and is not confined to a mere reading of the literal text of the Constitution.

All the above definitions of constitutional morality refer to a concept of morality that is closer to being the conscience or the spirit of the Constitution, and is necessary where the text is not specifically provided.

However, as against that, the concept of morality as has been laid down under Articles 25 and 26, debated by the Constituent Assembly and tested by the Supreme Court in various judgements, has stood the test of time. To introduce and replace the concept of 'morality' by that of 'constitutional morality' would be to undo the same.

The progressive tilt in favour of constitutional morality may in fact lead to watering down the protection provided to various rights under the Constitution. The Constitution in its original form is a pluralist document very carefully balancing the various rights and interests of the various sections of the new and the old world. The present exercise of testing a coded law on the anvil of constitutional morality will necessarily reverse the process of the challenge and will meet a predetermined fate. With such a wide ambit given to constitutional morality, the scope and width of the fundamental rights has reduced drastically.

In the context of constitutional morality, it is relevant to read the judgement of Justice Nariman with respect to public morality being treated as constitutional morality. He points to the distinction between Articles 25 and 26 of the Constitution. Article 25 makes that right subject to both public morality and all other fundamental rights. Article 26, on the other hand, is not specifically subject to the other fundamental rights. If fundamental rights, which inform the concept of constitutional morality, are to be read as part of 'public morality', that would amount to a back-door addition of restrictions to fundamental rights.[19]

I believe this view of Justice Nariman correctly demonstrates the flaws of imposing the burden of constitutional morality on public morality as far as the interpretation of the Constitution is concerned.

At this juncture it may be apt to refer to Justice Malhotra's view on constitutional morality, which could very well form the gist of this essay. Justice Malhotra ruled that constitutional morality in a pluralistic society with a secular polity would require that the followers of various sects have the freedom to practise their faith in accordance with the tenets of their religion. It is irrelevant whether the practice is rational or logical. Notions of rationality cannot be invoked in matters of religion by the courts.

Justice Malhotra further held that the followers of this denomination, or sect, as the case may be, submit that the worshippers of this deity in the Sabarimala Temple, even individually, have the right to practise and profess their religion under Article 25 (1) in accordance with the tenets of their faith, which is protected as a fundamental right.

Justice Malhotra holds that equality and non-discrimination are certainly facets of constitutional morality. However, the concept of equality and non-discrimination in matters of religion cannot be viewed in isolation. Under our constitutional scheme, a balance is required to be struck between the principles of equality and non-discrimination on the one hand, and the protection of the cherished liberties of faith, belief and worship guaranteed by Articles 25 and 26 to persons belonging to all religions in a secular polity, on the other hand. Constitutional morality requires the harmonization or balancing of all such rights, to ensure that the religious beliefs of none are obliterated or undermined.

THE ESSENTIAL PRACTICES AND THE RELIGIOUS DENOMINATION TEST

Part III of the Constitution of India deals with the Fundamental Rights. The chapter on rights, while protecting the basic human rights, also makes special provisions for protecting the right to freedom of religion.[20] The right to freedom of religion entails within its ambit several provisions, but for our purpose we are particularly concerned with Articles 25 and 26. As I have shared earlier in this essay, Article 25 deals with the freedom of conscience, free profession, practice and propagation of religion to all persons. Article 26 ensures freedom to manage religious affairs to every religious denomination and section thereof for the following: to establish and maintain institutions for religious and charitable purposes; to manage its own affairs in matters of religion; to own and acquire movable and immovable property; and to administer such property in accordance with law.

Religious Denomination

Like most provisions of the Constitution, both Articles 25 and 26 are not absolute. The rights are certainly subject to public order, morality and health. Specifically, Article 25 is also subject to other fundamental rights. However, as shared earlier, Article 26 is not by itself subject to the other fundamental rights. This would mean that the rights conferred under Article 26 to manage the affairs of a religious denomination is wider than the right conferred under Article 25.

Specifically, while the rights under Articles 14 and 15 (i.e. the right to equality) would clearly trump the rights under Article 25, in the case of Article 26, the Court would have to indulge in a balancing exercise. The right to equality and the right to manage and administer the religious affairs of a denomination would have to be harmonized rather than one simply yielding to the other. Therefore, an argument was made in the case that the followers of Ayyappa were a separate religious denomination and hence had rights under Article 26. This argument was rejected by the majority judgement, and I believe wrongly so.

One of the earliest judgements on Articles 25 and 26 of the Constitution of India was the case of *Commissioner, Hindu Religious Endowments v. Sri Lakshmindra Thirtha Swamiar of Sri Shirur Mutt.*[21] This case concerned itself with the settlement of a scheme (i.e. an effective takeover) in connection with a 'mutt' known as the Shirur Mutt. In history, the Shirur Mutt is stated to be one of the eight mutts situated at Udupi in the district of South Kanara, and reputed to have been founded by Shri Madhwacharya, the well-known exponent of dualistic theism in Hinduism. The judgement went on to decide many important issues of the day, but we are presently concerned with its exposition of the term 'religious denomination'. The Supreme Court held as follows:

> The word 'denomination' has been defined in the Oxford Dictionary to mean 'a collection of individuals classed together under the same name: a religious sect or body having a common faith and organization and designated by a distinctive name.

The Supreme Court observed that 'Each one of such sects or sub-sects can certainly be called a religious denomination, as it is designated by a distinctive name – in many cases it is the name of the founder – and has a common faith and common spiritual organization.' The judgement, a landmark judgement of that era, indicates a drift towards enhanced protection of the religious rights as contemplated under the Constitution. The term 'religious denomination' was read in a fairly liberal manner and could extend to not only a religious denomination but also any section thereof.

In another case pertaining to Auroville, a township of followers of Shri Aurobindo, the Supreme Court [22] retraced and reaffirmed the law as laid down in Sri Shirur Mutt (supra), and held as follows: 'The words 'religious denomination' in Article 26 of the Constitution must take their colour from the word 'religion' and if this be so, the expression 'religious denomination' must also satisfy three conditions. It must be a collection of individuals who have:

1. a system of beliefs or doctrines which they regard as conducive to their spiritual well-being, that is, a common faith;
2. a common organization; and
3. a designation by a distinctive name.

By application of these tests in the case of Sabarimala, Chief Justice Misra, Justice Chandrachud and Justice Nariman have all held that the group fails the religious denomination test.

Chief Justice Misra, speaking for Justice Khanwilkar and himself, held that the devotees of Lord Ayyappa do not constitute a separate religious denomination as they do not have common religious tenets peculiar to themselves, which they regard as conducive to their spiritual well-being, other than those which are common to the Hindu religion. The Chief Justice, therefore, held that the devotees of Lord Ayyappa are exclusively Hindus who do not constitute a separate religious denomination.[23] Justices Nariman and Chandrachud also held that the Ayyappans were not a religious denomination.

On the other hand, Justice Malhotra held that the meaning ascribed to 'religious denomination' by this Court in the Shirur Mutt (supra) case and subsequent cases is not a straightjacket formula, but a working formula. It provides guidance to ascertain whether a group will fall within a religious denomination or not. Justice Malhotra held that if there are clear attributes that there exists a sect, which is identifiable as being distinct by its beliefs and practices, and having a collection of followers who follow the same faith, it would be identified as a 'religious denomination'. In this view of the matter, she ruled that the worshippers of Lord Ayyappa at the Sabarimala Temple constitute a religious denomination, or sect thereof, as the case maybe, following the 'Ayyappan Dharma'.

At this stage, we may briefly discuss the scope of the religion of which the Ayyappans are to be a denomination. This is also relevant to understand why I agree with Justice Malhotra's view. The Hindu religion in its broadest form is incapable of a definition. In a celebrated Supreme Court judgement,[24] the Court considered the questions as to who Hindus are and what are the broad features of Hindu religion, and held thus:

> When we think of the Hindu religion, we find it difficult, if not impossible, to define Hindu religion or even adequately describe it. Unlike other religions in the world, the Hindu religion does not claim any one prophet; it does not worship any one God; it does not subscribe to any one dogma; it does not believe in any one philosophic concept; it does not follow any one set of religious rites or performances; in fact, it does not appear to satisfy the narrow traditional features of any religion or creed. It may broadly be described as a way of life and nothing more... Monier Williams has observed that 'it must be borne in mind that Hinduism is far more than a mere form of theism resting on Brahmanism. It presents for our investigation a complex congeries of creeds

> and doctrines which in its gradual accumulation may be compared to the gathering together of the mighty volume of the Ganges, swollen by a continual influx of tributary rivers and rivulets, spreading itself over an ever-increasing area of country, and finally resolving itself into an intricate Delta of tortuous streams and jungly marshes'... The Hindu religion is a reflection of the composite character of the Hindus, who are not one people but many. It is based on the idea of universal receptivity. It has ever aimed at accommodating itself to circumstances and has carried on the process of adaptation through more than three thousand years. It has first borne with and then, so to speak, swallowed, digested, and assimilated something from all creeds.

The above judgement shows that unlike, say, the Abrahamic religions, Hinduism is far more malleable and unstructured. There can be no hard and fast rules about determining what is or what is not a denomination. Ultimately, what must prevail is the Constitution's guarantee of religious freedom. There are few defined constituents of the Hindu religion. Denominations and sects in Hinduism are mostly found in post reformist and other movements. These denominations and sects recognized by the Supreme Court as a religious denomination in the *Shri Shirur Mutt* case (supra) and *Ramakrishna Mission*[25] are classic examples of the same.

However, can something more basic and rudimentary be brushed away without acknowledgement? The manifestation of Lord Ayyappa in the naishtik brahmachari form, for which an entire temple and practice was dedicated, must get its due. It is true that there are many temples devoted to Lord Ayyappa, but this particular manifestation – following the practice of refusing entry to women of age group 10–50 – is unique, and ought to be treated as a subsect for the purpose of religious denomination, and believers and worshippers must get the protection secured for them. Also, the travesty of denying to them the relevant protection will also lead to an attempt at only recognizing the reformist structures of the religion and protecting them while riding roughshod over the tenets of the religion themselves.

Parity may therefore be drawn with respect to the cases like the Shirur Mutt and Ramakrishna Mission with that of individual temples. Worshippers of Lord Ayyappa at Sabarimala Temple constitute a religious denomination, or sect thereof, as the case maybe, following the 'Ayyappan Dharma'. They are designated by a distinctive name wherein all male devotees are called 'Ayyappans'; all female devotees below the age of 10 and above the age of 50 are called 'Malikapurnams'. A pilgrim on his maiden trip to Sabarimala Temple is called a 'Kanni Ayyappan'. The devotees are referred to as 'Ayyappaswamis'. A devotee has to observe the 'vratham', and follow the code of conduct, before embarking upon the 'pathinettu padikal' to enter the temple at Sabarimala.

It may be apt to mention here that this is not a unique position in law. There have been many cases where the practices of individual temples were recognized and protected. Sri Venkataramana Temple at Mulki, Karnataka, was considered to be a denominational temple, and the Gowda Saraswath Brahmins were held to constitute a religious denomination. Similarly, in *Dr Subramaniam Swamy v. State of Tamil Nadu,*[26] the Podhu Dikshitars were held to constitute a religious denomination in the context of the Sri Sabanayagar Temple at Chidambaram.

Once the Ayyappans are a distinct denomination, they must get the full force of the Constitutional guarantee of freedom of religion. It is no part of the Court's, or society's, function to impose an allegedly reformist ideology on matters of faith. Rationality has no place in matters of belief.

Essential Practices Test

As per the judgement, the rights which are constitutionally protected only include the essential religious practices. Hence a question arose: Is the exclusion of women aged 10 to 50 an essential religious practice? If it was not an essential practice, there was no constitutional protection that the exclusion enjoyed. The majority held that the practice was in fact not an essential component of the Hindu religion and, as such, enjoyed no immunity.

The Supreme Court has held that the 'essential practices test' primarily means those practices that are fundamental to follow a religious belief. The test to determine whether a part or practice is essential to a religion is to find out whether the nature of the religion will be changed without that part or practice. If the taking away of that part or practice could result in a fundamental change in the character of that religion or in its belief, then such a part could be treated as an essential or integral part. There cannot be additions or subtractions to such a part because it is the very essence of that religion, and alterations will change its fundamental character.

It is such permanent essential parts, which are protected by the Constitution.[27] One more factor that is crucial for the determination of 'essential practice' is that it is to be determined from the perspective of its adherents. This principle was first laid down in the case of Shirur Mutt (supra). In that case, the Supreme Court held that 'What constitutes the essential part of a religion is primarily to be ascertained with reference to the doctrine of that religion itself.'

In the case of Sabarimala, Justice Nariman held that even assuming that there is a custom or usage for keeping out women of the ages of 10 to 50 from entering the Sabarimala Temple, and that the said practice is an essential part of the 'Thanthris' as well as the worshippers' faith, the said practice or usage would be clearly hit by Section 3 of the Kerala Hindu Places of Public Worship (Authorisation of Entry) Act, 1965. He ruled that the fundamental right claimed by the Thanthris and worshippers of the institution, based on custom and usage under Article 25 (1), must necessarily yield to the rights of women. Women between the ages of 10 to 50 also had a fundamental right to practise religion, which would be meaningless unless they were allowed to enter the temple at Sabarimala to worship the idol of Lord Ayyappa.

Chief Justice Misra held that that exclusion of women of any age group could never be regarded as an essential practice of Hindu religion and, on the contrary, it is an essential part of the Hindu religion to allow Hindu women to enter a temple as devotees and followers of the Hindu religion, and offer their prayers to the deity. Chief Justice Misra held so particularly in the absence of any scriptural or textual evidence to accord the exclusionary practice followed at the Sabarimala temple the status of an essential practice of Hindu religion.

Justice Chandrachud, also in the same manner, held that the exclusion of women was not an essential doctrine of the Hindu religion.[28]

In view of the above discussion on the scope and ambit of Hindu religion, I find it difficult to accept that the essential tenets of most temples of the Hindu religion can be imposed or serve as a yardstick for the practices of certain specific temples with variant practice. Each temple may have its own followers and come to have a custom that has been crystallized over centuries to become a practice for that holy site. To refuse it special status because there are temples in a country as vast as India, with a religion as malleable as Hinduism, would be to reduce the constitutional promise of Article 25 to a nought.

In regard to the preceding criticism, it would be relevant herein to refer to another issue raised by Chief Justice Gogoi in the review petition of this case: 'Whether the "essential religious practices" of a religious denomination, or even a section thereof are afforded constitutional protection under Article 26.'

It is pertinent at this stage to refer to an extract from the concurring judgement of Justice Chinnappa Reddy in *S.P. Mittal v. Union of India & Ors.* (supra) with respect to the approach to be adopted by courts whilst dealing with matters concerning religion:

> What is religion to some is pure dogma to others and what is religion to others is pure superstition to some others... But my views about religion, my prejudices and my predilections, if they be such, are entirely irrelevant. So are the views of the credulous, the fanatic, the bigot and the zealot. So also, the views of the faithful, the devout, the acharya, the moulvi, the padre and the bhikhshu, each of whom may claim his as the only true or revealed religion. For our purpose, we are concerned with what the people of the Socialist, Secular, Democratic Republic of India, who have given each of its citizens freedom of conscience and the right to freely profess, practise and propagate religion and who have given every religious denomination the right to freely manage its religious affairs, mean by the expressions 'religion' and 'religious denomination'. We are concerned with what these expressions are designed to mean in Articles 25 and 26 of the Constitution.
>
> Any freedom or right involving the conscience must naturally receive a wide interpretation and the expression religion and religious denomination must, therefore, be interpreted in no narrow, stifling sense but in a liberal, expansive way.

Justice Malhotra's dissenting view has correctly considered this question in an expansive way to uphold and secure the protections granted to the believers to uphold their faith. She has held that the only way to determine the essential practices test would be with reference to the practices followed since time immemorial, which may have been scripted in the religious texts of the temple. If any practice in a particular temple can be traced to antiquity, and is integral to the temple, it must be taken to be an essential religious practice of that temple.

The temple Thanthri, the Travancore Devaswom Board and believers of Lord Ayyappa have submitted that the limited restriction on access of women during the notified age of 10 to 50 years is a religious practice that is central and integral to the tenets of this shrine, since the deity has manifested himself in the form of a 'naishtik brahmachari'.[29]

CONCLUSION

In light of the above discussion I sum up my view as follows:

1. The Śabarimala Temple is a one-of-its-kind temple dedicated to Lord Ayyappa in his naishtik brahmachari form, and follows the practice of refusing entry to women of between the ages of 10 and 50. There are other temples of Lord Ayyappa where all Hindus go to worship; this one, however, is significant for its peculiar practices.
2. The 'Ayyappans' ought to necessarily qualify the test of the 'religious denomination test' as they are worshippers of Lord Ayyappa at Sabarimala Temple and constitute a religious denomination, or a sect as the case may be, following the 'Ayyappan Dharma'. They have distinct practices and ought to be recognized as a separate religious denomination.
3. The Hindu religion is vast and cannot be defined and confined with only a certain school of thought.
4. The peculiar practices of Hindus cannot be coloured with the same brush as the common practices of Hindus.
5. The essential practices of the religious denomination, or a set or even a subset of the Hindu religion must be protected.
6. The balance maintained by the Constitution between the various rights of the people must be maintained.
7. Holding otherwise, even if the outcome is meant to be reformative, will disturb the pluralist balance so maintained by the Constitution.
8. The question of constitutional morality ought to be preserved as the guiding principle, and not to be read into Articles 25 and 26.
9. The question of maintainability ought not to be treated as

a mere technicality particularly when on the same hinges the sensitive balance maintained by the Constitution.

10. The nature of this dispute, which means giving in to the question of religion, religious practices, essential practices and religious denominations alike, is akin to a minefield. The courts should be wary of wading into such controversies. By the very nature of the dispute, it is not easy to marshal the facts and apply the law. The Supreme Court in the case of *Krishna Singh v. Mathura Ahir*[30] had denied interfering in the religious custom that prohibited lower caste Hindus to take sanyas. The Court had held that the profession of religion should be a very personal choice. Just as the courts do not enter the 'political thicket', it would be wise not to enter the 'religious thicket' unless it is imperative.
11. I further reiterate that the need of the reference of the said judgement to a larger bench is an instance depicting that this Court was also of the opinion that that some facets of the said judgement need to be revisited.

As a general conclusion, I think it is time that we realize that short and pithy judgements go a long way in settling the law rather than long and winding judgements. One can take inspiration from the judgements of the Privy Council (dealing with Indian cases) in the 1930s and the 1940s.[31] Till date, there is no unanimity in the final conclusions rendered by the Bench in *Kesavananda Bharati v. State of Kerala*,[32] (the fundamental rights case) as separate opinions were delivered.

The Sabarimala judgement is an example of how lengthy judgements, rather than clarifying issues, can make them even more obscure. Judgements of the Supreme Court are not meant only for lawyers, but also for the lay public, and should be written in a simple and precise manner so as to be accessible to all.

The Growing Significance of Dignity Jurisprudence in the Field of Human Rights

JUSTICE A.K. SIKRI

Written constitutions in most democratic countries are of a recent origin which may, at the most, go back to a few hundred years. Most of these constitutions recognize and lay down specific provisions concerning human rights. Even those liberal democracies that do not have written constitutions, cherish and enforce human rights.[1] The main thesis of this essay is to demonstrate that the basis of human rights is *dignity*. The concept of dignity has not only added to known human rights, but has also led to the creation of a new genre of such rights.

Let it be clarified at the outset that there is no specific fundamental right in the Indian Constitution that expressly talks of human dignity. The word 'dignity' occurs only once in our Constitution, and that too in its Preamble. The Preamble proclaims that India is constituted into a 'SOVEREIGN SOCIALIST SECULAR DEMOCRATIC REPUBLIC', and it is aimed at securing to all its citizens 'JUSTICE, LIBERTY, EQUALITY and FRATERNITY'. While talking of fraternity, the Preamble states: '*FRATERNITY*, assuring the dignity of the individual and the unity and integrity of the Nation...'

Notwithstanding the absence of this expression in the fundamental rights chapter, certain rights like the right to equality (Article 14), certain freedoms (Article 19) and the right to life and personal liberty (Article 21), have been interpreted by the Supreme Court over the last four decades keeping in view the individual as the focal point of the Constitution. The concept of human dignity, in the process, has been recognized on the premise that it is the realization of individual rights that will lead to the collective well-being of the community. Thus, human dignity, as a value, has been the basis for giving various kinds of rights.

THREE MODELS OF HUMAN DIGNITY

Before chartering a discourse on such rights, let me first discuss three models of the human dignity doctrine, and their interconnection.

Insofar as the concept of human dignity is concerned, it dates back thousands of years. Historically, human dignity, as a concept, found its origin in different religions. Later, it was also influenced by the views of philosophers who developed human dignity in their contemplations.[2]

After the Second World War, constitutional and international legal texts began to adopt the concept of dignity, and in this manner, human dignity has come to be recognized as a constitutional value and as a constitutional right.[3] Thus, historically, three types of models for determining the content of the constitutional value of human dignity are recognized: The theological model; the philosophical model; and the constitutional model.

Legal scholars were called upon to determine the theological basis of human dignity as a constitutional value and as a constitutional right. Philosophers also came out with their views justifying human dignity as a core human value. Legal understanding is influenced by theological and philosophical views, though these two are not identical. Legal scholars have discussed the jurisprudential aspects of human dignity based on the aforesaid philosophies. Over a period of time, human dignity has found its way through constitutionalism, whether written or unwritten.

The manner in which historical progression has taken place, from a theological to a philosophical recognition of 'dignity' as a concept, and attained the coveted position as a constitutional right, makes for an interesting study. Before we talk of dignity in the present-day context, in order to understand its true complexion and contours, it would be worthwhile to trace this evolution.

Theological Model

Amritasya Putrah Vayam
(We are all begotten of the immortal.)

Every individual soul is potentially divine.
– Swami Vivekananda

Hinduism does not recognize human beings as mere material beings. Its understanding of human identity is more ethical–spiritual than material. That is why a sense of immortality and divinity is attributed to all human beings in Hindu classical literature. It is on the principle that the soul makes the body of all living organisms its abode and is, in fact, an integral part of the Paramatman, Divine Whole, that the Vedas declare unequivocally:

Ajyesthaaso Akanisthaasa Yete
Sam Bhraataro Vaavrudhuh Soubhagaya

(No one is superior or inferior; all are brothers;
All should strive for the
interest of all and progress collectively.)
– Rig Veda, Mandala 5, Sukta 60, Mantra 5

Even in Islam, the tradition of human rights became evident in the medieval ages. As per the tenets of the Quran, Islam preaches universal brotherhood, equality, justice and compassion. Islam believes that man has a special status before God. Because man is a creation of God, he should not be harmed. Harm to a human being is harm to God. God, as an act of love, created man, and He wishes to grant him recognition, dignity and authority. Thus, in Islam, human dignity stems from the belief that man is a creation of God – the creation that God loves more than any other.

In the Bible's Book of Genesis, Adam and Eve exist in a state of innocence until the serpent tempts Eve with a fruit from the Tree of the Knowledge of Good and Evil. After eating the fruit, both see their nakedness and, feeling ashamed, they try to cover up. God banishes them from the Garden of Eden for violating his commandment. The Christian concept of dignity has revolved around this capacity for 'moral choice'. It recognizes that human beings are able to distinguish between good and evil; they can choose to be good, even if they often do not do so. In this sense, in the Christian tradition, all human beings are fundamentally equal as they are endowed with an equal capacity for choice.

Christianity believes that the image of God is revealed in Jesus, and through Him to humankind. God is rational and determines His goals for Himself. Man was created in the image of God, and he too is rational and determines his own goals, subject to God as a rational creation. Man has freedom of will. This is his *dignitas*. He is free to choose his goals, and he himself is a goal. His supreme goal is to know God. Thus he is set apart from a slave and from all the creations under him. When a man sins, he loses his human dignity. He becomes an object.[4]

PHILOSOPHICAL MODEL

The modern conception of human dignity was affected by the philosophy of Kant.[5] Immanuel Kant, in fact, presented a secular version of the Christian understanding of dignity.[6] Kant's moral theory is divided into two parts: ethics and rights (jurisprudence). The discussion of human dignity took place within his doctrine of ethics, and does not appear in his jurisprudence.[7]

According to Kant, a person acts ethically when he acts by force of a duty that a rational agent self-legislates onto his own will. This self-legislated duty is not accompanied by any right or coercion, and is not correlative to the rights of others. For Kant, ethics includes duties to oneself (e.g. to develop one's talents) and to others (e.g. to contribute to their happiness). This ability is the human dignity of man. This is what makes a person different from an object. This ability makes a person an end unto himself, and prevents him from being a mere means in the hands of another.

Kant asserts that we can point to nothing as unconditionally good other than a good will – that is, the capacity for proper moral choice. But Kant did not see this in religious terms; moral choice for him consists of the ability to follow abstract rules of reason for their own sake, and not for instrumental reasons having to do with the outcomes such choices imply for human well-being or happiness. The human capacity for moral choice means that human beings are not machines subject to the laws of physics, as Hobbes suggested; they are agents and, for that reason, need to be treated not as ends to other means, but as ends in themselves. Morality is not a utilitarian calculus of outcomes that maximize human happiness, but about the act of choice itself. For Kant, human dignity revolves around human will, that human beings are genuine agents or uncaused causes.

Professor Upendra Baxi in his First Justice H.R. Khanna Memorial Lecture,[8] on the topic 'Protection of Dignity of Individual under the Constitution of India' has very aptly remarked that dignity notions, like the idea of human rights, are supposed to be the gifts of the West to the Rest, though this view is based on the prescribed ignorance of the rich traditions of non-European countries. He then explains the Eurocentric view of human dignity by pointing out that it views dignity in terms of personhood (moral agency) and autonomy (freedom of choice). Dignity here is to be treated as 'empowerment', which makes a triple demand in the name of respect for human dignity, namely:

1. Respect for one's capacity as an agent to make one's own free choices;
2. Respect for the choices so made;
3. Respect for one's need to have a context and conditions in which one can operate as a source of free and informed choice.[9]

Jeremy Waldron[10] opines that dignity is a sort of status-concept: It has to do with the standing (perhaps the formal legal standing or perhaps, more informally, the moral presence) that a person has in a society and in her dealings with others. He has ventured even to define this term 'dignity' in the following manner:

> Dignity is the status of a person predicated on the fact that she is recognized as having the ability to control and regulate her actions in accordance with her own apprehension of norms and reasons that apply to her; it assumes she is capable of giving and entitled to give an account of herself (and of the way in which she is regulating her actions and organizing her life), an account that others are to pay attention to; and it means finally that she has the wherewithal to demand that her agency and her presence among us as human being be taken seriously and accommodated in the lives of others, in others' attitudes and actions towards her, and in social life generally.

Constitutional Value

It is already discussed above that religions recognize all human beings as equal; they are God's creation, and God loves them equally. The entire world is one 'kutumb', family, where everyone has the right to grow and be meaningful to the society. That is where right of choice comes in. In Plato's *Republic*, one of the messages, and a central one, is that Socrates understood that 'desire' and 'reason' are component parts of the human psyche (soul), but a third part viz. thymus acts completely independent of the two.

Thymus is the seat of judgement of an individual's self-worth. This part prompts human beings to crave positive judgements about their worth or dignity. Although these judgements can come from within, human beings want other people in the society to 'recognize' their worth and to treat them with dignity. In that sense, they want that society recognizes their 'identity'.

Francis Fukuyama has used the term 'identity' in a specific sense in his book,[11] which is a discourse on contemporary identity politics and the struggle for recognition. He remarks:

> Identity grows, in the first place, out of a distinction between one's true inner self and an outer world of social rules and norms that does not adequately recognise that inner self's worth or dignity. Individuals throughout human history have found themselves at odds with their societies. But only in modern times has the view taken hold that the authentic inner self is intrinsically valuable, and the outer society systematically wrong and unfair in its valuation of the former. It is not the inner self that has to be made to conform to society's rules, but society itself that needs to change. The inner self is the basis of human dignity, but the nature of that dignity is variable and has changed over time.

By the early 19th century, most of the elements of the modern concept of identity showed their presence: The distinction between the inner and the outer selves; the valuation of the inner being above existing social arrangements; the understanding that the dignity of the inner self rests on its moral freedom; the view that all human beings share this moral freedom; and the demand that the free inner self be recognized.

Hegel pointed to a fundamental truth about modern politics – that the great passions unleashed by events such as the French Revolution were at the root struggles over dignity. The inner self was not just a matter of personal reflection; its freedom was to be embodied in rights and law. The democratic upsurge that would unfold in the two centuries after the French Revolution was driven by people demanding recognition of their political personhood, that they were moral agents capable of sharing in political power.

It is the aforesaid philosophical journey which has paved way for the constitutional recognition of the right to dignity. A liberal democratic regime, governed by rule of law and based on individual rights, enshrines the notion of equal dignity in law by recognizing citizens as moral agents capable of sharing in their own self-government.

The French Revolution led to the creation of two different versions of dignity: dignity of individuals; and dignity of collectivities. Dignity was a right recognized thereafter, and got constitutional recognition after the Second World War.

One of the most important lessons learnt as a result of the Second World War was the realization by the governments that human dignity needed to be cherished and protected. It is for this reason that in the UN Charter, 1945, adopted immediately after the Second World War, the dignity of the individual was mentioned as a core value. The almost contemporaneous Universal Declaration of Human Rights (1948) echoed the same sentiments.

Article 3 of the Geneva Conventions explicitly prohibits 'outrages upon personal dignity'. There are provisions to this effect in the International Covenant on Civil and Political Rights (ICCPR), (Article 7), and the European Convention of Human Rights (Article 3), though implicit. However, one can easily infer the implicit message in these documents about human dignity.

The ICCPR begins its preamble with the acknowledgment that the rights contained in the covenant 'derive from the inherent dignity of the human person'. Even if this is not a connection between dignity and law as such, it certainly purports to identify a wholesale connection between dignity and the branch of law devoted to human rights.

One of the key facets of 21st century democracies is the primary importance they give to the protection of human rights. From this perspective, dignity is the expression of a basic value accepted in a broad sense by all people, and thus constitutes the first cornerstone in the edifice of human rights. Therefore, there is a certain fundamental value to the notion of human dignity, which some would consider a pivotal right deeply rooted in any notion of justice, fairness, and a society based on basic rights.

The idea that dignity is rooted in human moral choice has received political recognition by becoming embedded in a significant number of modern democratic constitutions, including those of Germany, Italy, Ireland, Japan, Israel and South Africa. For example, Article I, Section 1, of the German Basic Law of 1949 states, 'The dignity of man is inviolable. To respect and protect it shall be the duty of all public authority.' Similarly, Section 10 of the South African Constitution states, 'Everyone has inherent dignity and the right to have their dignity respected and protected.' The South African Constitutional Court notes, 'A right to dignity is an acknowledgement of the intrinsic worth of human beings.'

Within two years of the adoption of the aforesaid Universal Declaration of Human Rights that all human beings are born free and equal in dignity and rights, India attained independence and, immediately thereafter, members of the Constituent Assembly took up the task of framing the Constitution of this country. It was but natural to include a Bill of Rights in the Indian Constitution and the constitution makers did so by incorporating a chapter on Fundamental Rights in Part III of the Constitution.

However, it would be significant to point out that there is no mention of 'dignity' specifically in this chapter on Fundamental Rights. It was the same in the American Constitution as well. In America, human dignity as a part of human rights was brought in as a judge-made doctrine. In India, the same course of action followed as the Indian Supreme Court read human dignity into Articles 14 and 21 of the Constitution.

RECOGNITION OF HUMAN DIGNITY AS AN ATTRIBUTE OF FUNDAMENTAL RIGHTS

Let me illustrate this by showing as how certain fundamental rights are expanded by translating human dignity.

1. The Supreme Court has given certain rights to prisoners with the assertion that they are to be treated with human dignity, and not be deprived of their rights merely because they are in prisons as undertrials or even as convicts. The judgements in *D.K. Basu v. State of West Bengal*[12] and *Sunil Batra v. Delhi Administration* are two examples that reflect this, though there is no specific mention of human dignity.

In *D.K. Basu*, the Court laid down the procedure that is to be followed even at the time of the arrest of a person to ensure that due dignity of the person arrested is maintained. Most notably among others, the Court directed that such a person shall not be handcuffed unless he is hardened criminal and, in that case also, the previous permission of the concerned Judicial Magistrate shall have to be taken.

In *Prem Shankar Shukla v. Delhi Admn.*[13], however, which arose from the handcuffing of the prisoners, Justice Krishna Iyer, speaking for a three-judge bench, specifically invoked the dignity aspect, and held:

> '...the guarantee of **human dignity** [emphasis supplied], which forms part of our constitutional culture, and the positive provisions of Articles 14, 19 and 21 spring into

> action when we realise that to manacle man is more than to mortify him; it is to dehumanise him and, therefore, to violate his very personhood, too often using the mask of 'dangerousness' and security... The Preamble sets the humane tone and temper of the Founding Document and highlights justice, equality and the dignity of the individual.

The aforesaid case law would amply demonstrate that the Court 'recognizes' that even prisoners are human beings and they have to be accorded the dignity they deserve.

In recent years, society, the Legislature, Executive and Judiciary have recognized the rights of those who are the victims of crime, in order to bring proper and just equilibrium between the rights of the accused/convicts and the rights of the victims. This approach, again, is in tune with the dignity of the victims, particularly those who are the victims of sexual offences.

2. Likewise, bonded labour is treated as that class of persons who also have the right to live with dignity. In *Bandhua Mukti Morcha v. Union of India,*[14] while dealing with individuals who were living in bondage, the Supreme Court again emphasized their right to live with human dignity and observed that:

> This right to live with human dignity enshrined in Article 21 derives its life breath from the directive principles of State policy and particularly clauses (e) and (f) of Article 39 and Articles 41 and 42 and at the least, therefore, it must include protection of the health and strength of the workers, men and women, and of the tender age of children against abuse, opportunities and facilities for children to develop in a healthy manner and in conditions of freedom and dignity, educational facilities, just and humane conditions of work and maternity relief. These are the minimum requirements which must exist in order to enable a person to live with human dignity, and no State – neither the Central Government nor any State Government – has

> the right to take any action which will deprive a person of the enjoyment of these basic essentials.

3. Rights given to the Scheduled Caste and Scheduled Tribe communities by Articles 15 and 16 are taken to a higher level by invoking the principle of human dignity.

Human dignity was construed in *M. Nagaraj* v. *Union of India*[15] by a Constitution Bench to be intrinsic too and inseparable from human existence. That was a case where reservation in promotions in cases of government employment was recognized on this principle upholding the Constitution (Seventy-Seventh Amendment) Act, 1995; Constitution (Eighty-First Amendment) Act, 2000; Constitution (Eighty-Second Amendment) Act, 2000; and Constitution (Eighty-Fifth Amendment) Act, 2001, in this behalf.

Constitutional dignity, the Court held, is not something that is conferred and that can be taken away, because it is inalienable. The Supreme Court asserted human dignity in the following manner:

> The rights, liberties and freedoms of the individual are not only to be protected against the State, they should be facilitated by it... **It is the duty of the State not only to protect the human dignity but to facilitate it by taking positive steps in that direction** [emphasis supplied]. No exact definition of human dignity exists. It refers to the intrinsic value of every human being, which is to be respected. It cannot be taken away. It cannot give (sic be given). It simply is. Every human being has dignity by virtue of his existence...

Interestingly, here the Court did not choose to deprive human dignity, and rested its approach by connecting it with the intrinsic value of every human being.

4. A person's autonomy is respected on the touchstone of human dignity. In *Smt. Selvi & Ors. v. State of Karnataka*, while

dealing with the involuntary administration of certain scientific techniques, namely, narcoanalysis, polygraph examination and the Brain Electrical Activation Profile test for the purpose of improving investigation efforts in criminal cases, a three-judge bench opined that the compulsory administration of the impugned techniques constitute 'cruel, inhuman or degrading treatment' in the context of Article 21.

5. Similarly, custodial torture or custodial deaths and fake encounters are deprecated by the courts as violating human dignity. Thus, even those who are accused of any offences and are subjected to investigation cannot be maltreated. The Supreme Court noted that inhuman treatment has many a facet. It fundamentally can cover such acts that have been inflicted with an intention to cause physical suffering or severe mental pain. It would also include a treatment that is inflicted that causes humiliation and compels a person to act against his will or conscience.

In *Arvinder Singh Bagga v. State of U.P. & Ors.*, it has been opined that torture is not merely physical but may even consist of mental and psychological torture calculated to create fright to submit to the demands of the police. It has even led to creating compensatory jurisprudence whereby exercising the powers in a writ jurisdiction, compensation is granted to those who suffered custodial torture or to the kith and kin of those who died in police custody or in fake encounters. (See *Dr Mehmood Nayyar Azam v. State of Chhattisgarh & Ors.*)

CONSTITUTIONAL EXPANSION OF DIGNITY JURISPRUDENCE: SEX AND THE SUPREME COURT

In the cases mentioned above, we find that human dignity as a constitutional value is recognized on the basis of which the contours of life and personal liberty in particular have been expanded vastly. In none of these cases had the Court defined the meaning and scope of 'human dignity' and what it would contain. The Supreme Court felt contented by describing human dignity to be the intrinsic value of every human being and acknowledging a person's autonomy as an attribute of dignity. At the same time, the jurisprudential basis of human dignity was not developed. However, in recent years, this task is being accomplished by various judgements.

If one looks at these recent judgements pronounced by the Supreme Court that touch upon 'dignity', it will not be an exaggeration to comment that the Supreme Court got these opportunities because of the fact that many important and fundamental issues touching upon the aspects of sex and gender were raised before it.[16]

In Plato's *Republic*, Socrates touched upon the third part of soul, that is, the thymos, which impels human beings to not only seek recognition, but also want other people to recognize their worth, for whatever they are. This attribute, coupled with the right of choice as a core concept of dignity, led various categories of human beings to project their dignity on the constitutional basis in the form of equality, non-discrimination and right to freedom. In the process, we have witnessed marginalized groups like the LGBTQ community, persons who are differently abled, and women who are denied their right of equality, coming forward to claim their rights, invoking 'human dignity'.

We can start by referring to the judgement in *National Legal Services Authority v. Union of India & Ors.*[17] where the Court embarked upon developing the concept of human dignity on a jurisprudential basis, as a constitutional value. In that case, while recognizing the right of transgender persons of self-determination of their sex, the Court explained the contours of human dignity in the following words:

> The basic principle of the dignity and freedom of the individual is common to all nations, particularly those having democratic set up. Democracy requires us to

> respect and develop the free spirit of human being which is responsible for all progress in human history. Democracy is also a method by which we attempt to raise the living standard of the people and to give opportunities to every person to develop his/her personality. It is founded on peaceful co-existence and cooperative living. If democracy is based on the recognition of the individuality and dignity of man, as a fortiori we have to recognize the right of a human being to choose his sex/gender identity which is integral to his/her personality and is one of the most basic aspect of self-determination, dignity and freedom. In fact, there is a growing recognition that the true measure of development of a nation is not economic growth; it is human dignity.

Thus, the right of choice and the right of self-determination were accepted as facets of human dignity. It was also emphasized that in certain cases like the case at hand (that of transgender persons), recognition of this aspect of human dignity would yield happiness to the individuals and, at the same time, also be in the public good.

The concept of dignity was developed and expanded further in *K.S. Puttaswamy & Anr. v. Union of India & Ors.*18, which is a recent path-breaking judgement recognizing right to dignity as a facet of Article 21 of the Constitution. The Court held that privacy postulates the reservation of a private space for an individual described as the right to be left alone as a concept founded on autonomy of the individual. In this way, the right to privacy has been treated as a postulate of human dignity itself. While defining so, the Court also remarked as under:

> Privacy of the individual is an essential aspect of dignity... The ability of the individual to protect a zone of privacy enables the realization of the full value of life and liberty. Liberty has a broader meaning of which privacy is a subset. All liberties may not be exercised in privacy. Yet others can be fulfilled only within a private space. Privacy enables the

> individual to retain the autonomy of the body and mind. The autonomy of the individual is the ability to make decisions on vital matters of concern to life. Privacy has not been couched as an independent fundamental right.

In *Navtej Singh Johar & Others v. Union of India*,[19] the Constitution Bench of the Supreme Court struck down a part of Section 377 of the Indian Penal Code as unconstitutional as it offended right to privacy. As noted in *K.S. Puttaswamy*, privacy has been treated as a fundamental right and a premise for this upliftment was that the privacy of the individual is an essential aspect of dignity. The Court held that Section 377 of the IPC insofar as it criminalizes consensual sexual acts between adults of whatever sexual orientation is an anathema to a constitutional order in which liberty must trump over stereotypes and prevail over the mainstreaming of culture. The following passage from the said judgement brings home the notion of dignity.[20]

> **155.** From the aforesaid, it has to be appreciated that homosexuality is something that is based on sense of identity. It is the reflection of a sense of emotion and expression of eagerness to establish intimacy. It is just as much ingrained, inherent and innate as heterosexuality. Sexual orientation, as a concept, fundamentally implies a pattern of sexual attraction. It is as natural a phenomenon as other natural biological phenomena. What the science of sexuality has led to is that an individual has the tendency to feel sexually attracted towards the same-sex, for the decision is one that is controlled by neurological and biological factors. That is why it is his/her natural orientation which is innate and constitutes the core of his/her being and identity. That apart, on occasions, due to a sense of mutuality of release of passion, two adults may agree to express themselves in a different sexual behaviour which may include both the genders. To this, one can attribute a bisexual orientation which does not follow the rigidity but allows room for flexibility.

Below are other passages from the said judgement that bring dignity into sharp focus:

> **561.1.** Sexual orientation is an intrinsic element of liberty, dignity, privacy, individual autonomy and equality;
>
> **561.2.** Intimacy between consenting adults of the same-sex is beyond the legitimate interests of the State;
>
> **561.3.** Sodomy laws violate equality by targeting a segment of the population for their sexual orientation;
>
> **561.4.** Such a law perpetrates stereotypes, lends authority of the State to societal stereotypes and has a chilling effect on the exercise of freedom;
>
> **561.5.** The right to love and to a partner, to find fulfilment in a same-sex relationship is essential to a society which believes in freedom under a constitutional order based on rights...
>
> **610.** Sexual orientation is integral to the identity of the members of the LGBT communities. It is intrinsic to their dignity, inseparable from their autonomy and at the heart of their privacy. Section 377 is founded on moral notions which are an anathema to a constitutional order in which liberty must trump over stereotypes and prevail over the mainstreaming of culture. Our Constitution, above all, is an essay in the acceptance of diversity. It is founded on a vision of an inclusive society which accommodates plural ways of life.

Another path-breaking judgement that decriminalized adultery is *Joseph Shine v. Union of India*,[21] where the Court touched upon the aspect of dignity in the following manner:

> The hypothesis which forms the basis of the law on adultery is the subsistence of a patriarchal order. Section 497 is based on a notion of morality which fails to accord with the values on which the Constitution is founded... Section 497 is based on the understanding that marriage submerges

> the identity of the woman. It is based on a notion of marital subordination. In recognizing, accepting and enforcing these notions, Section 497 is inconsistent with the ethos of the Constitution. Section 497 treats a woman as but a possession of her spouse. The essential values on which the Constitution is founded – liberty, dignity and equality – cannot allow such a view of marriage. Section 497 suffers from manifest arbitrariness.

In *Shayara Bano v. Union of India and Others,*[22] the Constitution Bench of the Supreme Court, by majority, struck down the practice of triple talaq – a Muslim husband's right to give divorce to his wife by pronouncing the word 'talaq' thrice was deemed unconstitutional. Though the concept of dignity has not been discussed specifically, I am of the view that this case, which is decided on the touchstone of Article 14 of the Constitution that ensures fairness and equality of treatment, recognizes the dignity of women, who have equal rights.

We may also refer to another recent judgement of the Supreme Court in *Indian Young Lawyers Association and Others v. State of Kerala and Others,*[23] popularly known as the Sabarimala case,[24] where the practice of not allowing menstruating women to enter the temple was held to be unconstitutional, by a majority of 4:1. The aspects of dignity are discussed by the Court in the said judgement as under:

> **201.** The Preamble to the Constitution portrays the foundational principles: justice, liberty, equality and fraternity… While recognizing and protecting individual *liberty*, the Preamble underscores the importance of *equality*, both in terms of status and opportunity. Above all, it seeks to promote among all citizens *fraternity* which would assure the *dignity* of the individual.
>
> **202.** The significance of the Preamble lies both in its setting forth the founding principles of the Constitution as well as in the broad sweep of their content. The Constitution was

> brought into existence to oversee a radical transformation... But the task which the Framers assumed was infinitely more sensitive. They took upon themselves above all, the task to transform Indian society by remedying centuries of discrimination against Dalits, women and the marginalised. They sought to provide them a voice by creating a culture of rights and a political environment to assert freedom. Above all, placing those who were denuded of their human rights before the advent of the Constitution – whether in the veneer of caste, patriarchy or otherwise – were to be placed in control of their own destinies by the assurance of the equal protection of law. Fundamental to their vision was the ability of the Constitution to pursue a social transformation. Intrinsic to the social transformation is the role of each individual citizen in securing justice, liberty, equality and fraternity in all its dimensions.

This evolving concept of dignity has encompassed *liberal individualism* as well as *collective identities* into 'we the people', thereby bringing the aspects of inclusiveness into our Constitution. Many other facets of dignity jurisprudence, pending before the courts in different forms, are going to enrich the concept of Dignity in times to come.

SUMMING UP DIGNITY JURISPRUDENCE

From the aforesaid discussion, it follows that dignity as a jurisprudential concept has now been well defined by the Supreme Court. Its essential ingredients can be summarized as follows:

1. The basic principle of the dignity and freedom of the individual is an attribute of natural law, which is manifested as basic or fundamental rights of all individuals in a constitutional democracy.
2. Dignity has a central normative role as well as constitutional value. This normative role is performed in three ways:

first, it becomes basis for constitutional rights; second, it serves as an interpretative principle for determining the scope of constitutional rights; and, third, it determines the proportionality of a statute limiting a constitutional right. Thus, if an enactment puts a limitation on a constitutional right and such a limitation is disproportionate, such a statute can be held to be unconstitutional by applying the doctrine of proportionality.

Professor Upendra Baxi explains that dignity is to be treated as 'empowerment', which makes a triple demand in the name of respect for human dignity, namely:

1. respect for one's capacity as an agent to make one's own free choices;
2. respect for the choices so made; and
3. respect for one's need to have a context and conditions in which one can operate as a source of free and informed choice.

His addition to the aforesaid theory commands acceptance when he says that idea of dignity is a metaethical one, that is, it marks and maps a difficult terrain of what it may mean to say being 'human' and remaining 'human', or put another way, the relationship between 'self', 'others' and 'society'. In this entire formulation, 'respect' for an individual is the fulcrum, which is based on the principle of freedom and the capacity to make choices. And a good or just social order is one which respects dignity via assuring 'contexts' and 'conditions' as the 'source of free and informed choice'.

Based on the above conceptualization, the Supreme Court held that though the chapter relating to Fundamental Rights in the Indian Constitution does not specifically mention human dignity, it is the essential attribute of Articles 14, 19 and, more particularly, Article 21. Article 21, which guarantees right to life and liberty, means the right to live life in a decent and dignified manner. The right of choice and the right of self-determination are the facets of human dignity.

We have come a long way insofar as the jurisprudence relating to the concept of dignity is concerned, and are now witnessing a democratization of dignity. The modern concept of technology unifies three different phenomena: thymos – a universal aspect of human personality that craves for recognition; the distinction between the inner and outer self and the raising of the moral valuation of the inner self over outer society; and the recognition that the concept of dignity is due not just to a narrow class of people but to *everyone*.

Along with the doctrine of constitutional morality, the concept of human dignity has been used by the Supreme Court in a series of progressive judgements. This jurisprudence of dignity has been one of the most useful tools used by the Supreme Court in ensuring justice and equality to women and sexual minorities. To hone the tool even more, the concept of dignity needs further elaboration and examination. This essay has hopefully set us on that path.

Notes and References

INTRODUCTION

1. Several enactments apply in the simple act of purchasing groceries. The Sale of Goods Act, 1930; the Contract Act, 1872; the Consumer Protection Act, 2019; the acts, rules and regulations relating to weights and measures, packaging, etc.
2. *Vishaka v. State of Rajasthan* (1997) 6 SCC 241.
3. *Navtej Singh Johar v. Union of India* (2018) 10 SCC 1.
4. *National Legal Services Authority v. Union of India* (2014) 5 SCC 438.
5. *Shafin Jahan v. Asokan KM* (2018) 16 SCC 368.
6. *Indian Young Lawyers Association v. State of Kerala WP* (Civil) 373 of 2006. It is important to note that the decision in this case came 12 years after the petition was filed in the Court. This also highlights the problems of judicial delays. No one suffers more from delays than a disempowered individual seeking recourse to justice.
7. The law before the enactment of the Hindu Marriage Act, 1955, permitted Hindu men to marry multiple women. The Hindu Marriage Act changed this, and prohibited polygamy among Hindus. This Act was part of a concerted effort to reform Hindu society through a series of legislations called the Hindu Code Bills. These were the Hindu Marriage Act, 1955, The Hindu Succession Act, 1956, the Hindu Minority and Guardianship Act, 1956, and The Hindu Adoption and Maintenance Act, 1956. At the time of their enactment, they were met with vociferous opposition from conservative elements in Hindu society. In fact, the President at that time, Dr Rajendra Prasad, went to the extent of suggesting that he, as President, was not obliged to sign the bills into law. For

more details, see Granville Austin's *The Indian Constitution: Cornerstone of a Nation*, pp. 176–178.

8. The provisions of the Indian Penal Code relating to adultery effectively deemed women to be the property of their husbands.
9. This refrain finds an echo in the judgement of Misra C.J. in the Sabarimala case where the opening words of his judgement are: 'The irony that is nurtured by the society is to impose a rule, however unjustified, and proffer explanation or justification to substantiate the substratum of the said rule. Mankind, since time immemorial, has been searching for explanation or justification to substantiate a point of view that hurts humanity.' Laws which give women limited inheritance rights are often invoked to show that a woman is not really a part of her father's family. The converse of this is that when special rights are given to women, they are often illusory. For instance, women may be given additional maternity leave. However, that is shown to be a disincentive to hiring women in the belief that they would not be available for the job as required.
10. The British were actually against enumerating rights in a written text other than being part of the judge-administered common law. For this reason, no rights were mentioned in the Government of India Act, 1935, which was the precursor to the Constitution. See Reports of the Joint Parliamentary Committee 1934, H.C.5 (1 Part I), pp. 215–216 and the commentary thereon in the *Indian Constitution* by Granville Austin, pp. 73–75.
11. For instance, various interventions by the Court to protect the forest cover in India are an instance of the enforcement of a positive right. The right to life has been interpreted to include the right to a clean environment. See various orders passed *TN Godavarman Thirumulpad v. Union of India* WP (Civil) 202 of 1995.
12. The Directive Principles of State Policy have been derived

from the Irish Constitution. Even though they are not enforceable in the Court, they are deemed to be fundamental in the governance of the country as well as a guide to the Legislature while enacting laws (Article 37). In fact, Article 31(c) of the Constitution even attempts to immunize certain laws that give effect to certain directive principles from constitutional scrutiny.

13. These three rights have been called the golden triangle of rights. See *Minerva Mills v. Union of India* (1980) 3 SCC 625. These rights have now been interpreted to be part of the basic structure of the Constitution. See *IR Coelho v. State of Tamil Nadu* (2007) 2 SCC 1.
14. Article 15 has also been interpreted to include sexuality as a facet of sex. Hence, any action that discriminates on the ground of sexuality will now be hit by Article 15 as well. See the NALSA and the Navtej Johar cases.
15. These same rights also have clauses that permit special rights and reservations to be made in favour of women, Scheduled Castes and Tribes and Other Backward Classes. While these special provisions were initially seen as exceptions to the general right to equality, later case law has interpreted these to be manifestations of a positive right to equality rather than as exception to the general right to equality. See *Indira Sawhney v. Union of India* (1992) Supp (3) SCC 217.
16. This was a particularly pernicious form of divorce where a husband could simply utter the words 'talaq, talaq, talaq' ('I divorce you, I divorce you, I divorce you') thrice for an irrevocable divorce to happen. There were many stories about its misuse (as noted in the chapter by Madhavi Divan in her essay in this anthology) and the practice was ultimately struck down as void by the Supreme Court in 2018.
17. *Shayara Bano v. Union of India* (2017) 9 SCC 1.
18. See *Navtej Singh Johar v. Union of India* (2018) 10 SCC 1. Sodomy is also possible between a straight couple, of course. Further, since the section was thought to prohibit oral sex as

well, its application was for heterosexual as well as homosexual couples.

19. Article 19 (1)(a).
20. Article 19 (1)(c).
21. Articles 19 (1)(d) and (e).
22. Article 19 (1)(g).
23. The right to freedom under Article 19 is different from the rights under Articles 14 and 21 inasmuch as these rights inhere only in citizens. Hence, a foreign national cannot claim the right to freedom. Equally, this right is restricted to humans and does not extend to juristic entities like companies. See *Barium Chemicals Ltd. v. Company Law Board* 1966 Supp SCR 311.
24. These restrictions are 'the sovereignty and integrity of India, the security of the State, friendly relations with foreign States, public order, decency or morality or in relation to contempt of court or incitement to an offence'.
25. In the case of Article 21, when the Constitution permits curtailment of liberty by 'procedure established by law', the Court has held that the procedure cannot be arbitrary or whimsical. In fact, since Article 14 mandates that all government action must be reasonable and rational, the procedure prescribed for curtailment of liberty must also be rational. This is called substantive due process. In fact, the Constituent Assembly debates reveal that these words were carefully chosen so that the power of the Court was restricted to examining whether it was a valid law that provided for any curtailment. This was also the original view taken by the Supreme Court in *A.K. Gopalan v. State of Madras* 1950 SCR 88 before this view was whittled down in a series of cases culminating in *Maneka Gandhi v. Union of India* (1978) 2 SCR 621. For an interesting exposition of the debates and the development of the law on this subject, see the judgement of Justice Nariman in *Mohd. Arif v. Registrar, Supreme Court* (2014) 9 SCC 737.
26. See *Palko v. Connecticut* 302 US 319 (1937) for a formulation

of this principle, even though the Court did not find any such right in that case.

27. *Bolling v. Sharpe* 347 US 497 (1954). This was the companion case of the more famous *Brown v. Board of Education* 347 US 483 (1954).
28. *State of West Bengal v. Committee for the Protection of Democratic Rights* (2010) 3 SCC 571.
29. See for instance *Bandhua Mukti Morcha v. Union of India* (1984) 3 SCC 161.
30. See *Virender Gaur v. State of Haryana* (1995) 2 SCC 577.
31. *Gobind v. State of Madhya Pradesh* (1975) 2 SCC 148, affirmed by the nine-judge bench in the case of *K.S. Puttaswamy v. Union of India* (2019) 1 SCC 1.
32. Article 32 of the Constitution gives each person a right to directly approach the Supreme Court to enforce and protect their fundamental rights. This right to approach the Court is itself a fundamental right that cannot be taken away even by amending the Constitution. This is because the Supreme Court has held that judicial review is part of the unamendable basic structure of the Constitution. See *Kesavananda Bharti v. State of Kerala* (1973) 4 SCC 225 followed in *L. Chandra Kumar v. Union of India* (1997) 3 SCC 261.
33. Each right in Article 19 has a set of conditions specific to it, which must be complied with by the restriction. These are enumerated in clauses (2) to (6) of Article 19. Interestingly, when the Constitution was first promulgated, the right to free speech did not require that any restriction to it be reasonable or otherwise. The reasonableness requirement was added by the First Amendment to the Constitution in 1951.
34. It is interesting to note that the former aspect was used most often by the Court in its early years when the right to property and the right to freedom of business were used to examine various aspects of agrarian reform and zamindari reform. It was only after the system of Public Interest Litigations was firmly entrenched that we see the use of the latter aspect, i.e., the

assertion of a personal right to question a social practice. This could be due to the evolution of the Court's jurisprudence and also the changing nature and needs of society. Fundamentally, it reflects the Court's view on its own function. Almost all the topics in the present book relate to the latter conception of the judicial function.

35. Article 13 of the Constitution.
36. Articles 32 and 226. Also, the power of the Supreme Court and the High Courts to hear matters and appeals under other provisions of the Constitution also vests them with substantial powers.
37. De, Rohit, *A People's Constitution: The Everyday Life of Law in the Indian Republic*, Princeton: Princeton University Press, 2018, p. 17.
38. Gandhi submitted two plans, one in January 1946 and the other in January 1948. See N.V. Rajkumar, *Development of the Congress Constitution*.
39. *Joseph Shine v. Union of India* (2019) 2 SCC (Cri) 84.
40. Tribe, Lawrence, and Michael Dorf, *On Reading the Constitution*, Cambridge: Harvard University Press, 1993.

PRIDE VERSUS PREJUDICE: THE STRUGGLE AGAINST SECTION 377

1. Section 377 of the Indian Penal Code states that 'Whoever voluntarily has carnal intercourse against the order of nature with any man, woman or animal shall be punished with imprisonment for life, or with imprisonment of either description for a term which may extend to ten years, and shall also be liable to fine.'
2. (2018) 10 SCC 1.
3. Puri, J., 'Concerning Kamasutra: Challenging Narratives of History and Sexuality', *Signs*, 27(3), 2002, p. 619.
4. *The Asiatic Journal and Monthly Register for British and Foreign India, China and Australasia*, 1838, p. 77.

5. The extract of this is given in: Gupta, A., 'Section 377 and the Dignity of Indian Homosexuals', *Economic and Political Weekly* 41(46), 2011, p. 4815.
6. *Noshirwan v. Emperor* AIR 1934 Sind 206 (a case relating to a neighbour intruding on the privacy of two men by peeping into the house and reporting them for attempting to commit sodomy), *D.P. Minwalla v. Emperor* AIR 1935 Sind 78 (a case relating to two men who were caught in oral activity at the back of a truck in a semi-public space).
7. *Government v. Bhapoji Bhatt* (1884) 7 Mysore LR. 280.
8. AIR 1925 Sind 286.
9. Preamble to the Criminal Tribes Act, 1871.
10. Section 24, Criminal Tribes Act, 1871.
11. Section 26 Criminal Tribes Act, 1871.
12. Sexual Offences Act, 1967 which decriminalized consensual sexual acts between members of the same-sex. This was followed in 2017 by the Policing and Crimes Act which gave ex post facto amnesty and pardon to persons who had been convicted of homosexual acts. Justice Nariman in his judgement in the Navtej case notes that 'the impetus for this law was the prosecution of Alan Turing in 1952. Alan Turing was instrumental in cracking intercepted code messages that enabled the Allies to defeat Germany in many crucial engagements in the War. Turing accepted chemical castration treatment as an alternative to prison upon conviction, but committed suicide just before his 42nd birthday in 1954.'
13. Quoted in: Joseph, Sherry, 'Gay and Lesbian Movement in India,' *Economic and Political Weekly*, 31(33), 1996, p. 2228.
14. Ironically, it was Bill Clinton who promulgated the 'don't ask, don't tell' policy in the military, and failed to veto the Defence of Marriage Act, 1996 which effectively prohibited states in the US from recognizing same-sex marriages held in other jurisdictions. The Act was finally struck down by the US Supreme Court in the case of *United States v. Windsor* 570 US 744.

15. Mentioned by Geetanjali Misra in her paper: 'Decriminalizing Homosexuality in India,' *Reproductive Health Matters* 17(34), 2009, p. 22.
16. In the context of the Emergency, refer to the speech of Ashok Desai on the occasion of the 150th anniversary of the Bombay High Court, reported in *The Wire* on 25 June 2019.
17. Interview of Anjali Gopalan published in *The Caravan* on 7 February 2016.
18. *Naz Foundation v. Govt. of NCT of Delhi* (2017) 15 SCC 619.
19. *Naz Foundation v. Govt. of NCT of Delhi* (2009) 111 DRJ 1.
20. See also *Frontline*, 18(18), published 1 September 2001.
21. *The National Coalition for Gay and Lesbian Equality v. Minister* (1999) 1 SA 6.
22. 'Impact of the Naz Foundation Judgement on the Gay, Bisexual and Transgender People in Delhi: An Empirical Investigation,' Centre for Health Law, Ethics and Technoloby, Jindal Global Law School, March 2012.
23. The Court at one point held that 'we are constrained to observe that the submission of the Learned ASG reflects rather poorly on his understanding of the Constitutional scheme', at paragraph 125 of the judgement. This chastisement did not lead the learned ASG to mend his ways. Before the Supreme Court he made the false averment that the Law Commission had recommended the retention of the provision, when in fact the 172nd Law Commission had recommended its abolition.
24. Though the Court does not allow for formal transcripts, the same were informally recorded and uploaded on the Net by the Lawyers Collective, a legal NGO which was also involved in the case. The transcripts can be founds online at: https://www.lawyerscollective.org/wp-content/uploads/2010/11/Proceedings-of-the-Final-Hearing-in-Section-377-Case.pdf
25. In the case of *Anil Rai v. State of Bihar* (2001) 7 SCC 318 the Supreme Court has held that in case a judgement is not pronounced within six months of it being reserved, the parties

will be at liberty to move the Chief Justice for rehearing by a different bench.

26. This deference to Parliament seems most curious. The same judge had no hesitation in striking down provisions of the Delhi Rent Control Act, which gave protection to commercial tenants, on the ground that it was violative of fundamental rights. It is apparent that property rights deserved more protection than personal liberty! See *Satyawati Sharma v. Union of India* (2008) 5 SCC 287.
27. Justice H.L. Dattu eventually became the Chairperson of the National Human Rights Commission.
28. *Rupa Ashok Hurra v. Ashok Hurra* (2002) 4 SCC 388.
29. *National Legal Services Authority v. Union of India* (2014) 5 SCC 438.
30. *K.S. Puttaswamy v. Union of India* (2017) 10 SCC 1. Justice Chandrachud, speaking for four of the nine judges, specifically held that the judgement in the Koushal case was wrong. Justice Kaul also held that the judgement in the Koushal case was wrong. Thus, a majority of five of the nine judges specifically held the Koushal judgement to be wrong.
31. *Naz Foundation v. Suresh Kumar Koushal* (2016) 7 SCC 485.
32. We cannot forget the contribution of Dr Menaka Guruswamy and Arundhati Katju. They had approached me in 2015 with the idea of filing a Writ Petition and it was largely they who convinced these five individuals to file the petition.
33. *Navtej Singh Johar v. Union of India* (2018) 1 SCC 791.
34. *Shakti Vahini v. Union of India* (2018) 7 SCC 192.
35. *Shafin Jahan v. Asokan K.M.* (2018) 16 SCC 368.
36. Paragraph 144 of the Navtej judgement.
37. Oscar Wilde denied that the term was a euphemism for homosexuality but as per him it referred to platonic love between two men. So willing was the jury to accept this interpretation that the trial resulted in a hung jury. He was, nevertheless, convicted when the case was tried finally and sentenced to two years in prison.

38. The last stanza of the song says, 'I love the country but can't stand the scene, and I'm neither left nor right... I'm junk but I'm still holding up this little wild bouquet.'

TRANSGENDER RIGHTS AND WRONGS

1. This case was brought to the Supreme Court by the National Legal Services Authority and has been dealt with later in this essay.
2. WP (C) No. 133/2012 filed in the Supreme Court of India.
3. Kidwai, Rasheed, 'Kamla Jaan to Kankar Munjare: Oddballs Whose Political Legacy Matters in Madhya Pradesh,' *DailyO*, 8 November 2018. https://www.dailyo.in/politics/kamla-jaan-to-kankar-munjare-eunuch-politicians-you-need-to-know-to-understand-what-s-at-stake-in-madhya-pradesh-assembly-elections-bjp-congress/story/1/27674.html
4. India TV, 'Shabnam Mausi-India's First Eunuch to Become an MLA,' 21 October 2014. https://www.indiatvnews.com/politics/national/shabnam-mausi-india-first-eunuch-hijra-politician-mla-inequality-18963.html/page/1
5. https://eci.gov.in/ByeElection/ByeFeb2000/bye_MP_AC85.htm
6. Chatterjee, Rituparna, 'History Is Made as Newly Elected Third Gender Mayor Won't Face Legal Hurdle,' *HuffPost*, 5 January 2015. https://www.huffingtonpost.in/2015/01/05/madhu-kinnar_n_6415540.html
7. Gupta, Suchandana, 'Eunuch's Election as Mayor Annulled,' *The Times of India*, 11 December 2019. https://timesofindia.indiatimes.com/city/bhopal/Eunuchamp39s-election-as-mayor-annulled/articleshow/ 11067274.cms
8. *Verve*, 'The (Em)Power List 2018: Madhu Bai Kinnar,' 3 July 2018. http://www.vervemagazine.in/people/the-empower-list-2018-madhu-bai-kinnar
9. Incidentally, anti-discrimination laws have been enacted in some countries in South Asia, such as the Philippines, Taiwan

and Thailand to protect the LGBT community. In Thailand, four transgenders have been elected as Members in the current Parliament. Two of them are transmen and the other two are transwomen. *The Nation Weekend* (Saturday–Sunday), 1–2 June 2019, Manila, The Philippines.

10. WP (C) No. 400 of 2012.
11. (1984) 3 SCC 161.
12. *National Legal Services Authority v. Union of India* (2014) 5 SCC 438.
13. Section 24 (a) of the Criminal Tribes Act, 1871.
14. Section 26 of the Criminal Tribes Act, 1871.
15. (1970) 2 All ER 33.
16. (1995) 1 NZLR 603.
17. [2003] Fam CA 94.
18. The NALSA judgement, paragraph 53.
19. The NALSA judgement, paragraph 81.
20. The NALSA judgement, paragraph 82.
21. The Yogyakarta Principles were adopted in an international conference held in Yogyakarta, Indonesia, in 2006. These principles are like a charter of rights for the sexual minorities.
22. 'On 6 April 2017, Today the European Court of Human Rights ruled that requiring sterilization of individuals seeking a change in their legal gender recognition violates human rights. Twenty two countries in Europe currently still require sterilization to access gender identity recognition, however this decision mandates that these countries amend their laws to reflect this positive ruling.'

    See OutRight Action International, 'European Court Ends Forced Sterilizations of Trans People,' 6 April 2017. https://outrightinternational.org/content/european-court-ends-forced-sterilizations-trans-people (accessed on 19 June 2019).
23. https://www.wpath.org/media/cms/Documents/Public%20Policies/2019/WPATH%20Letter%20to%20Japanese%20Gov%20Officials%20re%20Identity%20Recognition_May%20%2028%202019.pdf

24. https://www.wpath.org/media/cms/Documents/Public%20 Policies/2019/WPATH%20Letter%20to%20Japanese%20 Gov%20Officials%20re%20Identity%20Recognition_ May%20%2028%202019.pdf (accessed on 19 June 2019).
25. https://kerala.gov.in/documents/10180/46696/State%20 Policy%20for%20Transgenders%20in%20Kerala%202015 (accessed on 21 June 2019).
26. *The Economic Times*, 'In a First, Kochi Metro Appoints Transgenders as Its Staff,' 20 May 2017. https://economictimes.indiatimes.com/ news/politics-and-nation/in-a-first-kochi-metro-appoints-transgenders-as-its-staff/making-progress/slideshow/58764414. cms (accessed on 21 June 2019).
27. *Hindustan Times*, New Delhi, 3 June 2019.
28. *Hindustan Times*, New Delhi, 22 June 2019.
29. PTI, 'Delhi's Transgender Voters Excited at Voting for the First Time under Gender Identity of Their Choice,' *The Hindu*, 12 May 2019. https://www.thehindu.com/elections/ lok-sabha-2019/delhis-transgender-voters-excited-at-voting-for-the-first-time-under-gender-identity-of-their-choice/ article27108423.ece (accessed on 20 June 2019).
30. Tare, Kiran, 'Lok Sabha Polls: Transgender Candidates Coming to Fore in Maharashtra Politics,' *India Today*, 22 March 2019. https://www.indiatoday.in/magazine/nation/ story/ 20190401- transgender-candidates-lok-sabha-2019-maharashtra- 1484014-2019-03-22 (accessed on 21 June 2019).
31. Sharma, Betwa, 'Why Apsara Reddy, Congress's First Transgender Office Bearer, Chose Politics Over London,' *HuffPost*, 6 February 2019. https://www.huffingtonpost.in/entry/ apsara-reddy-congress-partys-first-transgender-office-bearer-on-life-love-and-politics_in_5c59b675e4b087104757e287 (accessed on 21 June 2019).
32. *Quint*, 'The Incredible Story of a Trans Woman Who Became a Single Mother,' 12 May 2019. https://www.thequint.com/ voices/women/transgender-single-mother-gauri-sawant (accessed on 20 June 2019).

33. *Business Standard*/IANS, 'As Transgender, Bringing Up Daughter Was Difficult: Activist Gauri Sawant,' 13 October 2018. https://www.business-standard.com/article/news-ians/as-transgender-bringing-up-daughter-was-difficult-activist-gauri-sawant-118101300226_1.html (accessed on 20 June 2019).
34. Dabas, Maninder, 'Meet Aishwarya Pradhan – India's First Transgender Civil Servant,' IndiaTimes, 1 July 2016. https://www.indiatimes.com/news/india/meet-aishwarya-pradhan-india-s-first-transgender-civil-servant-255688.html (accessed on 21 June 2019).
35. Qureshi, Imran, 'Padmini Prakash: India's First Transgender News Anchor,' BBC News, 29 September 2014. https://www.bbc.com/news/world-asia-india-29357630 (accessed on 21 June 2019).
36. Gentleman, Amelia, 'First Transsexual Celebrity, Rose, Makes a TV Debut,' *The New York Times*, 15 February 2008. https://www.nytimes.com/2008/02/15/world/asia/15iht-letter.1.10085268.html (accessed on 21 June 2019).
37. Shrikumar, A., 'Transgender Bharatnatyam Artiste Narthaki Nataraj Is Named for the Padma Shri,' *The Hindu*, 15 February 2019. https://www.thehindu.com/entertainment/dance/transgender-bharatnatyam-artiste-narthaki-nataraj-named-for-the-padma-shri-talks-about-her-love-for-classical-dance/article26280796.ece (accessed on 21 June 2019).
38. Quoted from http://164.100.47.193/lsscommittee/Social%20Justice%20&%20Empowerment/16_Social_Justice_And_Empowerment_43.pdf
39. *Hindustan Times*, 'Supreme Court Notice to Centre on Plea against Transgender Act,' 28 January 2020. https://www.hindustantimes.com/india-news/supreme-court-notice-to-centre-on-plea-against-transgender-act/story-HfBrPZBTFmusm9theecWoL.html
40. https://www.prsindia.org/billtrack/transgender-persons-protection-rights-bill-2016. Accessed on 25 June 2019. This does not include any analysis of the Bill of 2019.

41. WP (MD) No. 4125 of 2019 and WMP (MD) No. 3220 of 2019 decided on 22 April 2019.

FROM THE MARGINS TO THE MAINSTREAM

1. Milford, Michelle Renee, 'Hidden Battle.' https://hellopoetry.com/poem/1066986/hidden-battle/
2. Butler, Judith, 'Performative Acts and Gender Constitution,' *Theatre Journal*, 40(4), December 1988, pp. 519–531.
3. Mal, S., 'The Hijras of India: A Marginal Community with Paradox Sexual Identity,' *Indian Journal of Social Psychiatry*, 2018.
4. Policy Brief: 'Hijras/Transgender Women in India,' UNDP, 2010.
5. Deadname: This is the birth name of someone who has changed it. The term is especially used by transgender persons who go by their chosen name instead of their given name.
6. Collyrium: An ancient medicated ointment, meant to clear diseases of the eye.
7. Carl Jung.

LOVE AND MARRIAGE

1. Article 16 (6) which provides for reservation to the economically weaker sections was inserted vide amendment dated 12 January 2019. The word 'family' is included for the first time but not as a repository of any right. It merely provides that the benefits of reservation can be denied on the basis of, inter alia, family income.
2. (1973) 4 SCC 225.
3. *K.S. Puttaswamy v. Union of India* (2017) 10 SCC 1 ('the privacy judgement').
4. See para 107 of the privacy judgement.
5. *Asokan K.M. v. Superintendent of Police* WP Crl 25 of 2016 decided on 25 January 2016. It is interesting to note how the

composition of the Bench might significantly alter the outcome of a case. This order, permitting Hadiya to live as she wished, was passed by a Division Bench of C.K. Abdul Rehim and Shaji P. Chaly J.J. The ultimate judgement, which set aside her marriage to her husband, was passed by another Division Bench comprising of K. Surendra Mohan and K. Abraham Mathew J.J.

6. This fact is recorded in the High Court order. It is relevant to note that even this desire, though possibly comprehensible on the part of a parent, seems to be inexplicable on the part of the Court when dealing with a major with full mental capacity. It is no part of the role of the Court to come in as a knight in shining armour, rescuing people from fundamental decisions about their own lives! That freedom to make even a wrong decision is the very thing that separates the right to autonomy from the 'big brother' state. If the Court substitutes its own decision for that of an individual, the problem is graver for then the individual does not even have a judicial forum to approach to seek redressal of her grievances.
7. The Court directed that even her cell phone was to be taken away! See *Asokan K.M. v. Superintendent of Police* WP Crl 25 of 2016 order dated 21 February 2016.
8. See *Asokan K.M. v. Superintendent of Police* WP Crl 25 of 2016 order dated 30 January 2017. The High Court directed the parties to explain how the name was put on the matrimonial site. However, there is no record of what transpired further and hence it cannot be ascertained as to who actually put the name on the site.
9. This was further elaborated in the Section 377 case where, relying on Hadiya's judgement, the Court held that the right to choose a sexual partner was constitutionally protected even if it meant choosing a partner of the same sex. See *Navtej Singh Johar v. Union of India* (2018) 10 SCC 1.
10. '5 Percent of Indian Marriages Inter-caste; in Mizoram, 55 Percent (Special to IANS),' *Business Standard*, 11 May 2016.
11. p. 485.

12. p. 483.
13. *Madhavrao v. Raghavendrarao* ILR 1946 Bom 375.
14. Section 2 of the Act said that 'notwithstanding any text, rule or interpretation of the Hindu law, custom or usage, a marriage between Hindus, which is otherwise valid, shall not be invalid by reason only of the fact that the parties thereto belong to the same gotra.'
15. Third in the line of the mother and fifth in the line of the father.
16. This fact has been recorded by the Law Commission in its 242nd report – see, particularly, paragraphs 2.1–2.5.
17. As per one newspaper report this was because Sonia's family had promised her that they would accept her wedding if she came back to her parents' home. See '12 Get Life in Jail for 2009 Haryana Honour Killing,' *Indian Express*, Chandigarh Edition, 30 September 2011.
18. These facts have been taken from an article by Neha Dixit: 'A Taliban of Our Very Own,' *Tehelka*, 15 August 2009.
19. 242nd Report, Law Commission of India.
20. *Shakti Vahini v. Union of India* (2018) 7 SCC 192.
21. Ibid.
22. In fact, concentration of power in centralized institutions is possible as a necessary pre-condition for the creation of the modern state. See Francis Fukuyama's *The Origins of Political Order*.
23. This has been the general view of the Supreme Court. For instance, the Court while dealing with Shariat courts and organizations issuing *fatwas* held that 'In any event, the decision or the *fatwa* issued by whatever body (including Dar-ul-Qaza) being not emanating from any judicial system recognized by law, it is not binding on anyone including the person, who had asked for it. Further, such an adjudication or fatwa does not have a force of law and, therefore, cannot be enforced by any process using coercive method. Any person trying to enforce that by any method shall be illegal and has to

be dealt with in accordance with law.' *Vishwa Lochan Madan v. Union of India* (2014) 7 SCC 707.

24. Chapter 9.3: 'Her father protects (her) in childhood, her husband protects (her) in youth, and her sons protect (her) in old age; a woman is never fit for independence.'
25. *Manusmriti* 5.154.
26. Singh, Kirti, Law Commission on crimes and killing in the name of honour, 6 JILS (2014–15) 63.
27. As per Hindu belief, there are three human goals or purushartha – dharma, artha and kama, or piety, profit and pleasure. Each of these goals has separate texts. Kautilya's *Arthashastra* and Vatsyayana's *Kama Sutra* deal with the latter two goals and offer women a greater role in society. Dharma, on the other hand, had multiple texts. Of these, the *Manusmriti* is the best known, possibly because of the adoption of the text by the English rulers. As per this text, inter-caste marriages were greatly frowned upon. See for instance Chapter 3.4: '4. Having bathed, with the permission of his teacher, and performed according to the rule the Samavartana (the rite on returning home), a twice-born man shall marry a wife of equal caste who is endowed with auspicious (bodily) marks. Chapter 8.352 and 353: Those men who are addicted to intercourse with the wives of other men, the king shall banish after having branded them with terror-inspiring punishments. For out of that arises the admixture of castes among people; whence follows root-rending unrighteousness, tending to total destruction.'
28. See *Marriage: A History; How Love Conquered Marriage*, Stephanie Coontz.
29. Rao, Prakasa, *Marriage: The Family and Women in India*, 1982, p. 17.
30. An interesting study of matrimonial advertisements in the newspaper shows these societal shifts. See 'Changing Pattern in the Indian Arranged Marriage Market: A Longitudinal Study' by Aparajita Chattopadhyay and Debashis Ganguly at https://iussp2005.princeton.edu/papers/51840

31. See, for instance, the Protection of Women from Domestic Violence Act, 2005.
32. *Navtej Singh Johar v. Union of India* (2018) 10 SCC 1.
33. Ibid., p. 116.
34. (2014) 3 SCC 220. This was the judgement whereby the Supreme Court first reversed the Delhi High Court judgement decriminalizing homosexuality, i.e. *Naz Foundation v. Union of India* (2009) 111 DRJ 1.
35. p. 499. Three other judges joined in the judgement of Justice Chandrachud, i.e. Chief Justice Jagdish Khehar and Justices R.K. Aggarwal and Abdul Nazeer.
36. See the privacy judgement, p. 635.

FROM ADULTERY TO SEXUAL AUTONOMY

1. (2018) 10 SCC 1.
2. ((2019) 11 SCC 1.
3. (2019) 2 SCC (Cri) 84.
4. Section 498A of the Indian Penal Code makes criminal conduct that amounts to cruelty as well as harassment for the purposes of seeking dowry.
5. AIR 1954 SC 321.
6. *State of Madhya Pradesh v. Gopal D. Thirtani* (2003) 7 SCC 83.
7. *Air India Cabin Crew Association v. Yeshwaswni Merchant* (2003) 6 SCC 277.
8. 1985 Supp SCC 137 (*Sowmithri Vishnu* judgement).
9. Ibid.
10. (2014) 1 SCC 1.
11. *Sowmithri Vishnu* judgement.
12. Ibid., para 12.
13. 1988 2 SCC 72 (*V. Revathi* judgement).
14. Ibid., para 5.
15. Ibid.
16. *Indian Hotel & Restaurant Association (AHAR) v. State of Maharashtra* (2019) 3 SCC 429. The Supreme Court struck

down allegedly regulatory measures relating to dance bars in Mumbai as being excessive, and merely a device, to force a prohibition on dance performances.
17. *Joseph Shine v. Union of India*, para 105.
18. Ibid., para 189.
19. Ibid.
20. Ibid.
21. Ibid., para 274.
22. Ibid., paras 29 and 30.
23. Ibid., para 103.
24. Ibid., paras 141 and 142.
25. Ibid., para 29.
26. Ibid., para 35.
27. Ibid., para 168.
28. Guruswamy, Menaka, 'Lesser Citizenship of Indian Wives,' *Tehelka*, 8 May 2015.
29. *Joseph Shine*, para 182.
30. 84th Report, Law Commission of India.
31. 172nd Report, Law Commission of India, p. 22.
32. Report of the Committee on Amendments to Criminal Law, pp. 113–118.
33. *C.R. v. U.K.* Publ. ECHR, Ser. A., No. 335-C.
34. 167th Report on the Criminal Law (Amendment) Bill, 2012; Department-Related Parliamentary Standing Committee on Home Affairs, Rajya Sabha Secretariat, New Delhi, March 2013, p. 44.
35. Ibid., pp. 47–48.
36. *Independent Thought v. Union of India* (2017) 10 SCC 800.
37. The Court clarifies that 'it has not dealt with the larger question of marital rape of adult women, since that issue was not raised before us by the petitioner or intervenor,' at para 108.
38. See note 36, p. 845.
39. Ibid., p. 846.
40. Ibid., p. 897.
41. Ibid., p. 855.

42. MANU/GJ/0291/2018.
43. (2014) 1 SCC 1.
44. Ibid.
45. Ibid.
46. Ibid.
47. Ibid.
48. Ibid.
49. *Navtej Singh Johar v. Union of India* (2018) 10 SSC 1.

THE BEAST IN OUR MIDST

1. The strange spelling could be attributed to a numerologist guiding the film's fate. Regardless, the error is not mine.
2. 'Actual 2008 footage of how Tanushree Dutta was attacked when she walked out of Nana Patekar song,' YouTube: https://www.youtube.com/watch?v=lfEeoCPJ7j4
3. Shankar, Karthik, 'Why I Published a List of Sexual Predators in Academia,' *BuzzFeed*, 25 October 2017.
4. Menon, Nivedita, 'Statement by Feminists on Facebook Campaign to Name and Shame,' *Kafila*, 24 October 2017.
5. Author interview with Anoo Bhuyan.
6. Ibid.
7. Author interview with Paromita Vohra.
8. Author interview with Bhanwari Devi.
9. Pandey, Geeta, 'Bhanwari Devi: The Rape That Led to India's Sexual Harassment Law,' BBC News, 17 March 2017.
10. The same Justice J.S. Verma would go on to head a committee named after him, formed by the then UPA government in the aftermath of the gang rape and murder of a young student in Delhi in December 2012. The Verma Committee was tasked with suggesting changes in the law dealing with sexual assault and violence.
11. Mody, Zia, *10 Judgments That Changed India*, New Delhi: Penguin Random House, 2013.
12. Ibid.

13. Comments made at an open meeting on MeToo organized at Jamia Milia Islamia by the Network of Women in Media in January 2019.
14. Mody, Zia, *10 Judgments That Changed India*, New Delhi: Penguin Random House, 2013.
15. Author interview with Bhanwari Devi.
16. Auerbach, Taylor, '"Bucks Night for 1200 People": Families Horrified by Cruise Bender,' 9News, 1 October 2018.
17. Author interview with Mahima Kukreja in December 2018 in Mumbai.
18. Ibid.
19. 'Report Garima, Sexual Harassment at Workplace,' INBA and Netrika Consulting, Indian National Bar Association.
20. The postscript to this story came a year later in November 2019 when Utsav Chakraborty took to Twitter to ask, 'Why would so many women lie about one person?' His contention was that as many as four women who had previously spoken up, including Kukreja herself, were lying or editing mutual flirting on text, or sexting, as non-consensual.

He claimed that an exchange with Kukreja was edited to reveal only one side. He dredged out another conversation with a woman whom he admittedly asked for topless photographs but added that after that episode, she had stayed in touch, even wishing him on his birthday. A third woman was dismissed as a 'garden variety fake accuser'.

He also stated that in the course of a phone conversation with Kukreja and her sister, a lawyer, in November 2018, he was threatened with legal action if he publicly released any information that could damage Kukreja's reputation.

The conversation was recorded without Kukreja's permission, or knowledge. Threatening legal action against a possibly illegal act is not against the law anyway. But the question remained: If the women had been lying, why had he apologized a year earlier? 'It wasn't a real admission,' Chakraborty said. 'I did it because I felt like I had no choice. I had no lawyers, no PR team to guide me. That's why I deleted it later.'

Regardless of the veracity of Chakraborty's belated explanation, he remains silent about why his videos were taken down by AIB – presumably after an exercise of due diligence. But the he-said-she-said stalemate led to larger questions about the credibility of the MeToo movement. 'It's always women who come under scrutiny,' Kukreja told me on the phone three months after Chakraborty's accusations on social media. 'Frankly, I am exhausted.'

21. I worked with *Sunday* from 1991 to about 1999. My editor was Vir Sanghvi. Akbar had moved on.
22. Wahab, Ghazala, 'M.J. Akbar, Minister and Former Editor, Sexually Harassed and Molested Me,' *The Wire*, 10 October 2018.
23. Bhandare, Namita, 'My #MeToo Moment Goes Back 30 Years and I Have the Right to Be Angry,' *ThePrint*, 8 October 2018.
24. Ramani, Priya, 'To the Harvey Weinsteins of the World,' *Vogue*, 12 October 2017.
25. Author interview with the complainant in the *Tehelka* case.
26. http://www.knowyourlaw.com/tarun-tejpal-sex-scandal-facts-the-fingertips/
27. Ibid.
28. Author interview with the journalist.
29. *News18*, 'The Complete Email Trail of the Tarun Tejpal Sexual Assault Case,' 28 November 2013.
30. Ibid.
31. *The Times of India*, 'Tarun Tejpal Faces Arrest after Being Booked on Rape Charge,' 22 November 2013.
32. Ohri, Raghav, 'RK Pachauri Case: Teri Internal Probe Backs Complainant,' *The Economic Times*. Last Updated: 23 May 2015.
33. Aiyar, SA, 'RK Pachauri Needs to Go,' *The Economic Times*, 22 July 2015.
34. Bhandare, Namita, 'Trial by Public Opinion,' *Livemint*, 24 July 2015.

35. Ibid.
36. Vidal, John, 'Rajendra Pachauri Speaks Out Over Sexual Harassment Claims,' *The Guardian*, 26 March 2016.
37. Author interview with Vinta Nanda.
38. Interview with Paromita Vohra.
39. Supreme Court notice dated 20 April, signed by the additional registrar.
40. *Nemo judex in causa sua.*
41. Beard, Mary, *Women and Power: A Manifesto*, Profile Books, 2017.
42. Author interview with Justice Sujata Manohar.
43. Ibid.

TRIPLE TALAQ

1. (2017) 9 SCC 1.
2. See reference to the *Shah Bano* case later in this essay.
3. Dhavan, Rajeev, 'Why J.S. Khehar Was Arguably One of the Worst Chief Justices of India,' *DailyO*, 21 August 2017.
4. Rajagopal, Krishnadas, 'Once Again, Supreme Court Upholds Chief Justice of India as "Master of Roster",' *The Hindu*, 6 July 2018.
5. Sharma, VVP, 'Religious Diversity of Triple Talaq Bench Justices Only a Coincidence,' *News18*, 11 May 2017.
6. *Shayara Bano v. Union of India*, (2017) 9 SCC 1, para 141, p. 202. Interestingly, on 14 November 2019, at the time of writing, in *Kantaru Rajeevaru v. Indian Young Lawyers Association*, Review Petition (C) No. 3358/2018 (the *Sabarimala Review*), the Supreme Court referred certain important questions arising out of the interpretation of Articles 25 and 26 of the Constitution, including 'whether the "essential religious practices" of a religious denomination, or even a section thereof are afforded constitutional protection under Article 26'.

7. *Suresh Kumar Koushal v. Naz Foundation* (2014) 4 SCC 1. Subsequently, overruled by *Navtej Singh Johar v. Union of India* (2018) 1 SCC 791.
8. *The Times of India*, 'Why Media Got the Triple Talaq Order Wrong – Initially,' 22 August 2017.
9. *Hindustan Times*, 'Triple Talaq: AIMPLB Says SC Verdict "Huge Victory" As It Protects Muslim Personal Law,' 22 August 2017.
10. Agnes, Flavia, 'Whose Fight Is It Anyway,' *Indian Express*, 12 June 2017.
11. See sub-section (2)(a) of Article 25.
12. 1985 (2) SCC 556.
13. Mulla, *Principles of Mohammedan Law*, 22nd ed., Lexis Nexis, 2013: 'Mahr or Dower is a sum of money or other property which the wife is entitled to receive from the husband in consideration of the marriage.'
14. The Muslim Women (Protection of Rights on Divorce) Act, 1986.
15. *Danial Latifi v. Union of India*, (2001) 7 SCC 740 (5J).
16. Hussain, Sabiha, 'A Socio-historical and Political Discourse on the Rights of Muslim Women: Concerns for Women's Rights or Community Identity: (Special reference to 1937 and 1939 Acts),' *Journal of International Women's Studies*, 16(2), pp. 1–14.
17. Muslim Personal Law (Shariat) Application Act, 1937.
18. Hussain, Sabiha, 'Muslim Women's Rights Discourse in the Pre-Independence Period,' Centre for Women's Development Studies, 2006.
19. Ibid.
20. Mulla, *Principles of Mohammedan Law*, 22nd ed., Lexis Nexis, 2013.
21. (2016) 2 SCC 36.
22. Ibid.
23. (2016) 2 SCC 36.
24. Kumar, Niraj, and Akhilendra Pratap Singh, *Invalidating*

Instant Triple Talaq: Is the Top-down Approach of Reforming Personal Law Prudent?, 11 NUJS L. Rev 2 (2018).

25. Pathak, Sushant, and Jamshed Ali Khan, 'Exposed: How Maulvis Take Money for One Night Stand with Divorced Women Trying to Save Marriage,' *India Today*, 16 August 2017.
26. (2002) 7 SCC 518.
27. (2003) 8 SCC 369.
28. (1995) 3 SCC 635.
29. Hameed, Syeda Saiyidain, *Voice of Voiceless: Status of Muslim Women in India*, National Commission for Women, 2000.
30. Ibid., pp. 23–24.
31. Ibid., p. 25.
32. Ibid., p. 26.
33. Kirmani, Nida, 'Mobilising for Muslim Women's Right in India,' *Open Democracy*, 14 January 2011.
34. Goradia Divan, Madhavi, 'A Civil Crime,' *Indian Express*, 25 September 2018.
35. AIR 1952 Bom 84.
36. Ibid.
37. Ibid.
38. See Article 13 of the Constitution.
39. (1981) 3 SCC 689.
40. (1994) Supp (1) SCC 713.
41. (2001) 7 SCC 740 (5J).
42. (1985) 2 SCC 556 (5J).
43. (2003) 6 SCC 611 (3J).
44. (1996) 8 SCC 525.
45. Ibid., paras 26 and 15.
46. *Indian Young Lawyers Association v. State of Kerala* (2019) 11 SCC 1, paras 276, 278.
47. (1996) 9 SCC 548, para 87.
48. (2003) 8 SCC 369, paras 49 and 50.
49. AIR 1952 Bom 84, paras 5 and 7.
50. (2004) 12 SCC 770, para 9.

51. This was what formed the basis of Justice Indu Malhotra's dissenting judgement in *Indian Young Lawyers Association v. State of Kerala*, (2019) 11 SCC 1.
52. *Shayara Bano v. Union of India*, (2017) 9 SCC 1.
53. Mohammed, Tahir, *Statues of Personal Law in Islamic Countries*, 2nd ed., Universal Law Publishing, 1995.
54. Haider, Nadya, 'Islamic Legal Reform: The Case of Pakistan and Family Law,' *Yale Journal of Law and Feminism*, 12(2), 2000.
55. The Report of the Commission on marriage and family laws, 1956. Reprinted in *Studies in the Family Law of Islam*, Vol. 39.
56. *The Economic Times*, 'ET View: Passage of Triple Talaq Bill a Moment of Great Importance for India's Legislative History,' 31 July 2019.
57. Ibid.
58. Nair, Sangeeta, 'Triple Talaq Bill Gets President's Assent,' *Jagran Josh*, 1 August 2019.
59. Section 4 of The Muslim Women (Protection of Rights on Marriage) Bill, 2019.
60. Hall, Jerome, 'Interrelations of Criminal Law and Torts,' *Columbia Law Review*, 43(6), September 1943, pp. 753–779.
61. Indian Penal Code, 1860.
62. *Shayara Bano v. Union of India*, (2017) 9 SCC 1.
63. Office of Registrar General and Census Commissioner, India, 2011 Census Data.
64. Ibid.
65. Justice Rajinder Sachar Committee, *Report on Economic and Educational Status of the Muslim Community of India*, 2006.
66. Doepeke, Mithhias, Michele Tirtilt and Others, 'Women's Empowerment and Development: The Family Connection,' *VoxDev*, 3 October 2017.
67. Bernasek, Alexandra, 'Banking on Social Change: Grameen Bank Lending to Women,' *International Journal of Politics, Culture and Society*, Vol. 16, no. 3, 2003, pp. 369–385.

UNDERSTANDING MUSLIM LAW IN THE MODERN CONTEXT

1. The Delhi High Court had in 2007 held that the instantaneous triple talaq was not an immediate irrevocable divorce. Instead, as per the judgement, the talaq was to be construed as a single, revocable talaq. Effectively, even after the pronouncement of the term 'talaq, talaq, talaq', the divorce could be revoked during the period of the *iddat*, i.e. during the three monthly periods of the wife. *Masroor Ahmed v. State* (NCT of Delhi): ILR (2007) 2 Del 1329: 2007 SCC Online Del 1357.
2. The Supreme Court held that *talaq-e-biddat* was unconstitutional in 2017. *Shayara Bano v. Union of India*: (2017) 9 SCC 1.
3. 'For many Muslims therefore, the word "Shariah" simply means "justice", and they will consider any law to conform to the Shariah as long as it promotes justice and social welfare.' See Vikør, Knut, 'Muslim Journeys, Item #226: "Sharia" from Oxford Islamic Studies Online,' 4 June 2014.
4. Nasr, Seyyed Hossein, *The Study Quran*, Harper One, 2015.
5. The expression 'reverence God' is a statement of affirmation of faith and trust in God and it signifies the approval of God that the debtor should dictate and the creditor should not remove or weaken the debtor's covenants.
6. Nasr, Seyyed Hossein, *The Study Quran*, Harper One, 2015.
7. There are several collections of *hadis* – such 'Sahih Al Bukhari', 'Sahih Muslim', Imam Malik's Muwatta, etc.
8. Nasr, Seyyed Hossein, *The Study Quran*, Harper One, 2015.
9. Al-Imam Muhammad ibn Idris al-Shafi'i: Founder of the Shafi'i school of law.
10. *Al-Shafi'i's Risala: Treatise on the Foundations of Islamic Jurisprudence*, translated by Majid Khadduri, pp. 111–112.
11. Here 'the Apostle' is a reference to Prophet Muhammad.
12. Nasr, Seyyed Hossein, *The Study Quran*, Harper One, 2015.

13. See *M. Siddiq (dead) through LRs v. Mahant Suresh Das & Ors*, (2020) 1 SCC 1, particularly paras 998 to 1018 for a historical perspective of the application of the doctrine in India.
14. Section 37 of the Bengal, Agra and Assam Civil Courts Act, 1887 (which is applicable even today) is an example. There are other similar enactments covering other states and territories in India. The said Section 37, for ready reference, reads as follows:

    37. Certain decisions to be according to Native law.

    (1) Where in any suit or other proceeding it is necessary for a Civil Court to decide any question regarding succession, inheritance, marriage or caste, or any religious usage or institution, the Muhammadan law in cases where the parties are Muhammadans, and the Hindu law in cases where the parties are Hindus, shall form the rule of decision except in so far as such law has, by legislative enactment, been altered or abolished.

    (2) In cases not provided for by sub-section (1) or by any other law for the time being in force, the Court shall act according to justice, equity and good conscience.
15. An excellent but simple explanation of *ijtihad* and how it is to be exercised is given in Al Risala (supra) at pp. 302–303:

    And he asked: How is ijtihad [to be exercised]?

    [Shafi'i] replied: God, Glorified and Praised be He, has endowed men with reason by which they can distinguish between differing viewpoints, and He guides them to the truth either by [explicit] texts or by indications [on the strength of which they exercise ijtihad].

    He asked: Will you give an example?

    [Shafi'i] replied: God erected the Sacred House and ordered men to face it [in prayer], when it is in sight, and to seek its direction [by ijtihad] when they are at a distance from it. And He created for them the heaven and the earth and the sun and the moon and the stars and the seas and the mountains and the wind [as guiding indications by which they can exercise ijtihad]. For God said:

It is He who has appointed for you the stars, that by them you might be guided in the darkness of land and sea [Q. VI, 97].

And He said:

And landmarks and by the stars they might be guided [Q. XVI, 16].

Thus [God] instructed men to be guided by the stars and [other] indicators, and by His blessing and help they know the direction of the Sacred House. So those who can see it from their places [may perform the prayer] and those who cannot see it should either be informed by those who have seen it or seek guidance by means of certain indications such as a mountain, which might point to [the direction], or a star indicating the north and south, or the sun, whose rising and setting is known, pointing out the direction for him who performs the evening [prayer], or the seas [which might also be a guiding indication] and the like.

Thus men should seek, through the reasoning power which God has implanted in them, the direction in which He made it incumbent for them to face [during prayer]. If it is thus sought, through their reasoning power and their knowledge of the indications [pointing to it], men can fulfil their duty.

[God] has made it clear that the duty He imposed on them is [to pray in] the direction of the Sacred Mosque, not always to face the House [al-Kaba] itself. If the right direction is not known with the same certainty as is possessed by those who see it, it is not permissible to hold that one can face any direction one wishes without [a guiding] indication.

16. See, Sunan Abu Dawud, *Kitab al-Aqdiyah*, Vol. III, Chapter 1348, Translated by Prof. Ahmad Hasan, Kitab Bhavan, 1990 reprint.
17. That is, the roots of jurisprudence: (i) the Quran; (ii) the *Hadis*; (iii) *Ijma*; and (iv) *Qiyas* (analogy) or *Aql* (systematic reasoning).

18. Faruqi and Faruqi, *The Cultural Atlas of Islam*, Macmillan, 1986, pp. 267–268.
19. Hodgson, Marshall G.S., *The Venture of Islam*, The University of Chicago Press, Volume 1, 1974, p. 335.
20. One definition of *mufti* and *fatwa* is as follows: A *mufti* is a specialist on law who can give an authoritative opinion on points of doctrine; his considered legal opinion is called a *fatwa*. Schacht, Joseph, *An Introduction to Islamic Law*, Clarendon Press, 1982, p. 73.
21. A *qazi* (or *qadi*) is a judge appointed by the political authority or state. He or she may pass judgements in his or her jurisdiction in respect of many legal matters, including divorce, inheritance, property, contractual disputes, etc. Ibid., p. 188. A *qaza* or *kada* is a judgement, which must be given according to the *madhab* to which the *qadi* belongs. Ibid., p. 196.
22. The ruling of a *qazi* settles a dispute between two parties. The ruling is binding, although if the *qazi* is not a jurist, he should on all legal questions consult a *mufti*. Abdur Rahim, pp. 171–172, 370. The *fatwa* of a *mufti* is an advisory decision, while a *qaza* of a *qazi* is a binding court judgement. Hodgson, Marshall G.S., *The Venture of Islam: Volume 1, The Classical Age of Islam*, The University of Chicago Press, 1974, p. 338.
23. Rahim, Abdur, *The Principles of Islamic Jurisprudence*,' 2nd Revised Ed., Kitab Bhavan, p. 172 (in respect of qazis).
24. In *Vishwa Lochan Madan v. Union of India*, (2014) 7 SCC 707.
25. See *Satappa v. Mahomed-Saheb*: AIR 1936 Bom 227.
26. See, Statement of Objects and Reasons of Kazis Act, 1880 (Act XII of 1880), which reads as follows:

    Under the Mohammadan Law the Kazi was chiefly a Judicial Officer. His principal powers and duties are stated at some length in the Hedaya, Book XX. He was appointed by the State, and may be said to have corresponded to our Judge or Magistrate. In addition, however, to his functions under the Mohammadan Law, the Kazi in this country, before the advent of British rule, appears to have performed certain other duties, partly of a secular and partly of a religious nature. The principle of these seems to have been preparing, attesting and registering deeds of transfer of property, celebrating marriages, and performing other rites and ceremonies.

Certain of his duties having thus survived the passing of Act XI of 1864, the Kazi is still a functionary of considerable importance in the Mohammadan community. What was originally in some sense an accidental adjunct of his judicial office has become his principal and only duty, and in some parts of the country at least, the presence of a kazi at certain rites and ceremonies appears now to be considered by Mohammadans essential from their point of view.

27. Faruqi and Faruqi, *The Cultural Atlas of Islam*, Macmillan, 1986, pp. 267–268.
28. It is believed by some scholars that the ability to use the process of *itjihad* ended around 900 CE. Wael B. Hallaq, quoting Joseph Schacht, says '[about 900 CE], however, the point had been reached when the scholars of all schools felt that all essential questions had been thoroughly discussed and finally settled, and a consensus gradually established itself to the effect that from that time onwards no one might be deemed to have the necessary qualifications for independent reasoning in law, and all future activity would have to be confined to the explanation, application, and, at most, interpretation of the doctrine as it had been laid down once and for all'. See, 'Was the Gate of Itjihad Closed,' *International Journal of Middle East Studies*, 16(1), 1984, pp. 3–41. The article goes on to argue that this closure is, in fact, a misconception. There was sufficient historical evidence, as per the author, to prove to the contrary.
29. '*Taqlid* means following the opinion of another person without knowledge of the authority for such opinion.' See: Abdur Rahim, supra, p. 164.
30. For example, it is generally perceived that interest is prohibited

under the Shariah. This is based on the understanding that '*riba*', which is clearly forbidden in the Quran, means usury or charging of interest on money lent. The Arabic word *riba*, however, simply means 'increase'. Interest does not necessarily mean *riba*. For example, if the rate of interest is equal to the rate of inflation then, in real terms, there is no increase (i.e., no *riba*). This makes it clear that charging of interest, *ipso facto*, does not amount to *riba*. It would be *riba* if it results in increase in real terms. Thus, it is necessary to understand the full meaning of Arabic words used in the Quran and the context in which they are used.

31. Muslim law operates in this sphere since the general law of the land specifically permits this.
32. The territory of the erstwhile princely state of Awadh (of Nawab Wajid Ali Shah fame), of which the capital was Lucknow.
33. By virtue of Section 3(b) of the Act.
34. This effectively implied that statutory enactments would take precedence over the applicable personal law.
35. See Section 2 of The Muslim Personal Law (Shariat) Application Act, 1937 which reads as under:

    2. Application of Personal Law to Muslims – Notwithstanding any customs or usage to the contrary, in all questions (save questions relating to agricultural land) regarding intestate succession, special property of females, including personal property inherited or obtained under contract or gift or any other provision of Personal Law, marriage, dissolution of marriage, including *talaq, ila, zihar, lian, khula* and *mubaraat*, maintenance, dower, guardianship, gifts, trusts and trust properties, and *wakfs* (other than charities and charitable institutions and charitable and religious endowments) the rule of decision in cases where the parties are Muslims shall be the Muslim Personal Law (*Shariat*).

36. Nasr, Seyyed Hossein, *The Study Quran*, Harper One, 2015.
37. Ibid., p. 192.

38. This was a case where the custom was less favourable to women than the Shariah. The law stepped in and custom was overridden by the Shariah.
39. Section 2 of the 1939 Act includes grounds such as desertion, impotence, insanity, certain specified grounds of cruelty, etc.
40. Certain segments of the Muslim community always considered the *talaq-e-biddat* to be immoral or even illegal. There was no consensus on its applicability. In the case of *Masroor Ahmad*, the Delhi High Court has noted that the Shia schools do not recognize this as a valid form of divorce.
41. See note 2.
42. See note 1.
43. For example, by the process of interpretation that had been given in the *Masroor Ahmad* case rendering the process into one of a single revocable divorce.
44. Muslim Women (Protection of Rights on Marriage) Act, 2019.
45. See the note above dealing with the closure of the gates of *ijtihad*.

AN AXIS SHIFT

1. *Indian Young Lawyers Association v. State of Kerala* (2019) 11 SCC 1 ('Sabarimala judgement' by Justice Chandrachud).
2. Paragraphs 20–22 of the Sabarimala judgement.
3. *S. Mahendran v. The Secretary, Travancore Devaswom Board, Thiruvananthapuram* AIR 1991 Ker 43.
4. See the Kerala High Court judgement, footnote 3.
5. Paragraph 25, part B of Judgement dated 28 September 2018 by Justice D.Y. Chandrachud in Writ Petition (Civil) No. 373 of 2006.
6. 1981 Supp (1) SCC 87, p. 210.
7. *Adi Saiva Sivachariyargal Nala Sangam v. State of Tamil Nadu* (2016) 2 SCC 725.
8. Paragraph 446 of the Sabarimala judgement.
9. *The Commissioner, Hindu Religious Endowments, Madras v. Sri*

Lakshmindra Thirtha Swamiar of Sri Shirur Mutt, (1954) 1 SCR 1005.

10. Paragraph 447 of the Sabarimala judgement.
11. Paragraph 106 of the Sabarimala judgement.
12. Paragraph 110 of the Sabarimala judgement.
13. (2014) 9 SCC 1.
14. (2018) 10 SCC 1.
15. (1973) 4 SCC 225.
16. Article 356: Provisions in case of failure of constitutional machinery in the State.
17. See note 13.
18. See note 14.
19. Of course, the fundamental right under Article 26 will have to be balanced with the rights of others contained in Part III as a matter of harmonious construction of these rights as was held in *Sri Venkataramana Devaru*. But this would only be on a case-by-case basis, without necessarily subjecting the fundamental right under Article 26 to all other fundamental rights contained in Part III. This is discussed further in the section relating to the religious denomination test.
20. Under Articles 25 to 28 of the Constitution of India.
21. *Shirur Mutt* case, (1954) 1 SCR 1005.
22. Para 80, *S.P. Mittal v. Union of India* (1983) 1 SCC 51.
23. Para 96 of the Sabarimala judgement.
24. *Shastri Yagnapurushdasji v. Muldas Bhundardas Vaishya*, AIR 1966 SC 1119.
25. *Sidheswar Shai v. State of West Bengal* (1995) 4 SCC 646, a similar structured aspect of the Hindu religion was examined, and the Supreme Court held that the Ramakrishna Mission or Ramakrishna Math is 'a religious denomination'.
26. (2014) 5 SCC 75.
27. *Commissioner of Police v. Acharya Jagadishwaranand Avadhuta*, (2004) 12 SCC 770.
28. Para 122 of Judgement dated 28 September 2018 in Writ Petition (Civil) No. 373 of 2006.

29. Justice Malhotra noticed that the practice of restricting the entry of women belonging to the age group of 10 to 50 years was challenged as being violative of Articles 15, 25 and 26 of the Constitution before a Division Bench of the Kerala High Court in *S. Mahendran v. The Secretary, Travancore Devaswom Board, Thiruvananthapuram & Ors*, AIR (1993) Ker 42. Justice Malhotra observed that in that case, the High Court held that the restriction on the entry of women between the ages of 10 to 50 years was in accordance with the practice prevalent since time immemorial, and was not violative of Articles 15, 25 and 26 of the Constitution. Justice Malhotra also observed that since the judgement of the Kerala High Court was not challenged any further, and has attained finality, the findings contained in the judgement of the Kerala High Court deciding a Writ Petition under Article 226 were findings in rem, and the principle of res judicata would apply.
30. AIR 1980 SC 707.
31. Notable among them are the following:

    King Emperor v. Khwaja Nazir Ahmad [(1943–44) 71 IA 203] is known for its celebrated dictum of *'if a thing has to be done, it should be done in accordance with law or otherwise not'*.

    Hanooman Prasad Pandey v. Babbooee Munraj Kunwaree, (M.L.A. 393) is known for its decision on the issue of the power of the widow or the limited heir to alienate the estate inherited by her.

    Barendra Kumar Ghosh v. King Emperor, AIR 1925 PC 1 is known for its famous dictum that '*they also serve who only stand and wait*'.
32. (1973) 4 SCC 225.

THE GROWING SIGNIFICANCE OF DIGNITY JURISPRUDENCE IN THE FIELD OF HUMAN RIGHTS

1. The United Kingdom and Israel would be such examples.

2. Though Western thinking is that the concept of human dignity has a history of 2,500 years, in many Eastern civilizations including India, human dignity as a core human value goes back much longer.
3. Barak, Aharon, *Human Dignity: The Constitutional Value and the Constitutional Right*, Cambridge University Press, 2015.
4. Based on the approach of Thomas Aquinas (1225–1274) in his work *Summa Theologia*.
5. See Hill, Thomas E., 'Humanity Is an End in Itself,' *Ethics*, 91(1), October 1980, pp. 84–99.
6. Kant, Immanuel, *Critique of Practical Reason* and *Groundwork of the Metaphysics of Morals*.
7. See Pfordten, Dietmar von der, 'On the Dignity of Man in Kant,' *Philosophy*, 84(329), July 2009, pp. 371–391.
8. Delivered on 25 February 2010 at the Indian Institute of Public Administration, New Delhi.
9. To the aforesaid, Professor Baxi adds: 'I still need to say that the idea of dignity is a metaethical one, that is, it marks and maps a difficult terrain of what it may mean to say being "human" and remaining "human", or put another way, the relationship between "self", "others", and "society". In this formulation the word "respect" is the keyword: dignity is respect for an individual person based on the principle of freedom and capacity to make choices, and a good or just social order is one which respects dignity via assuring "contexts" and "conditions" as the "source of free and informed choice". Respect for dignity thus conceived is empowering overall and not just because it, even if importantly, sets constraints state, law, and regulations.'
10. Waldron, Jeremy, 'How Law Protects Dignity,' *The Cambridge Law Journal*, 71(1), March 2012, pp. 200–222.
11. Fukuyama, Francis, *Identity: The Demand for Dignity and the Politics of Resentment*, Farrar, Straus and Giroux, 2018.
12. (1997) 1 SCC 416.
13. (1980) 3 SCC 526.
14. (1984) 3 SCC 161.

15. (2006) 8 SCC 212.
16. The Vishaka judgement (*Vishaka v. State of Rajasthan* AIR 1997 Supreme Court 3011) would always be remembered in this context.
17. (2014) 5 SCC 438.
18. (2017) 10 SCC 1.
19. (2018) 10 SCC 1.
20. See the judgement in the case of *Navtej Johar v. Union of India* above.
21. (2019) 3 SCC 39.
22. (2017) 9 SCC 1.
23. (2019) 11 SCC 1.
24. This case is now a subject matter of a seven-judge bench where the issues pertaining to religious faith vis-à-vis individual rights are going to be taken up.

Notes on Contributors

Justice B.D. Ahmed is a former judge of the Delhi High Court and the Chief Justice of the Jammu and Kashmir High Court. He is a renowned scholar of Islamic law. He authored the judgement in the case of *Masroor Ahmad* in 2007, which had declared that instant triple talaq ought to be considered as a single revocable divorce, thereby mitigating its harshness.

Namita Bhandare has a master's degree in journalism from Stanford University and close to 30 years of reporting experience. She was appointed India's first gender editor for the newspaper *Mint* and, as an independent journalist, continues to write on issues relating to women and gender.

Ritu Dalmia is a noted chef with restaurants spread across India as well as Italy. She, along with Navtej Johar, was the petitioner in the lead petition which led to the reading down of Section 377.

Madhavi Divan is a Senior Advocate and the current Additional Solicitor General for India. She appeared for the Government in the *Shayara Bano* case, which led to the invalidation of the practice of triple talaq.

Dr Menaka Guruswamy is a Senior Advocate at the Supreme Court of India. Her litigation practice includes successfully seeking reform of the bureaucracy in the country through fixed tenure, defended federal legislation that mandates that all private schools admit disadvantaged children and, most recently, the overturned Section 377, the colonial-era law which criminalizes consensual same-sex relations. Dr Guruswamy is *amicus curiae* appointed by the Supreme Court in a case concerning 1,528 alleged extra-judicial killings by security personnel. Dr Guruswamy's most recent publications include a co-edited volume of essays on *Founding Moments in Constitutionalism* (Hart/Bloomsbury, 2019), an essay on constitution-making in South Asia in the *Handbook on Constitution-Making* (Edward Elgar, 2019) and an essay titled 'From the Movement Party to Movement Court' in *Revolutionary Constitutionalism* (Hart/Bloomsbury 2020). Dr Guruswamy was educated at Oxford University, Harvard Law School and the National Law School of India. She was the B.R Ambedkar Research Scholar and Lecturer in Law at Columbia Law School from 2017 to 2019 where she taught constitutional design in post-conflict democracies.

Arundhati Katju is a lawyer in the Supreme Court of India, practising white-collar defence, civil and commercial law. In 2018, Arundhati successfully represented the lead petitioners in the Indian Supreme Court's judgement in *Navtej Singh Johar and others v. Union of India*, where the Court struck down India's 157-year-old sodomy law. She holds a BA LLB (Hons.) degree from the National Law School of India University, Bangalore, and an LLM from Columbia Law School, where she was a Human Rights Fellow, Herman N. Finkelstein Memorial Fellow and a CLAGS Duberman-Zal Fellow. In 2019, she was named one of *TIME* Magazine's 100 Most Influential People of the Year. Alongside her litigation practice, she is presently a Senior Fellow at the Center for Contemporary Critical Thought at Columbia University.

Justice M.B. Lokur is a former judge of the Supreme Court of India and is currently a judge of the Supreme Court of Fiji. He was a member of the Social Justice Bench in the Supreme Court and is the author of many landmark judgements, including the judgement that declared that sex with a wife who was a minor amounted to rape.

Zainab Patel is a transgender woman and human rights activist. She impleaded in the NALSA judgement, where the Supreme Court recognized transgender persons as a distinct gender and constitutionally guaranteed their social and political rights.

Mukul Rohatgi is a Senior Advocate in the Supreme Court of India and is a former Attorney General for India. He appeared for the government in the triple talaq case and for the petitioners in the *Navtej Johar* case.

Justice A.K. Sikri is a former judge of the Supreme Court of India and is currently a judge at the Singapore International Commercial Court. He was the author of many path-breaking judgements, including the case of NALSA where the Court recognized transgenders as a separate gender.

Keshav Suri is the youngest executive director at The LaLiT Suri Hospitality Group. He is involved in the Group's expansion, quality management, building marketing strategies, operations and F&B revenues. A firm believer of responsible entrepreneurship, Keshav Suri has been working with several NGOs and activists to help mainstream marginalized communities. He is also one of those who petitioned to revoke Section 377 in the Supreme Court of India. Under his leadership, the Group has provided opportunities to more than 100 queer people, and has established itself as one of the safest places in the country. Having taken up the cause of building an inclusive nation, he launched the Keshav Suri Foundation, with a mission to embrace, empower and mainstream the LGBTQ+ community. He was also instrumental in setting up the D&I task force with FICCI, which he co-chairs.

Acknowledgements

As will obviously be the case in any anthology, my thanks are also due to each of the contributors for this book. They are authors who come from disparate backgrounds and beliefs. However, they are all deeply committed to the cause of bettering the life of the most oppressed and marginalized communities. The eagerness with which they accepted the writing assignment and the zeal and promptitude with which they wrote the essays made my task as editor considerably easier.

I must also thank Hachette India and, in particular, Rukmini Chawla Kumar. She not only planted the idea of the book in my head, but also diligently pursued and encouraged me through the writing.

Finally, this book would not have been possible without my family members: My father, Justice B.N. Kirpal, who imbued in me the love for the law and the desire to use it to make real change; my mother, Aruna Kirpal, who encouraged and supported me in my studies, in my career as well as my personal life; my partner in love and life, Nicolas Bachmann, who put up with my tantrums when I was writing this book. I hope we see an India where all of us are full citizens.